THREE WISE MONKEYS

THREE WISE MONKEYS

Mizaru – 'See No Evil'

The Makings of an African Economic Tragedy: Mozambique, circa 1500–1960

Charles van Onselen

Jonathan Ball Publishers
Johannesburg · Cape Town

© Text: Charles van Onselen (2023)
© Published edition: Jonathan Ball Publishers (2023)

Published in South Africa in 2023 by
JONATHAN BALL PUBLISHERS
A division of Media24 (Pty) Ltd
PO Box 33977
Jeppestown
2043

ISBN 978-1-77619-244-1
ebook ISBN 978-1-77619-245-8

Every effort has been made to trace the copyright holders and to obtain their permission for the use of copyright material. The publishers apologise for any errors or omissions and would be grateful to be notified of any corrections that should be incorporated in future editions of this book.

jonathanball.co.za
twitter.com/JonathanBallPub
facebook.com/JonathanBallPublishers

Cover and slipcase design by MR Design
Design and typesetting by MR Design Proofreading by Paul Wise
Index by George Claassen
Set in Garamond

CONTENTS

THE THREE WISE MONKEYS IN IMPERIAL AND
COLONIAL SOUTHERN AFRICA

The origins of the three wise monkeys, some speculate, lie in Hinduism, and the maxims surrounding them made their way into the wider world via the Silk Road. Confronted with the choice of going east or west, the monkeys went east, where, they believed, they were more likely to find succour than in the west. Their wisdom was readily adopted, perhaps adapted, by Confucius, making an early appearance in his *Analects* hundreds of years before the Christian era. In the 16th century, Buddhist monks, valuing their lessons, ferried them silently across the South China Sea to take up residence in Japan.

By then seasoned travellers, the monkeys moved easily through the forest of ancient religions abounding on Honshū Island. It was with Koshin, God of the Roads, a friend to Buddhist, Shinto and Taoist wanderers alike, that they felt most at home. Fittingly, they are honoured on a carved wooden panel at the Toshogu Shrine, at Nikkō, in the region where they were widely respected.

How, why or by whom the three were smuggled into the Anglophone world is unclear, but it took some time. Only in the 20th century did they put in an appearance in Western popular culture. An air of mystery clung to them and, perhaps incongruously, they were occasionally reported as having been seen in military arenas where notions of discipline and obedience are always de rigueur. By then, however, their wisdom may already have undergone a rather subtle cultural twist.

In their earliest Eastern setting, the messages of the primates may have come across as a positive proactive injunction to those seeking to live the good life and cultivate a sense of tranquillity. Evil in its many forms existed; it was rooted in place, totem-like. Those in search of wisdom should be pre-emptive and *do something* to avoid it by averting their eyes, not listening to it or speaking of it. Evil was fixed, but intelligent people could navigate their way around it. By acknowledging its existence and acting, the potential for evil could be minimised.

But something had been lost in translation by the time that Mizaru, Kikazaru and Iwazaru got to whisper to English speakers in their customary hushed tones. Wickedness still existed, as it did, always, everywhere, but it was no longer static; it was mobile and on the move towards people. And so, instead of being proactive and doing something, as back in the East, folk needed to sit tight and *do nothing* – see no evil, hear no evil and speak no evil. It was as if people were urged to recognise the presence of evil, and then promptly to deny its existence.

The wisdom of the Three Wise Monkeys came to southern Africa via English, from the West, replete with a cultural coding that encouraged settler ideologies of denial, rootedness and silence when confronted by moral ambiguities. In a setting where colonialism and imperialism posed questions of profound ethical importance about issues of conquest, occupation and gross dispossession, the willingness to see no evil, hear no evil and speak no evil held some appeal. How those ancient directives – in both their old active and new passive form – helped shape the deeply entangled social history of 20th-century South Africa and Mozambique is the subject of these three volumes. Only by seeing, hearing and speaking honestly about the past can we hope to understand a troubled present.

INTRODUCTION TO THE TRILOGY

INTERSECTIONS OF CHURCH, NATION AND STATE: SOUTH AFRICA AND MOZAMBIQUE, CIRCA 1650–1970

We must be strict with ourselves and lenient with our neighbours. For we know not their difficulties and what they overcome.
MK GANDHI

... a union of government and religion tends to destroy government and to degrade religion.
JUSTICE H BLACK, US SUPREME COURT, 1964

Historians, unlike scientists, do not preside over laboratories. Because their findings cannot readily be replicated, their results can be dismissed as being subjective and ideologically, or politically, tainted to a degree determined by the competence of the practitioner of what remains more of a craft than a science. Scientists tend to collaborate in research teams more readily than do historians, which adds to the rigour of the scientific method and militates against the easy dismissal of their findings. Historians are far more likely to pursue their craft individually, which often renders them more vulnerable to subjective criticisms.

But that superficial description of the difference between the practitioners of science and the arts, or science and the social sciences, will not withstand too much interrogation. It eventually collapses beneath the weight of unstated similarities, including such elusive elements as creativity and the imagination, discipline and patience, or knowledge and wisdom. So, before we abandon the comparison entirely, let us pause briefly to slow down, if not stop, the implosion, albeit just enough to outline a few of the complexities that come with writing history.

Historians, too, engage in 'experiments' using evidence, the authenticity of which can be verified independently. But because there is no single, universally accepted methodology governing historical research, historians can be loath to invite outsiders into the laboratories of the mind to witness their 'experiments' before they arrive at an assessment of the value of their always contested findings. Professional historians are reluctant to explain how they go about their work.

What follows is an invitation into a historian's 'laboratory', to catch a glimpse of how the experiment around the *Three Wise Monkeys* originated, and of the struggle to isolate the critical variables capable of achieving two objectives. First, to demonstrate that there are advantages to be gained by abandoning the customary use of the 'nation-state' as a primary unit of analysis, even when attempting to understand its development on its own terms. Second, that by placing two 'nation-states' side by side and exploring the explicit or implicit ways in which their institutions and structures competed with or complemented one another, it is possible to emerge with a heightened appreciation of how regional history helped shape some dynamics and structures of colonial rule.

The historian's laboratory

First, an admission of guilt. The full list of charges is much longer than that which appears here; those cited relate almost exclusively to the *Three Wise Monkeys.*

A historian is trapped within the four points of a quadrilateral from which escape is impossible. First, the author is, to a greater or lesser measure, confined to the existing historiography and the inherited explanations and interpretations of 'the past' that this offers. Second, chronicling the past can only be done from the vantage point of the present, which, consciously or unconsciously, invites the historian into seeing 'real', or 'imagined', links between the past, remote or proximate, and the present.[1] Third, because historians cannot avoid linking the past to the present, they cannot – in the mind's eye – avoid extrapolating and sneaking a glimpse, 'true' or 'false', at what they think the future might hold. Like the past, the present crowds in on the future. All three form part of a single continuum. Fourth, and we will return to this challenge directly below, the historian consciously or unconsciously sets his narrative within a real or imaginary spatial dimension that influences explanation.

The situation may be dispiriting but is not hopeless. All historians are confined to the same quadrilateral, but within it they are seldom held communally, and a prison is not a cell, even if a prison is collectively constituted of its cells. Within the diminished space and seclusion of a cell, an inmate with a historical imagination can interrogate, manipulate and play with the fixity of the four points of the quadrilateral that define the limits of his or her experimental freedom. He or she is free to create an expanding or contracting universe capable of generating new questions that may inform different ways of seeing and, in so doing, help add to the expanding store of historical knowledge.

Historians are at liberty to define the time span of their experiments as they see fit, hence the use of the prefixes 'ancient', 'medieval' or 'modern' history in publishers' catalogues even before casting them within subdisciplines such as 'political', 'economic' or 'social' history and then, ultimately, delineating the specific topic that falls within the ambit of such boldly stated parameters. But, as Fernand Braudel reminded us, time itself is a complex concept and, if necessary, can be disaggregated into 'a geographical time, a social time, and an individual time'.[2]

Braudel's greatest misgiving, if not scorn, about the way that time is deployed by most conventional historians, in what he terms 'traditional history', lies in their preference for tightly bracketed, chronologically restricted histories. For him, short-span studies tend to elevate the transitory, to lift 'events', which, in turn, encourage historians to indulge in narrative to the detriment of deeper understandings of what transpired. 'The historian', Braudel writes, 'is naturally only too willing to act as theatrical producer. How could he be expected to renounce the drama of the short time span, and all the best tricks of a very old trade?'[3] His stark warning is, for obvious reasons, of special importance for social historians, who have an understandable tendency to foreground human agency in events.

One of the more trusted ways of guarding against the intrinsic appeal that events and narrative hold for authors and readers alike,

Braudel suggests, is to slide out the interlocking compartments of the historian's spyglass until they are fully extended, and then to take in the longer sweep of history: '[T]he way to study history is to view it as a long duration, as what I have called the *longue durée*.' 'It is not', he cautions, 'the only way, but it is one which by itself can pose all the great problems of social structures, past and present.'[4] His willingness to concede that the longer view allows the historian to address the great problems of social structures, past *and* present, holds out the prospect of social historians' being able to use the *longue durée* to situate events and narrative in a more accurate and persuasive context. In theory, it should be possible to reconcile long and shorter time spans in ways that ultimately deepen and enhance historical explanation.

But if the *longue durée* helps historians situate *when* events and narratives that interest them unfold in a putatively causative, chronologically informed sequence, then it does not simultaneously address the question of *where* the determinative processes and structures were located. For Braudel, like Edward Said, history and geography are inextricably linked. Geography is not 'an end in itself but a means to an end. It helps us to rediscover the slow unfolding of structural realities, to see things in the perspective of the very long term'.[5] In this, Braudel's thinking was akin to that of David Hume, who argued that notions of space and time should remain coupled when searching for persuasive explanations.[6]

But this raises as many questions as answers for historians intent on testing the strength of the hinges of their cell doors. The cartographic representation of the space occupied by a continent or a country, for example, can vary over time according to the 'changing constellations of power, knowledge and geography' that influence patterns of cognition.[7] The radical changes that places undergo over time for any number of reasons, ranging from the environmental to a myriad of interventions attributable to human agency, thus demand a *spatial* as well as a historical imagination from the analyst. For the dislocated and the disrupted, the exiled or the homecoming, the migrant or the visitor, time, space and liminality all combine to necessitate and inform 'imaginative geographies'.[8]

The contemporary chronicler is locked into time and space just as surely as was Marco Polo when he recorded his experiences on the Silk Road. And just as Polo had to engage the 13th-century world of kings and kingdoms, tribes and territories, warriors and women, while moving through space and time, so historians in the post-Napoleonic world must deal with presidents and parliaments, borders and bureaucrats, a few trappings of the modern 'nation-state'. But what exactly is that?

In its purest form, Eric Hobsbawm argues, the 'nation' precedes the 'state', the latter of which, by the 20th century, also necessitated 'a totally independent, territorially and linguistically homogeneous, *secular* – and probably republican/parliamentary state – for each "people"'.[9] For those championing the idea of the 'nation-state', he suggests it also has to be cast as being 'progressive', that is, 'capable of developing a viable economy, technology, state organization and military force'.[10]

But, since modern nationalism underwent its most significant ideological and political development between 1880 and 1914, and acquired additional momentum outside Europe as the Western imperial powers waned, there have been instances where the 'state' has preceded the 'nation'.[11] Thus, on the old imperial margins and elsewhere, where the terms 'nation' and 'state' are now often used interchangeably in the mistaken belief in the existence of the nation-state, the underlying problems are often exposed through programmes of 'nation-building'. In truth, 'nations' can, and do, give rise to 'states', but in newly independent countries, erected over former arbitrarily defined colonial territories, 'states' are more frequently called upon to construct 'nations' than the other way round.

In countries in the making, the eldritch voices of nationalists in pursuit of a nation-state or state-nation emanate from two swamps that grip the patterns of latter-day thinking about how space and time relate to the present. The first is how convenient it is to forget that the often-contrived borders of ersatz states were a parting gift from the imperialists. Braudel has a warning for historians and nationalists alike: 'To draw a boundary around anything is to define, analyse, and reconstruct it ... [to] select, indeed adopt, a philosophy of history.'[12] Nationalists may be wise to speak no evil of the borders and maintain a discreet silence about the origins of their inheritance, but historians hoping to understand the social dynamics of a region need to be mindful of the hidden philosophy that comes from an uncritical acceptance of borders recently drawn, and how they shape and inform structures and processes that play out in real or imagined geographies.[13]

Second, in old and new states alike, 'the nation', as Benedict Anderson reminded us, is 'an imagined political community – and imagined as both inherently limited and sovereign', and is 'conceived of as a deep, horizontal comradeship'. For such 'limited imaginings', he tells us, millions are ready 'willingly to die'.[14] The present is at least as dangerous for the historian as the past. Historians need to be deeply suspicious of the 'nation-state' and the 'state-nation'; they are neither self-standing nor are their inner workings self-evident.

These theoretical concerns and warnings are of some importance to those who, within the confines of their cells in the quadrilateral prison, wish to erect makeshift laboratories of the mind in which they can conduct historical experiments. The real test, however, comes when abstract notions are forced to address the evidential realities that make for a convincing epistemology. How far can these theoretical considerations be turned into a workable methodology, and can cultural, social history be spatialised in the manner after Edward Said?

From abstraction to practice

Rendering time and space tractable for the purposes of writing history calls for choices with political implications for the practitioner. Undefined, the *longue durée* is of variable length, and so defining it becomes the historian's choice. So, too, with determining how time and space will be linked. 'Africa', that integrated, mythical entity that slides so easily off the tongues of some American tourists and nestles so tightly in the minds of nationalists intent on constructing an ideological entity, has a history that predates, and that will postdate, European imperialism.

There is, however, a crude logic in commencing a historical study in the age of imperialism and confining it to *southern*, as opposed to South Africa. From the 16th to the 20th century, southern Africa, a land mass pressed between two oceans, with a reasonably mountainous and better-watered east coast, was a poorly defined zone for a few competing and expanding European powers. For centuries a mere geographical footnote on an intervening continent for those in search of the greater prizes that lay to the east or west, it was, at various moments, of but passing interest to British, Dutch, German and Portuguese imperialists.

In southern Africa, the earliest imperial interventions along the east coast were by-products of explorations to discover a route to India and dated back to the 15th century. But it took two more centuries of trading in the Indian Ocean for the Cape of Storms – or 'Cape of Good Hope', if you are that way inclined – to be taken seriously as a potentially viable point for permanent European settlement. The extent, intensity and nature of rival European interventions, however, accelerated in the 19th century as the economic potential of the mineralised African interior was reassessed for possible realignment with the needs of the industrialising northern and western hemispheres. These fundamental settings of geography and history had enduring consequences for later developments in southern Africa that extended into the colonial era, and that will persist long into the post-colonial.

The same realities, truths of the *longue durée*, account for how 'different empires emerged, competed, and forged governing strategies, political ideas, and human affiliations', before the emergence of accepted and formalised boundaries of colonies, let alone nation-states.[15] Without an imperial perspective it is difficult to account for some of the features and historical dynamics that put the region on the path to modernity in the 20th century. How else is one to account for the ways in which, say, capital and labour were mobilised in southern Africa?

In what eventually became 'South Africa', capital was drawn into the country via the European and Atlantic Ocean networks, from the northern and western hemispheres. By contrast, unskilled and semi-skilled manual labour came from the Indian Ocean and beyond, from the near northern and eastern hemispheres. Slaves and indentured workers of colour were dispatched to the Cape, Natal and Transvaal from Madagascar, Mozambique, India, Indonesia, Malaysia and China in their hundreds of thousands to augment relatively small and pricey domestic sources of labour, long before the settlers joined economic forces to become the 'Union of South Africa'. The Union then manufactured its own black proletariat.

When thus viewed by social historians, over the *longue durée* and through a wider-angled lens, a slightly different perspective of contemporary southern Africa emerges. It allows one to see the cultural complementarities and conflicts between 'nations' and 'states' in a deeper and more meaningful context. It renders the brutal, short 20th century in episodic fashion that allows for a fascinating reconciliation of the historical concerns of Braudel and Hobsbawm.

For those examining regional dynamics, 20th-century southern Africa is best viewed not as a latticework of 'nations' and 'states' or free-standing, independent entities, as the finished products of an imperial history that has not yet passed. It is not the borders of 'states' that have failed, or are in the throes of failing, that should be taken too seriously but what happens across and between them, covertly and overtly. Southern Africa should be viewed, primarily, as a zone of transactional economic activity where interconnectedness and interdependence over the *longue durée* have given rise to asymmetric cultural, demographic, social and political exchanges. Transitional in nature, those exchanges, and especially those that took place 'despite rather than because', those that were less formal or institutionalised and more hidden than manifest, also contribute to its being seen as a liminal zone, a place squirming in the present, one forever in the making but never arriving. And to understand more fully how *that* applied to the proximate past, we need first to examine more closely the properties of the hollow colonies, 'nations' and 'states' that determined their modes of interaction over the troubled 20th century.

'Nation' and 'state' as reagents in South African history

For purposes of the *Three Wise Monkeys* collection, 'southern Africa' comprises what is now South Africa, Mozambique, Botswana, Eswatini, Lesotho, Namibia and Zimbabwe. But since dealing with so large an expanse over the *longue durée* is not feasible for a single researcher, the focus is drastically reduced. Our inquiry will be confined to an examination of the dynamics of the historical relationship that developed between the post-1910 Union of South Africa and the republic that followed it – an aspirant 'nation-state' – and southern Mozambique, part of a Portuguese colony that later acquired a few severely restricted nation- and state-like features before winning its own version of a full 'nation-state' in 1975. As we shall see below, this foundational asymmetry between the two territories was in and of itself of some significance.

Of the many temporal divides possible to draw when studying the history of southern Africa, few if any transcend the seminal distinction that can be made between the period prior to the mineral discoveries of 1867–1886 and the industrial revolution that they unleashed. Before Kimberley and Johannesburg, the future of the region lay on the land, in agriculture, and thereafter deep beneath it, in mining and in the emerging connections between the sectors.

In agrarian, pre-revolutionary southern Africa, in the late 1830s, several thousand indigenous Afrikaners, propelled by the schismatic politics that grew out of their strong dislike of the 'enlightened' Cape Colony, moved on to the Highveld, manifesting some of the cultural, religious and linguistic unity capable of informing a nation in the making. Indeed, if the black majority is ignored, then the Boer republics of the mid-19th century – agrarian and financially weak – vaguely resemble the more integrated 'nation-states' that emerged in Europe. A shadowy status, as 'states', was tacitly conceded by British imperialists who, after the discovery of diamonds and for much of the 1870s, sought, unsuccessfully, to coax the Boer republics into a confederation of white southern African states.[16]

It was British imperial military intervention, after the emergence of Kimberley and Johannesburg, in what Afrikaners cast as two 'wars of independence', that separated the Boer 'nations' from their 'state', thereby fuelling renewed nationalist resentment and the desire to re-establish an expanded, integrated republic in which the nation – ethnically defined – would be reunited in a stronger state.

After the British defeat of the republicans in the Anglo-Boer War of 1899–1902 (also known as the South African War), the division between rurally based Afrikaans/Dutch-speaking nationalists and city-dwelling, imperial-sympathising English speakers bedevilled white 'nation-building', except when it could be advanced at the expense of the marginalised African majority. But while sinister imperial music left politics and nation wary of attending any dance promoting unity, economics and the state soon got close enough to risk a waltz. The unlikely matchmaker was the recession of 1906–1908.

Imperial proconsul Alfred Milner's hope for the unification

of southern Africa had not been achieved by the time he left the Transvaal, in 1905, but the idea was alive if not well. His former assistant colonial secretary, Lionel Curtis, embraced the idea, spelling it out in a memorandum in 1906. It was followed, in 1907, by an even more famous memorandum by Milner's successor, Lord Selborne, that pointed in the same direction. By then, financial realities flowing from seriously faltering customs and railway revenues right across southern Africa, and cross-threaded by the ongoing regional threat posed by a competitive rail outlet at Delagoa Bay, in Mozambique, trumped many softer political imaginings. Curtis launched 'Closer Union Societies' across the country, along with a monthly journal named, significantly, *The State*.[17] The Union of South Africa, born in 1910, was neither a white 'nation' nor a 'state', just a swampy foundation for both.

For those Afrikaners believing that they were, if not already a 'nation' sharing a culture, language and religion, then one well in the making, the emergence of a 'nation-state', in republican form, would remain elusive until the 'state' was shorn of all constitutional links to the resented imperial order. In 1919, in the aftermath of World War I, they sent a 'freedom deputation' to Paris to seek 'complete independence' for a country not yet ten years old. In the 36 months that followed, the country acquired a gold refinery, a branch of the Royal Mint and a reserve bank – all signs of hurried state-making. Another big push and limited progress were achieved when, in 1926, the country gained autonomy through the Dominion status accorded it at that year's Imperial Conference.[18]

But, for hard-core Afrikaner nationalists, on a quest for sovereign independence, Dominion status was only one more shaky step on the long road to the republican state they aspired to. It took 35 years for them to reach their destination. Whites of differing inclinations were persuaded to provide the mandate for the declaration of a republic that eventually came in 1961. South Africa, or at least the white part of it, had the sovereign independence that it desired, along with a republican constitution. But even within that racially exclusive format, it was not yet supported by an identifiable culturally homogeneous 'nation'. Indeed, so profound was the challenge to this contrived republic from African nationalists that by the late 1960s, and in the decades that followed, South Africa, economically prosperous and politically bankrupt, was, arguably, more 'police state' than state.

An increasingly diversified and successful economy, backed by modern, sophisticated technology, an impressive transport infrastructure, a tolerably competent and reasonably uncorrupt civil service and a much-feared police force, along with an air force, army and navy fit for purpose, made for a strong state. As Simon Schama once noted, in a different context, 'States are built with hardware, but nations run on software.'[19] South Africa's first three state-building prime ministers had all been generals, and a militaristic sequel was not out of keeping with its historical trajectory. A country with a name derived only from its geographical position was still a state in search of a 'nation'. It had long since lost its way.

Like a dachshund wobbling along behind a whippet, the idea of 'the nation' – always conceived of as white – could never keep up with the 'state' through a revolutionary century that started with the bloodiest imperial war Britain had known. 'Unification' was followed by a rural rebellion by Afrikaner nationalists in 1914, mobilisation for the imperial war effort in 1914–1918 and an urban revolt by radicalised, mainly English-speaking miners in 1922. Collectively, these events failed to lay some of the groundwork necessary for the emergence of a broader 'national' identity underpinned largely by a common racial identity.

It took decades to wear down the sharper edges of angular imperialist and nationalist sentiments that continuously rubbed up against one another. In 1925, 15 years after Union, Afrikaans received official recognition as a national language and the following year saw the publication of 'Die Stem van Suid-Afrika'. Eighteen years after Union, in 1928, the country acquired a national flag. Ten years after that, in 1938, it adopted 'Die Stem' as a national anthem that could be sung along with 'God Save the King' to the irritation of both parties. Some union, some nation! The country was being held together by mere dabs of state glue.

The core of an authentic idea of a white 'nation' sharing a common culture, language and religion rested almost exclusively in Afrikaner hands. It remained part of a project to gain political power in ethnically exclusive fashion, which would facilitate growing racial separation in ways that their secretive ginger grouping, the Afrikaner Broederbond, and the Dutch Reformed churches never let go of.

And the more strident they became in their demands and ideals, the less were the chances of cultivating a more organic, socially rooted national identity among whites, let alone their African, Asian or coloured countrymen and -women.

Except for brief moments of pride deriving from great sporting triumphs, or from closer involvement in two world wars, it was difficult to detect the voice of a truly national choir rising above parties singing from different song sheets. It was, still is and may always be like that. In 1941, amid the travails of World War II, an author with an eye on the nationalist vanguard in a racist whites-only 'democracy' published a book under the provocative title *There Are No South Africans*.[20] When asked, in 1952, how they self-identified, Broederbonders came up with the wisdom of Solomon. They were both 'Afrikaners' and 'South Africans', but what distinguished them from English speakers was a 'strong Calvinist character'.[21]

After 1990, some urban black South Africans began referring fondly to the country of their birth as Mzansi – now a term much loved by African radio personalities. For those hoping that the word might have moved beyond the familiar prison of geography, it may have come across as a touch disappointing. The term has little inherent emotional or linguistic resonance. It means 'south' in isiXhosa. Not surprisingly, militant African nationalists looked to a more distinctive name, advocating 'Azania', perhaps not realising that Evelyn Waugh had used it for a fictional east African country in his 1932 novel *Black Mischief*.

Nor did the advent of democracy, in 1994, sow the seeds for a more encompassing, lasting national identity other than for a transient moment after a Rugby World Cup triumph that was put to good use by Nelson Mandela, in 1995. Beneath all the bonhomie of a 'new' South Africa lurked profound old ethnic, if not racial, sentiments. Archbishop Desmond Tutu sought to square the circle for a fevered press with his idea of a 'rainbow nation'. The preferred national anthem of African nationalists had long since been '*Nkosi Sikelel' iAfrika*', a plea for God to bless Africa that had, conveniently, tagged on to it part of a hymn in Sesotho. A year later, in 1996, Mandela's successor, Thabo Mbeki, made his famous 'I am an African' speech to a 'nation' composed of those of African, Asian, coloured and European descent. Not much evidence of a primary loyalty to South Africa there, prompting yet another frustrated author to ask, *Do South Africans Exist?* at a time when the state was already clearly failing.[22] Things had, apparently, not gone all that well.

A historian of southern Africa may therefore be forgiven for not taking the concepts of 'nation-state' and 'state-nation' too seriously when examining the arc of regional political dynamics in the 20th century. Neither is a consolidated, self-evidently meaningful notion capable of yielding definitive, stand-alone explanations. For sceptics, they are perhaps better understood as liminal longings. And if that is true for South Africa, then how much more so for Mozambique?

Mozambique: Ersatz colony, settler 'state' and 'nation'

The search for, and discovery of, a passage to India as a trading destination ensured that, for 150 years, from circa 1500 to 1650, tropical Mozambique was of greater interest to the European powers than was the remote, temperate Cape of Storms. In the age of sail, the inhaling and exhaling of the monsoon across the Indian Ocean presented Mozambique with a seasonal geographical advantage that the cooler Mediterranean climate of southern Africa, trapped between the Atlantic and the Indian oceans, could never match fully.

While the spice trade was almost as important as that in gold, if not more so, Portugal had an enduring stake in coastal Mozambique but took, almost literally, only passing notice of southern Africa. Monsoon winds locked Mozambique and India into a trading template of inestimable value, while the stormy Cape, where ships paused for basic reprovisioning, led to nowhere of known interest. Initially, Portugal administered its would-be African colony from Goa, in India, and then, from the 16th century on, from a northerly fortress erected on Ilha de Moçambique (Mozambique Island).

For centuries, Mozambique looked out over the Indian Ocean, to the northeast, when trading in ivory and other commodities, while over the same period it bled hundreds of thousands of African men, women and children as chattel slaves into the rapidly developing plantation economies of the Atlantic world. The 19th-century discoveries of diamonds and gold inverted the gaze of the still ill-defined coastal strip, and especially its southernmost part, the Sul do Save – the area south of the Save River. By the mid-1890s, once primary resistance by Africans had at last been fully overcome by the Portuguese, the territory had taken on more of the appearance of a colony and was governed from Lourenço Marques.

Braudel leads the way to understanding what happened next. 'Assuming that there are entities, economic zones with relatively definite boundaries', he writes, 'would not a method of observation based on geographical location prove useful?' Mozambique's historical flip, from looking to the north and east for its material benefit to looking to the south and west, may have been unusual but was not without historical precedent. Eighteenth-century France, turning its back on its Mediterranean trade, wheeled around and faced the Atlantic, transforming its 'trade routes, markets, and cities'.[23] What *was* unusual was that southern Mozambique was subjected to not one but two successive bouts of colonisation – the first by Portugal and commerce, the second by South Africa and industry. The Sul do Save became, in effect, South Africa's fifth province, the subject of a form of sub-imperialism both bedevilling and retarding 'state' formation in a colony.

The importance of the flip was not immediately evident to Lisbon's commercially minded elite. Even as the South African diamond fields began attracting significant fixed investment, and telltale urban patterning became evident on the Highveld, the government in Portugal continued to see Mozambique as little more than a coastal strip distantly linked to its own fortunes in Goa. Indeed, were it not for hesitancy on the part of Lord Kimberley, Britain could have acquired Delagoa Bay for £12 000 in 1872. Twenty-five years later, Cecil Rhodes arrived in Lourenço Marques, cheque book in hand, still believing that he could buy the finest harbour on the east coast. The idea of perhaps selling parts of the continent or, if not, subletting huge swathes of it to chartered companies on a scale that beggared belief remained central to thinking in influential Lisbon circles well into the 20th century. Mozambique was so much African real estate.[24]

The illusory western borders of a territory more actively imagined than presided over by the ambitious Lisbon Geographical Society acquired slightly more meaningful proportions a decade or more later.

It was the great continental carve-up by the imperial powers, at the Berlin Conference of 1884–1885, that settled on 'effective occupation' as being the *sine qua non* for legitimate colonisation. Even then, not much happened on the ground, and it took the infamous British ultimatum of 1890 for Lisbon to prompt more rigorous demarcation of the western boundaries of a 'colony' that the African majority often chose to ignore.

A ribbon of coastline of indeterminate standing, aspiring to become a colony comparable to others on the continent, meant that a vulnerable Mozambique continued to occupy a prominent place in the political imaginations of imperial powers and the increasingly assertive state on its southwestern border well into the 20th century. Even before World War I, Germany and Britain had reached a cynical agreement that, should Portugal ever fail, they would split Mozambique in two, with the United Kingdom appropriating the southern half, abutting South Africa, and the Germans the northern half. For its part, South Africa was quite open about its desire to acquire Delagoa Bay well into the 1920s. Indeed, that decade was marked by several intense – bullying, unequal – economic, diplomatic and financial exchanges between South Africa and the Mozambican administration.[25]

The Mozambique 'state', financially starved for much of the 20th century, was all bone and no muscle. It lacked the resources to make the transition from a spectre-like 'colony' to something more closely approximating a 'state'. Throughout the interwar years, the South African Police (SAP) regularly sent detectives to Lourenço Marques to monitor what it considered criminal activity, without so much as a by-your-leave to the local administration. Until the threat posed by insurgent African nationalists in the mid-1960s, Lourenço Marques lacked the capacity to enforce its authority or laws evenly across the vast domains that it laid claim to. In the closing decade of colonial rule, it was the PIDE, Portugal's feared secret police, that provided the state with the increased powers of surveillance necessary for more widespread control and oppression of a functioning colony destined to become a different type of 'state'.[26] The armed forces, too, struggled.

In 1895, a Portuguese military force defeated Ngungunyane, an exceptional effort putting paid to the last of the Gaza chiefdoms, but successful mobilisation and victory on that scale was unusual. Quotidian rule, even in the heart of the Sul do Save, was difficult to maintain with any conviction. The disturbances in Lourenço Marques in 1895 may have been unusually challenging given what was happening elsewhere, but Stanley Hollis, the veteran United States consul, described army, police and navy attempts to enforce some order as 'quite useless'.

Lacking anything approaching a modern rail or road transport network in the countryside, the administration's hold on the Sul do Save was largely fictional, other than when collecting taxes. For many decades the Witwatersrand Native Labour Association (WNLA), the recruitment agency for the Transvaal mines, had more uniformed personnel on the ground than did the colonial administration. A Portuguese official readily conceded that the WNLA ran a 'parallel administration' and constituted 'a state within a state'.[27] From the turn of the 20th century and into the 1920s, South Africa 'stole' the province's black male labour by paying wages that declined steadily in value, while at least a third of all cash remittances to the Sul do Save sent by black migrant miners were misappropriated or simply purloined by postal officials or other corrupt, poorly remunerated civil servants.[28]

Without a central bank that accounted solely to the Lourenço Marques administration, the colony's financial fortunes were overseen by a privately owned bank, in Lisbon. It was a financial drain and contributed to the chronic weakness of local and metropolitan currencies, which could not compete successfully with their British and South African rivals. It took the 1926 coup in Portugal, and the long-term dictatorial rule of António Salazar, to provide the colony with a better-regulated regime of poverty. By the late 1950s, Mozambique had barely acquired the stark outline of a severely underdeveloped colonial state. The 'state', resented by settlers for its inbuilt metropolitan bias, was poorly positioned to build a 'nation'.

There was, in any case, insufficient by way of economic progress and urban development to nurture a positive identification with the colony by many if not most Portuguese settlers. They were more inclined to have negative sentiments directed at far-off Lisbon, or at South African predations in the regionally skewed market for cheap black labour. In 1911, there were fewer than 10 000 Portuguese in the colony, a number that did not grow markedly during the interwar period when a few thousand women – always at a premium – chose

Mozambique as their destination. By 1955, the number of settlers had crept up to around 110 000 and by 1970, probably at its peak, stood at just about 200 000.[29]

In the opening decades of the 20th century, complaints of neglect by Mozambican settlers and the political shortcomings of the Lisbon or Lourenço Marques administrations tended – in order of preference – to be ignored, suppressed through the deportation of individuals or, when all else failed, inadequately accommodated.[30] Organised settler resentments were at their most pronounced throughout the financially strained 1920s. Small-scale farmers resented the WNLA's recruitment practices, while others, such as the 'fascist-like' Liga de Defesa e Propaganda de Moçambique, hoping to promote agriculture on a much larger, commercial scale, objected to the dominance of the chartered companies.[31]

In urban Lourenço Marques, poorly remunerated state railway employees led the resistance to a parsimonious administration, culminating in a notably violent strike in 1925–1926. But it was the dictator, Salazar, who effectively put paid to organised political resistance by local whites. Between 1961 and 1974 Salazar and his successors in the Estado Novo resolutely refused to delegate political powers to the Mozambican settlers, contributing to escalating political tensions throughout the empire.[32] When the Armed Forces Movement overthrew the Lisbon government in the Carnation Revolution of April 1974, it heralded the end of Portuguese colonialism in Africa. In Mozambique, it helped set off an unsuccessful settler countercoup in which the state's former law enforcement officers were prominent, resulting in the loss of 3 000 lives – mostly African.[33]

Violent settler eruptions in the urban south were, however, few and far between. A weak sense of national identity usually went hand in hand with transient political organisations that tended to come to the fore only during periodic crises, such as in the 1920s, or in other moments of extremis.[34] Distance, isolation and small numbers simultaneously undermined and contributed to the social solidarity of a confused, inchoate, part-Mozambican/Portuguese, part-colonial/national identity.

White Mozambicans drew a distinction between those born and raised in the country, so-called *naturais da colónia*, and recent immigrants with stronger ties to metropolitan Portugal. To the extent that the former constituted the core of an emerging 'national' identity, it was rendered corporeal through widespread miscegenation. In the absence of large numbers of white women of marriageable age, many Portuguese males, urban and rural, acquired African mistresses or wives, giving rise to a sizeable coloured or *mestiço* population. The important 'mixed race' element within the population, authentically and indubitably Mozambican in nature, added a little stiffening to the weak settler nationalism.[35]

Coloured females occupied an important subliminal place in the white male colonial imagination. Mulatto women were perceived as beautiful, seductive and sexually charged, contributing to the image of Mozambique and Angola as being places that were both exotic and erotic – a view shared by many white males across the region.[36] It was part of the settler mindset and ostensibly directly at odds with the purported beliefs about race and sex held by white South Africans.

The seemingly easy-going accommodation of the offspring of white male and black female couplings or marriages was never wholly incompatible with the pervasive racist beliefs and values of settlers. Miscegenation and racist attitudes were not necessarily drawn from different universes; in truth, they were blood brothers, coexisting uneasily alongside one another.[37] In Mozambique, *mestiços* were often as readily marginalised in the wider society and the workplace as were Africans. At various historical moments the Lourenço Marques administration and settlers openly expressed their admiration for certain notoriously oppressive and racist South African institutions and practices, such as compounds, job reservation and segregation.[38] Indeed, in some instances, they went out of their way to accommodate the prejudices and practices of their southern neighbours.

Yet, for all their willingness to play host to South African visitors and, where necessary, pander publicly or privately to racist attitudes, the Portuguese administration and settlers remained officially committed to an ideology of assimilation and non-racialism. For much of the 20th century, then, and more especially so after the advent of apartheid in 1948, Portuguese and South African ideologies and political postures were – formally, at least – at variance. It meant that for the better part of half a century, but more noticeably so in the economically buoyant

1960s, some white South Africans, although lacking an easily identi-fiable national identity, became increasingly arrogant, demanding or openly racist when visiting 'non-racial' southern Mozambique.

Cultural clashes and misunderstandings between Mozambican entrepreneurs and white South African visitors in the tourist sector over Portuguese bureaucracy, currency and exchange rates, a 'Mediterranean' lifestyle and race relations had long been features of their interactions.[39] Two slowly developing, partly overlapping, partly conflicting 'national' identities rubbed up against one another, necessitating consistent reminders to the South Africans of the need to be more relaxed, tolerant and understanding of their Portuguese-Mozambican hosts. It was a rea-sonably constant theme in tourist guides through much of the century.

Having alerted his readers to some of the awkwardness arising from different lifestyles in Johannesburg and Lourenço Marques shortly after World War I, the author of an article in the *South African Railways & Harbours Magazine* urged his countrymen and women to 'be charitable and give our Latin neighbours the benefit of the doubt!' Portuguese ways, it seemed, needed to be tolerated rather than embraced. By 1960, the difference in the professed political outlooks and national identities of the two countries had become sufficiently stark for the officially endorsed *Lourenço Marques Guide* (which ran to several editions) to devote an entire chapter to 'Human Relations in the Portuguese World'.[40]

Confronted by visitors from an industrial powerhouse, the *Guide* acknowledged that although the Portuguese were 'sometimes unable to compete with others in material progress', this did not equate to 'moral progress'. A poor translation from the original Portuguese reminded apartheid-supporting white South Africans that they were increasingly out of step with the modern world. They were now in a particular time and place, in 'a global society where there will be no place to dom-inative exclusivisms' (*sic*) and in which Mozambique was a part of Portugal, where 'the colour of an individual does not count in human relations'. In cafés, restaurants and tea rooms, visitors would have to sit 'side by side' with 'different races' who would be served 'without the least distinction'. But tourists need not be too fearful; colonial culture had not completely disappeared: 'Observe also the correctness of the Portuguese African with his frank and respectful smile.'[41]

But, if the guidebooks are to be believed, South African visitors appear to have learnt little if anything. A decade after assuming republican status, and in the face of growing international isolation, their individual and collective behaviour towards civil servants, the police and operatives in the Mozambican tourist industry seems to have deteriorated. To the extent that they were manifesting a 'national' identity, there were several troublesome characteristics on display that needed curbing. In 1971, *Holiday in Mozambique: A Guide to the Territory* contained a few explicit warnings to tourists from across the region.

It was asserted that the 'Portuguese, like all Latin people, are a cheerfully philosophical and unhurried lot', but resented being pushed too far. It was 'a crime to use words offensive to Portuguese currency' and 'impolite South Africans had faced such charges'. 'Impatience and discourtesy', especially by young people, caused friction, and 'insulting the local constabulary' had seen a few adolescents being sent to the cells for the night. Indulged to excess, even a playground for the imagination could result in some psychological damage.[42]

The racist beliefs shared by Mozambican settlers of Portuguese origin and white South Africans were insufficient to guarantee good relations among people of European descent drawn from across the region. Obviously, most interpersonal or group clashes could be attributed to manifest differences of class, culture and language among the whites. But, important as those considerations were, they could not account fully for several other mass-based interactions and phenomena that characterised the simultaneously accommodating and rejecting historical relationship between South Africa and Mozambique. There were other things at work, things that now seem obvious, things hidden within plain sight.

Hidden catalysts in a regional dynamic

If the history of Protestant southern Africa commenced with the arrival of Jan and Maria van Riebeeck at the Cape, in 1652, then that, too, is an event that requires placing within the *longue durée*. It was not yet 150 years since Luther had nailed his 95 theses to the Castle Church door, in Wittenberg, signalling his break from the Roman Catholic

Church and the start of the Reformation. In 1688, only 36 years after the van Riebeecks had landed, the first Huguenots, refugees from a resentful Catholic France, arrived to bolster the number of Christians as encouraged by the VOC, the founding Dutch East India Company,

The European settlement at the Cape of Storms came with an open and official invitation to Protestantism, and a sullen rejection of Catholicism, which had first appeared on the Mozambican coast with the Portuguese explorers in 1498 – 200 years earlier. For 400 years, from the 17th to the 20th century, and on into the present, Protestants and Catholics have held different views about God's earthly dispensation, the strengths and weaknesses of human nature and the one route to salvation. Differing mindsets, formal and informal, shaped the ways (of which there could only ever really be one) that 'true believers' cast one another and their colonised African subjects, behaved towards each other and found business opportunities that were in accordance with their theological tenets.

Religious beliefs, catalysts of greater or lesser strength, acting singly or reacting collectively, preceded 19th-century attempts at constructing nation-states or state-nations. The questions that then arise for historians of southern Africa are how, when and where did the Afrikaner 'nations' and 'states' of the 19th and 20th centuries accommodate, entrench or promote the legal standing of Protestantism on the Highveld, and Portuguese colonialists Catholicism on the east coast? Furthermore, how well, or poorly, did the resulting legal dispensations articulate with the subsequent revolutionary arc of economic history across the region?

Calvinism and the long march north

For a century and a half, as post-Reformation Dutch settlers moved slowly inland, neither their Netherlands Reformed Church, heavily influenced by the teachings of Jean Calvin (1509–1564), nor the less long-lived VOC (until 1795), tolerated the public expression of other faiths in the colony, Christian or non-Christian. In effect, the colony for some time had all the makings of a slowly expanding, Dutch, Protestant 'state' supported informally by an 'established' church.

The annexation of the Cape by the British in 1806 did little to change two sets of underlying Calvinist beliefs for adherents, one 'positive' and dangerous, the other negative, deriving from fear of Napoleonic France and any residual Catholicism.

First, most Cape Dutch colonists had confidence in Calvinist notions of the elect and predestination. These inherently problematic ideas carried within them the potential for assuming greater importance and a different, more overtly political trajectory when confronted by non-believers in contested colonial situations.[43] Second, a fear of the Catholic Church might be transported north by those moving beyond the colony's borders, manifesting itself as religious intolerance.

The freeing of the enslaved in the Cape by the British, in 1838, combined with other factors to provide added impetus for those Dutch settlers intent on creating new lives for themselves by trekking north and onto the plateau that dominates the southern African interior. The resulting small-scale scattered populations encouraged parochialism and political conflict among the trekkers, tensions that were occasionally also overlain by developing religious schisms. By 1860, the mother church, the Cape-centred Nederduitse Gereformeerde Kerk (NGK), had seen the emergence of two new northern sister churches, the slightly less dogma-driven Nederduitse Hervormde Kerk and the smaller, more sect-like, ultra-conservative Gereformeerde Kerk, whose adherents were popularly known as 'Doppers'. All three churches, however, remained staunchly Calvinist in outlook.[44]

Living up to the austere measures of social and self-discipline demanded by Calvinism, as first enforced and practised in Geneva, was never easy. Abstinence, frugality and sobriety, forgoing cursing, dancing and gambling, along with the need for strict Sunday observance, were demanding habits and virtues requiring great application by individuals, who were then subjected to communal surveillance and vigilance. The disciplinary revolution that Calvinism set off was predicated partly on 'self-observation, mutual observation, [and] hierarchical observation' that, over time, could also be harnessed for the purposes of 'political power and domination'.[45] The state, operating in a different sphere and plane, was God's creation, one of its primary functions being to facilitate the salvation of the elect. Personal freedoms were less important than religious freedoms.[46]

A daunting Calvinist regimen, along with its need to fend off the threat of its long-standing bogey, Catholicism – together with its English cousin, Anglicanism – was, arguably, more easily accommodated in agrarian, commercial, ethnically confined and sparsely populated southern Africa during the first half of the 19th century than it was in the latter half, when the country had to contend with challenges arising from industrialisation, urbanisation and an increase in population drawn from different faiths. Farms and hamlets such as Calvinia (founded in 1850) or small market towns were unlikely hosts to the most notorious vices to which humanity fell prey, and were more inclined to pulse to diurnal and seasonal rhythms than those of the clock or the calendar. Yet, despite the relative absence of temptation, small communities were subjected to rigorous moral policing by the dominee (pastor) and his deacons, reinforced through the twins of fear and respect that came with *huisbesoek* – regular home visits.[47]

North of the Vaal River, the constitution of the South African Republic specifically forbade the establishment of Roman Catholic churches, a provision that was repealed in 1870, shortly after the start of the mineral revolution, then still well to the south.[48] Self-regulation by Calvinists, in a rural universe, required little external intervention by the state in the form of legislation, but the rise of Kimberley, in the 1870s, and Johannesburg, in the 1890s, posed new challenges to the church, a Dutch-Afrikaner 'nation' in the making and the state.

In the new mining towns of the interior, the Afrikaner-Dutch Reformed churches and the Anglophone Methodist, Presbyterian and Lutheran churches – each insistent on doctrinal specificities that could not readily be reduced to 'Calvinist' – met on a new battleground for souls. Yet, for all the differences between the various Protestant denominations, they frequently allied themselves with the militantly Calvinist NGK when it came to presenting a united front against the social excesses of an encroaching industrialising order. For good reason, the Afrikaner faithful of the late 19th century were wont to refer to Johannesburg as *Duiwelsdorp* – Satan's City. For Protestant ministers, the most egregious and visible violation of the commandments, the Mosaic command most in need of reinforcement by the state, was the injunction to observe the Sabbath. Not only was it a self-serving canon that supposedly encouraged – when all it really did was to try and stabilise – attendance at church, but it lent itself to visible policing.

Nowhere can the transition from Calvinism-of-the-countryside to Calvinism-of-the-city be tracked more readily than through the passing of Sunday observance legislation. The contrast between pre- and post-industrial legislation in this regard is as stark as it is revealing. Prior to the discovery of diamonds, in 1867, colonial white southern Africa was subject to but one law enforcing Sunday observance. Act 1 of 1838 in the Cape Colony dated back – perhaps not entirely coincidentally – to the year that saw the first exodus of Afrikaner-Dutch discontents and the freeing of the enslaved. Neither of the agrarian Boer republics, the Orange Free State or the Transvaal, saw the need for such a law.

Once the country began pulsing to the beat of industrial time and machinery as demanded by continuous operation of diamond and gold mines, however, the need to safeguard the Sabbath proceeded apace across much of the country. True, in the farming towns of the Orange Free State, Calvinists slept on peacefully. Indeed, the legal klaxon only sounded there through Ordinance 21 of 1902. But in Natal, mills producing sugar destined for the diamond fields were governed by the new, selectively applied Law 24 of 1878. The original Cape Act was amended twice, in 1883 and 1886, and by 1895 things in Kimberley had reached such a pitch it took the Lord's Day Observance Act 19 of 1895 to prevent dancing in public on Sundays. But it was at the heart of the new order, in the Transvaal, where the emerging gold-mining industry ran slap-bang into President SJP Kruger's Dopper-dominated government, that legislation was demanded most urgently and passed in the wake of the boom of 1895 – the formidable Act 28 of 1896.[49]

The importance of these late-19th-century enactments, which remained on the statute book for more than a century, and were enforced on a discretionary basis in the four provinces of the Union and republic, has attracted almost no attention beyond that of a few legal scholars.[50] The Sunday laws have been studiously ignored by most historians and sociologists. Sunday observance and other legislation, born of the disquiet experienced by Afrikaner-Dutch ministers of religion accustomed to a Calvinism-of-the-countryside, came to occupy a position of some importance in shaping the industrial discipline, social lives and recreational preferences of South Africa's mainly white, English-speaking urban proletariat in the 20th century, where they were widely resented, albeit quietly endorsed, by many of the leading Anglophone Protestant churches.

The grip of the churches on the legislature and the agencies of the state was unrelenting until well into the 20th century. At the behest of the Calvinists, parliament passed the Prohibition of the Exhibition of Films on Sundays and Public Holidays Act 16 of 1977.[51] 'In the pre-1994 era of South African history', writes a legal scholar, 'its political authorities never even pretended to be religiously neutral; nor did the law of the country seek to isolate law from religion or to uphold the separation of Church and State.'[52] More intriguingly, many strictures governing Sunday observance linger on in 21st-century statutes.[53]

But, as Highveld Protestants discovered soon enough, applying Calvin's precepts, as unfolded in commercial Geneva in the 16th century, was less easily achieved in the industrial cities of the 19th century. Underground mining and milling operations, pumping water out of shafts and other safety precautions were part of continuous, integrated, ceaseless production processes not readily compatible with rigidly enforced Sunday observance legislation. Nor could the mining industry's requirements be isolated fully from ancillary activities, such as the generation of electricity or the running of rail services. In the countryside, ministers of religion and elected representative had relatively direct, unmediated access to small numbers of craft workers, farmers, shopkeepers and townsfolk when attempting to enforce respect for the Sabbath. But in cities they were confronted by a powerful third party when they sought to enforce Sunday observance – industrial capitalists who bent the knee to profit rather than prophet.

In short, there was a world of difference between enforcing Calvinism-in-the-countryside and Calvinism-in-the-city. Strict Sunday observance in sparsely populated rural constituencies, where the proximity of 'church' and 'nation' made for a natural, almost organic alliance at election time, allowed them to speak with one voice to the state. In densely populated industrial constituencies, however, where the hold of the church was uncertain and the idea of the 'nation' contested, the 'state' was forced to pay additional attention to the capitalists and workers.

The mining revolution confronted urban Protestants and their rural political allies with an insoluble problem. How were they to arrive at a coherent policy capable of reconciling the demand of the capitalists for continuous industrial production with the need to enforce Sunday observance, or for white employees who were, often simultaneously, struggling to limit the number of hours in the working week and increase their leisure and recreational time? The entire exercise required a double standard that 'church', 'nation' and 'state' came to be as willing to embrace as they found it awkward to manage. The Calvinists and their friends would see, hear and speak no evil when it came to the needs of industrial capitalists but would remain ultra-vigilant in ensuring the Sabbath was observed by white workers. It was a messy outcome that mirrored the Protestant churches' approach to the issue of gambling. Horse racing, the sport of kings, and of the capitalists, would go largely unchallenged, but other forms of working-class gambling needed to be curbed.

Calvinism was up against capitalism. From Kruger's ultraconservative Doppers in the late 19th century to the belated liberalisation of the other Dutch Reformed churches in the later part of the 20th, Sunday observance legislation groaned beneath contradictions, exemptions and incoherence. The Doppers were at first as concerned with rural brethren as they were with urban interlopers. Law No. 2 of 1888, amended by Act 16 of 1894, informed burghers responding to new markets that they were not to shoot game on Sundays, attend to their gardens or fields needlessly, or transport goods across urban boundaries.

But the mining boom of 1895 witnessed such an increase in the tempo of urban capitalism that Kruger's legislature felt the need for renewed intervention. Law No. 28 of 1896, which replaced the previous Sunday laws, reinforced provisions aimed at those Boer transgressors heading for the market but, grudgingly, accommodated a few of the needs of the new deep-level mining operations. Sunday observance no longer applied to 'working with machinery in the public service, viz. on railways, and for lighting and for the pumping of water for public use'. The noisy crushing of quartz, which disturbed churches and citizens alike, was prohibited, but the pumping of water on mines was allowed. Social excesses were curbed when *all* public entertainments, including dog- and cockfighting, were banned.[54]

Following the Anglo-Boer War, the Milner reconstruction administration, set on reviving the economy via the mining industry in the face of growing militancy on the part of Anglophone white miners, could not afford to intervene too directly in the question of Sunday observance. The birth of the Union of South Africa in 1910, however, provided rural Calvinists, well represented in the new parliament, with the opportunity of linking up with urban trade unionists to advance the cause of Sunday observance, to the disadvantage of mine owners and industrialists.[55] The new parliament had been seated for barely a year when, in August 1911, it appointed a wide-ranging Sunday Observance Commission. It became a watershed moment in the clash between Calvinism-in-the-countryside and Calvinism-in-the city, giving rise to the historic compromise that we have already noted – going softly on the requirements of capitalists and hard on those of the workers.

Under the chairmanship of HJ Hofmeyr, five commissioners were empowered to examine the existing legislation, determine the extent to which Sunday labour was being performed in the provinces and how changes in legislation might affect it and, if necessary, make recommendations 'as to the necessity or otherwise' of new legislation to govern the observance of the Sabbath. It was a fudge commission and, like most such commissions, came up with fudged findings two years later.[56]

The commissioners reported that examining the subject 'under modern industrial conditions' in all its 'ethical, humanitarian, religious, eugenic, and financial bearing might well occupy the time and energy of a number of commissions' since it 'bristles with difficulties'. Not the least of their problems was that the state was, by far, the largest employer of labour in the country. The private and public sectors of the economy simply did not lend themselves to ready separation. The commissioners were firmly of the opinion that while 'there *should* be no direct connection between the Church and the State', the religious aspect of the [Sunday observance] question could not be 'a matter of indifference to the State'.

They criss-crossed the country, convening 54 formal meetings and taking evidence from every major institution of relevance and 175 witnesses. Aware of the danger of speaking with too pronounced a Calvinist accent when addressing Christians, the commissioners were at pains to challenge the popularly rooted idea that 'the Roman Catholic Church does not concern itself greatly with the observance of Sunday', and were eager to receive the blessing of Pretoria's Catholic bishop. There was no reason to sound out the opinions of Africans, Hindus, Jews or Muslims. South Africans were at work constructing a white Christian 'nation' and 'state'.

The most important vectors of an integrating economy were reported on, in laundry-list fashion, documenting the nature and quantum of labour engaged in Sunday work, from mining, railways and harbours to domestic service. The published report ran to 50 pages, with an appendix containing a 'Declaration on the Observance of Sunday', providing the churches with the authoritative voice demanded by Christians. The recommendations dished up little more than a tired old status quo stew, spiced so mildly that no one had cause to reach for water.

'On the whole, the Sunday observance laws of this country have worked satisfactorily', the report intoned. An 'ideal law' would stipulate that no person 'be allowed to carry on his occupation for more than six consecutive days', but the 'chief difficulty of legislating on these lines is the financial one'. 'The running of mills, or other machinery used for crushing ore, and erected before the Mines and Works Act No. 12 of 1911, [should] cease within a period of three years' if any new legislation was forthcoming. No coaling of ships should be allowed on Sundays and the state should 'endeavour' to 'limit the running of Sunday goods trains'.

'Financial' considerations determined that the functioning of the public and private sectors of the economy should not be jeopardised by proscribing Sunday work. But, in deference to Calvin and the other Protestant churches, the same tolerance was not extended to that part of the economy catering to the need for leisure, recreation or sport of white workers after six days of labour. In keeping with the already established, two-decade-old Dopper view of the world and that of their Anglophone Protestant church allies, it would be unlawful 'to carry on, advertise, engage in, or be present at any public performance, spectacle, exhibition, game, contest, competition, or other entertainment of whatever kind at which any fee or payment is charged or demanded [on Sundays]'.[57]

The recommendations and the spirit, if not the letter, of the Sunday laws shaped much of South African social life throughout the 20th century. Laws that underwrote the rhythm of the working week and helped ensure productive labour on Monday mornings were silently approved of by employers keen to eliminate the after-effects of any excesses among white workers arising from drinking or gambling over the weekend. Capital marched in lockstep with the churches.[58] And, as the century unfolded, this and other notions of social discipline, pioneered by the Dutch Reformed churches and followed by English-speaking Protestants, became embedded in the fusion of neo-Calvinist ideas with Afrikaner nationalist political aspirations after World War II.[59] They made for a 'civil religion' championed by the insurgent National Party intent on shaping a 'nation' within a republic.[60]

And just as notions of stricter Sunday observance could be traced back to the Reformation, so, too, could the condemnation of idleness and the injunction to work – ideas central to Max Weber's famous 'Protestant ethic'. God, it was believed, smiled on work, and those who refused to engage freely in it could, if necessary, be forcibly subjected to corrective treatment. In England, the Bridewell Hospital was converted into a workhouse, of Dickensian fame, in 1557, and in the Netherlands, correcting indolence or vagrancy could be traced back to the House of Discipline, or *Tuchthuis*, founded in 1596.[61] Both institutions, it might be noted, bore a passing resemblance to the *kampong*, or compound – a confined workspace, or a village – that entered the Cape lexicon via the southeast Asian slave trade in the 17th century and was later applied, primarily, to the housing of black workers in the labour-repressive diamond and gold mines of the north.

Hard manual labour was almost exclusively the province of black men, as slaves, indentured labourers in the countryside and urban industrial or mine workers restrained by oppressive pass laws in the colonial economies. But, by insisting that *work* was the only legitimate way of acquiring the comforts of wealth, Calvin, if not God, had shown himself to be colour-blind. In southern Africa, the predestination of the self-elected imposed a burden on the governing classes, requiring them to set an example to 'idle' blacks that was beyond moral reproach.

Flagrant, persistent white drunkenness or indolence was intolerable. In 1893, the 'mother church', the NGK, set up the first white work colony intent on rehabilitating those suffering from social pathologies attributable to the growing landlessness that accompanied the mineral revolution. Over time, the short-circuiting of neo-Calvinist religious precepts and political ideals dear to Afrikaner nationalists fused, giving rise to the same 'civil religion' that allowed the state to foreclose on space previously dominated by the church. Acts 20 of 1927 and 25 of 1949 saw the state assume control of the work colonies that were only abandoned in the 1960s, once the rise of the police state and the extension of military conscription for young men made new demands on white manpower.[62]

The shortcomings of hundreds of work-shy individuals suffering from mental or physical inabilities paled, however, beside the lot of hundreds of thousands of ordinary men and women searching for way out of routinised drudgery, and for a life free of work, through the purchase of lottery tickets. It was not only the lottery that appealed to the mass of white workers and their wives and children but several other forms of gambling, including card-playing, chain letters, dog and horse racing, football pools and the detested pinball machines. Gambling, a 'social evil' once confined to the mining camps, had mutated and infected metropolitan areas, tormenting the Calvinist faithful in the cities. The war against gambling, led by Methodists and Presbyterians in Anglophone mining towns on the East Rand, was, as with their determination to enforce Sunday observance and restrict smoking and drinking, fought relentlessly and well into the mid-1960s.

Again, Kruger's Doppers had shown the way with the passing of the Gambling Act 6 of 1889, at a time when the goldfields were in their infancy. As with Sunday observance, legislation that originated from a small, essentially rural Calvinist church was pressed into the service of an emerging Afrikaner 'nation' and then an industrialising state intent on enforcing social discipline on an unruly, seemingly profligate white working class composed largely of English speakers who took the country to the brink of a revolution in 1922. By World War I the number of days on which horse racing was permitted on the Witwatersrand had been severely curtailed. In the late 1930s pinball machines offering cash prizes were prohibited. In 1947 dog racing was abolished, and in 1949 football pools were eliminated. But what Calvinist militants really craved was not piecemeal provincial legislation that discouraged financial windfalls, other than those earned through the sweat of the brow, but a consolidated law applicable nationwide. Act 51 of 1965 rendered *all* gambling, other than horse racing, illegal.

Here again – as with the later banning of film shows on Sundays – the timing of the Calvinist dream come true is worth noting. It came about as the country slipped into an authoritarian state increasingly governed by ministerial diktat, so that playing cards for cash within the privacy of your home became an offence punishable by a fine. It was as if vociferous Afrikaner nationalists and a growing number of their silently thankful English-speaking supporters, both parties increasingly reliant on the army and the security police to protect the borders of 'their' nation and state, were intent on seeing the militarisation of the country being matched by a commensurate degree of social discipline on the home front.[63]

Calvinist-contrived social fettering of the white working classes was a marked feature of white rule in South Africa during the first half of the 20th century. But the Protestant churches' insistence on social discipline compatible with industrial capitalism never went uncontested by workers. Some of the roots of that everyday resistance to an increasingly joyless existence lay, as we will see, in nearby Catholic Mozambique. Afrikaner and English-speaking ministers of religion may have walked hand-in-hand down the aisle of history when it came to moulding the social lives of white workers already living in racially segregated areas, but from the mid-1930s that partnership – seldom celebrated too publicly or noisily – began to take strain for reasons born of politics derived from a skewed reading of the scriptures. Afrikaner nationalists, in alliance with the three Dutch Reformed churches, building on the civil religion that they had been cultivating assiduously over several decades, sought to advance and protect the white 'nation' and its privileged way of life through rigidly enforced social and political segregation. Activists moved freely between the Broederbond, the Dopper church and the National Party. Indeed, leadership of these organisations sometimes overlapped.[64]

A decision by the synod of the NGK, in 1857, permitted converts of colour to be accommodated in segregated facilities where necessary. Although born of pragmatism and not intentionally formulated to enforce rigid racial separation, the ruling nevertheless created an opening for those wanting to see more distance between black and white Christians.[65] The increasing industrial, racial and social separation of the races that scarred the mineral revolution provided added impetus to those Calvinists set on entrenching and legalising segregation. Afrikaans- and English-speaking white workers in mining towns and other urban areas provided electoral endorsement for a project that started out as a supposedly benign form of protective segregation in the first half of the 20th century, only to mutate into the consciously ultra-exploitative apartheid policies of the latter half.

Before the widespread distribution of the Bible, first translated fully from the Dutch into Afrikaans in 1933, Protestant ministers had an important role in unpacking segregationist thinking not only for less-fortunate congregants but also for fiery nationalists in the Broederbond and other pressure groups. 'A distinctive interpretation of Dutch neo-Calvinism', notes one authority, 'gave a theological underpinning to the ideology of apartheid.' But, just as a take on the writings of the Dutch Calvinist theologian and prime minister (1901–1905) Abraham Kuyper helped propel apartheid thinking to its apogee, so did readings by other theologians of André Biéler and others later deny that Calvin had endorsed racial segregation.[66]

Where precisely the tipping point in that theological dispute lay is a matter for debate. What is beyond doubt is that it was Calvinists, the church and white Christians who paved the way for a political ideology that helped set South Africa on a destructive path. On that we have the word of no less than National Party leader DF Malan, himself a minister of religion, who once said: 'It was not the state but the church who took the lead with apartheid.'[67]

But for those tracking the role that religion played in the regional dynamics of modern southern Africa, it is not only the way Calvinists underwrote the rising tide of racist politics that is of interest but how its socially oppressive forays were accompanied by sustained attacks on the old enemy, the Catholic Church. The Protestant onslaught followed a familiar trajectory, gathering steam in the first part of the

20th century and then petering out as authoritarian rule and a police state became the major source of oppression in the 1960s and 1970s.

The NGK, the Cape Town-based Protestant Association and the Stellenbosch Theological Seminary were the boiler rooms from which issued a stream of hysterical pamphlets, constantly warning about *Die Roomse Gevaar* – the Catholic Menace. And since the Catholic Church was often portrayed as being almost timeless and unchanging, there was no reason to change or update the titles of pamphlets. *Die Roomse Gevaar* became dogma, a mantra within the church and Afrikanerdom. The NGK's catechism manual, first printed in 1927 and reprinted 30 times, still contained two pages of warnings about supposedly sinister Catholicism in 1968.[68]

That handbook for the true believers was an extension of a much older genre of anti-Catholic rhetoric going back to the 19th century, directed at the curious or those wavering in their faith. 'The Roman Catholic Church', a 1917 booklet announced, 'is anti-Afrikaans.' 'Its whole bearing is foreign and in conflict with the Afrikaner tradition.' The year of the Great Trek celebrations, 1938, was the occasion for more dark warnings about the imminent danger and 'how to combat it'.[69] In neighbouring Mozambique, it was alleged, Catholicism was by then so well protected by the regime that the NGK had effectively been expelled from the country. But all was not lost. Protection against papal influence could still be acquired through the outlay of one or two pennies by requesting tracts such as 'Convent Life Unveiled', 'The Jesuits and their Crimes' or 'Why I am not a Roman Catholic'. By World War II, it was 'The Romans and Our Children' being threatened in Catholic schools, in small urban centres. In 1962, after the founding of the republic, the Rev Jeffree James warned any complacent English-speaking compatriots: 'In South Africa the chief target of Rome's new approach is the Dutch Reformed Church – the main bastion of Protestantism in our land.'[70]

An underlying paranoia about the dangers that aggressive forms of Catholicism in general, and its sluggish Mozambican variant, supposedly held for white South Africa had a peculiarly dated ring to it. It was as if Calvin and Luther were alive and well and living in Cape Town. It was a perception difficult to align with the realities of the Catholic Church or the missionaries of Portuguese East Africa. Plateau

Protestants and coastal Catholics were, by the mid-20th century, sparring in a hopelessly asymmetrical contest. Maybe the Calvinists needed to pause and ask the question attributed to Joseph Stalin: 'How many divisions has the Pope?'

The Catholicism of the coast – intermittent, scrambled defences

The presence of Dominican and Jesuit missionaries in northern and central Mozambique dated back to the 15th century and the creation of a bishopric in Goa in 1534. But the modern history of Christian clashes in southern Mozambique can conveniently be traced to the Berlin Conference of 1884–1885 that rounded off the Scramble for Africa. The discoveries on the Witwatersrand 12 months later prised open further the minds, and coffers, of the imperial powers. But the deeper roots of the latter theological thrust harked back to the late 18th century.

In Britain, the Slavery Abolition Act of 1833 was driven largely by the churches. Thereafter, the space occupied domestically by imperialist politicians had, to an increasing extent, to be shared between the church and an electorate bolstered by the modest extensions of the franchise that came with the Reform Acts of 1867 and 1884. At the Berlin Conference, and at an anti-slavery conference in Brussels in 1889, and in other treaties entered into before 1919, ecclesiastical concerns were mirrored in the insistence that missionaries should enjoy freedom of religious movement in the African colonies.[71] In Mozambique, the Protestant presence, born of imperialism, was underpinned by a nearby industrial revolution.

The three-way link between religious fervour, imperialism and the mining upheaval expressed itself geographically; it was southern Mozambique, with its strong migrant labour links to South Africa, that called loudest to the missionaries. Not only were black Mozambicans the preponderant ethnic grouping among African mineworkers on the Rand, but the missionaries had access to them twice over – first within the prison-like compounds while they were at work and then back home, in their family villages, after they had completed their contracts. It was a privileged setting for carrying on an evangelical tradition born of the first industrial revolution, but here Protestant missionaries could speak to a black working class in the making both as peasants *and* as proletarians. And, in town and countryside alike, colonial authorities controlled and monitored the faithful.

In the shadows of industry, Methodists, Presbyterians and other lay preachers and missionaries relayed the linked virtues of discipline, literacy, thrift and work to black men whose earnings were destined for investment in the sandy soils of the Sul do Save. Back home, in Gaza and Inhambane provinces, and in and around Lourenço Marques, the missionaries preached other virtues – chastity, monogamy, patriarchy and sobriety – compatible with the emergence of a domesticated, urban, working-class nuclear family, which, in that case, would not be allowed to root or reproduce itself at its place of employment.[72]

In this state-cultivated and -entrenched twilight world, halfway between an increasingly impoverished peasantry and a proletariat whose cash earnings from mine labour declined for most of the 20th century, Protestant missionaries worked away for the love of their God. In the first half of the century, despite many breakaways by African evangelists seeking indigenous pathways to salvation for their communities, and despite the disapproval of the Portuguese administration, American Congregationalists, Dutch Reformed Calvinists, Swiss Presbyterians and Methodists of at least three stripes made modest gains south of the Save River.

Some of the appeal that Protestantism and its variants had for Africans in the southern reaches may have come from the country to which hundreds of thousands migrated during the agonisingly long 20th century. Protestant South Africa's greatest virtue, it seemed, was that it was not Catholic Mozambique. Both countries were disfigured by forms of gross racial and class oppression, but within South African borders there was an absence of mass institutionalised forced labour, a comparatively free labour market beyond mine properties, better wages to be earned in a stronger currency and the rudiments of an education and health system for blacks, as well as some opportunities for women to earn wages even more modest than those of their husbands. If the Catholics saw the Protestants as their enemies, and they did, then surely Protestantism could not be all bad? If the logic of 'my enemy's enemy is my friend' did apply, it may have run deep, well into the black liberation struggles of the late 20th century. '[A] very high proportion of nationalist leaders in Mozambique', one scholar notes, 'were drawn from the ranks of the persecuted protestant elite', while another reminds us pertinently that the first president of the Mozambique Liberation Front (Frelimo), Eduardo Mondlane, was from 'a Protestant school for boys at Cambine, not from a Catholic one'.[73] That the Frelimo government itself was opposed to all forms of religion was another, later, irony.

The fact that the Mozambican Protestant elite was so small historically may have facilitated its persecution by a Portuguese administration intent on retaining the colony. In 1950, black Catholics outnumbered Protestants by three to one, and the gap then widened. In 2000, 54 per cent of Africans in Mozambique still followed traditional religions, 27 per cent were Roman Catholics and only 7 per cent belonged to Protestant denominations.[74] As was often the case in southern Africa, early clashes between Protestants and Catholics, as we will come to note, were predictably toxic and asymmetrical.

Seen over the *longue durée*, the history of the Catholic Church in Mozambique was neither linear, in the sense that its presence was continuous or dense, nor bilateral, in the sense that its fate was defined exclusively or primarily by its interactions with the Vatican. Indeed, its vicissitudes, secondary in nature in the larger scheme of things, can be traced to forces that lay in the northern hemisphere, in the triangle between the Catholic Church in Lisbon, the Portuguese state along the Tagus and the Vatican. The church's early history falls into three periods of which only two, post-Napoleonic, phases need concern us here.[75] On the east coast, the Pope's divisions were never large or well-coordinated.

In Portugal, important political changes within the state, starting in 1750 and followed nine years later by the expulsion of the Jesuits from the country, ushered in a long 'anti-clerical century'. The change in ecclesiastical fortunes in Lisbon was matched by the decline of the Catholic Church in Mozambique, where the number of missionaries fell from 24 in 1781 to 10 in 1825, by which time the country was without a prelate. Napoleon's invasion of the Iberian Peninsula set the church back further; the liberal but nationalist regimes that followed on a civil war abolished the tithe in 1832, stopped the recruitment of novices in 1833 and then, in 1834, expelled all Catholic religious orders from the country. By 1855, barely four years after the founding of Calvinia, in the northern Cape Colony, there were just four Catholic missionaries spread out along the entire Mozambican coastline.[76] Southern African Protestants may have had doctrinal reasons for fearing Rome but, closer to home, in terms of numbers, Portuguese Catholics posed little threat.

The long decline in the numbers of Catholic clergy and religious institutions on the east coast ended in the 1850s. It was followed by a 60-year period of ecclesiastical regeneration, though coming off a very low baseline. The origins of the recovery in Mozambique lay in the old northern triangle of power.

Between 1848 and 1886, Portugal and the Vatican edged closer to one another through a series of ground-breaking conventions and concordats, easing tensions dating back to earlier liberal excesses. The Jesuit and Franciscan orders were allowed back into the country and the Lisbon administration agreed to the construction of a seminary for the training of secular missionaries. The first graduates of the seminary at Cernache do Bonjardim, filled with a potent mixture of religious enthusiasm and nationalist zeal, arrived on the east coast in 1875. In the two decades that followed, around half of the few score secular missionaries who arrived in Mozambique were drawn from the founding seminary.[77]

The revival was partly, attributable to António Barroso, who, in 1891, was chosen by the Vatican to head the prelacy of Mozambique. As fervent a nationalist as he was a believer, Barroso, oversaw the arrival of several more Catholic orders on the east coast. There was, however, no need for the night watch in Protestant southern Africa to sound the alarm. At the high point of the second period, in 1909, there were only 'seventy-one fathers and tens of sisters' in the country – 'a figure never reached before in Mozambique and never to be reached again before 1939' – another year of seminal importance for the church on the east coast.[78]

If 1890–1910 constituted some sort of minor 'golden age' for the Catholic clergy in Mozambique, then, ironically, it coincided with a period in which the Portuguese state was virtually bankrupt and industrialising southern Africa preparing for political consolidation and economic take-off. The expansion or contraction of church, nation and state in greater southern Africa, either singly or in unison, bore little direct relation to the strength of the economy. In Mozambique, the church made modest progress amid near bankruptcy, while in South Africa during the same period, one of profound economic progress, the Catholic Church made almost no headway at all. Indeed, in what became 'South Africa' organised Catholicism got off to a notably belated and slow start, and in its economic heartland, the Witwatersrand, the church was beset by a serious shortage of priests throughout the years between the end of the Anglo-Boer War and World War I. Catholic missionaries numbered barely 300.[79]

For Catholics on the east coast, the overriding importance of temporal power, as refracted through Lisbon and the Vatican, was brought home in the starkest way possible in 1910. A republican coup in Portugal ushered in another anti-clerical era, a third iteration, that lasted into the 1920s. The Jesuits were once again expelled and religious dress prohibited. The anti-clerical backlash was further facilitated by the 1911 'Law of Separation'. Among many other restrictions, the state determined the hours at which mass might be celebrated and the clergy were paid by state administrations rather than the church. It took a decade for the state to relax its grip on the clerical collar in the metropole, but in Mozambique, although the missionaries had already been expelled, the prohibitions were eased within 36 months. Nevertheless, by 1927 there were still only 56 regular priests, as opposed to missionaries, up and down the length of Mozambique.[80]

Endless bouncing appeared part of the wild politico-religious see-saw ride that Lisbon and the Vatican were engaged in. But then, unexpectedly, it eased. Yet another coup in Portugal, in 1926, curtailed the violence of the movement when the military straddled the fulcrum, slowing the movement and giving the partners time to catch their breath. Two new accords improving relations between church and state were signed within 48 months of the coup and then, in 1930, the Colonial Act handed the responsibility for 'civilising' and educating Africans in overseas territories to the Catholic missions.[81] Antagonisms were subsiding.

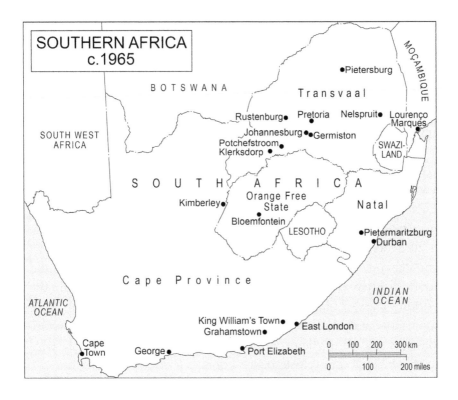

The deepest healing, however, commenced in 1932, when Salazar was appointed prime minister and operated as dictator of a quasi-fascist state until his death in 1970. Portugal soon appealed to wartime Afrikaner nationalists and neo-Nazis in South Africa, including Oswald Pirow, hoping for a New Order.[82] Salazar proceeded to pave the way for the Concordat of 1940, when the Catholic Church was recognised as both an ecclesiastical and legal entity, thereby rendering it liable to 'service the needs of imperial unity and the civilization of the peoples in the colonies'.[83] It was the formal coming together of politics and religion in the Concordat of 1940, in Portugal, and the informal alliance between the Dutch Reformed Church and the National Party, when the latter assumed power in South Africa in 1948, that infused an underlying affinity between the two countries.

After 1950, Portugal and South Africa both indulged their civil religions – a 'bizarre blend of nationalist sympathy and subservient religiosity'.[84] Important elements within both ruling classes were wont to cast themselves as (white) peoples chosen by God to lead a civilising mission in (black) Africa.[85] In both cases the church, God, 'the people' and their politics were in alignment, making for an awkward, seldom articulated but useful silent ideological symmetry that culminated in military agreements during the liberation struggles of the 1970s.

In southern Africa, then, Calvinism and Catholicism could make for either contestation or cooperation in the economic or social domains. And while conflict may have manifested itself more frequently in their relationship, there was no certain way of telling which of the two was more likely to show itself. In that greatest of all explanatory phrases, 'it all depended'. But on what exactly did deal-making for material gain depend? In retrospect, the locus of conflict or cooperation did not lie directly within the ranks of the respective elites, but within the working classes, black and white. Calvinism and Catholicism were important catalysts in regional dynamics, but identifying the precise role they played in the economic and social changes that they triggered demands some closer observation.

The processes activated – some observations

In 1875, a decade before the discovery of gold on the Highveld, at a time when the needle on Mozambique's shaky economic compass pointed to India, the South African Republic entered a Treaty of Commerce with Portugal. The treaty allowed for the duty-free exchange of commodities originating within the two agrarian economies. In essence, it was an agreement entered into out of financial weakness rather than strength, and the economic disparities between the parties were not overwhelming. The Kruger administration was in no hurry to seal the deal and Portugal was not renowned for its nervous energy.[86]

But when gold was discovered in the eastern Transvaal, in the early 1880s, the agreement assumed added importance. The Treaty of Commerce was ratified in 1882, and two years later the parties agreed to the establishment of a rail link between Lourenço Marques and Pretoria. By the time the link was completed, however, in 1895, the relationship between the South African Republic and Portugal's east coast colony had changed radically. The Transvaal economy was no longer dominated by commerce but by a booming gold-mining industry linked into the most advanced Western financial markets. The old logic underpinning the treaty of commerce and the rail link had changed; the economies of the South African Republic and Mozambique were not comparable.

The discovery of vast gold deposits on the Witwatersrand and the triumph of British imperialism in the Anglo-Boer War changed the economic dynamic of southern Africa irrevocably. The eastern main line and the treaty, originally thought of as being of mutual benefit to the Transvaal and Mozambique, assumed a different trajectory and outcome. Instead of constituting the steel spine that would encourage the development of economic muscles in both countries, the Pretoria–Lourenço Marques railway became the primary instrument for the sustained impoverishment of Portugal's perpetually cash-strapped east coast colony. The imperially backed 'modus vivendi' of 1902, and the Mozambique Convention of 1909, conveniently settled in the year before Union, guaranteed the Witwatersrand monopolistic access to cheap black labour from the Sul do Save. The railway helped suck the lifeblood out of a chronically anaemic east coast colony condemned to a commercial rather than an industrial future.[87]

In theory, the Convention guaranteed Mozambique a fixed percentage of South Africa's rail traffic to the coast, which would contribute to the development of the harbour and rail infrastructure of Lourenço Marques. But in practice the harbour infrastructure was captured by South African interests, and it was only after World War I that Portugal could lay claim to the most essential facilities and equipment in the port. By then, however, South African mining-house capital – either directly or indirectly – had already embedded itself in other sectors of the port economy. The forwarding agencies, the shipping industry and the sprawling timber yards forwarding lumber to the collieries and mines of the interior were all operated and owned by South African companies. It was another asymmetrical arrangement.

In tense relationships, disagreements can manifest themselves in many ways, including unpleasant noisy vocalisations or prolonged silences. The geographically forced marriage between Protestant South Africa and Catholic Mozambique was characterised more by sulking than by shouting. It is true that things got a bit boisterous in the early

1920s, when economically strong South Africa tried to bully financially strapped Mozambique into a political union, but that eventually passed. Neither government, however, ever chastised the other publicly, even indirectly, about their differing systems of belief. The great silence around issues of Calvinism and Catholicism was, in part, ensured by the valuable dowries that the parties had exchanged in the opening decade of the 20th century. It was the big deal: money trumped ethics, moderating behaviour.

Central to South Africa's material well-being was the gold-mining industry, which, through the modus vivendi and the Mozambique Convention, ensured that its recruiting arm, the WNLA, had a monopoly on the wholesale importation of cheap, indentured black labour from the Sul de Save. In return, fully a third of all Mozambique's paltry external earnings depended on taxes extracted from returning migrant workers. The exploitative, forcibly policed, repressive, secretive, transnational labour regime was, arguably, one of the biggest scandals in southern Africa. Yet, for the better part of the 20th century the Chamber of Mines and the church leadership on both sides of the border, along with the administrations in Pretoria and Lourenço Marques, were at best extremely discreet – if not somewhat muted – when it came to expressing their reservations about the functioning of a pernicious system. Why would a couple, already silently resentful of one another, agree to kill the golden goose that ensured their individual and collective well-being in exchange for airing a few of their religious differences? Better, like the three wise monkeys, to see, hear and speak no evil.

But if the couple were reluctant to be seen or heard quarrelling about religion in public, then in private they fought like hell. It was not the open lounge window at the front that witnessed the most painful and telling exchanges but the rooms at the back of the house, where privacy supposedly reigned. And, as sometimes happens, when divorce proceedings threaten, it was wealth that did most to ensure discretion. It was the impecunious black and financially stretched white working classes who had to listen to the most egregious of religious disputations.

In the first three momentous decades of the gold-mining industry, it was A W Baker's 'South African Compounds and Interior Mission' that was the standard bearer for Calvinism, which, the Randlords appreciated, did no ideological harm to capitalism or a black working class in the making. Most of Baker's energies, and those of his co-religionists – 'Methodist evangelicals' – focused on conversion that derived from sincere personal efforts at salvation. They imposed missionary time on participants who, as on another frontier of 'civilisation', were subjected 'to a continuous regime of instruction, veneration, and surveillance'.[88] By spelling out familiar Protestant virtues, Baker and others, working in 20 compounds along the Reef, sought to establish the social foundations of sustainable Christianity.

But tucked in among the good news for men and mine managers were a few lessons that failed to underscore Christian charity or religious tolerance. In the face of competition from an energetic Portuguese graduate of Cernache do Bonjardim and his assistants along the Rand, Baker's men were not beyond indulging in occasionally pugnacious anti-Catholic outbursts, which were reflected in *Africa's Golden Harvests*, a publication circulating in America, Australia, the United Kingdom, South Africa and elsewhere. The least offensive of its rhetoric, aimed at subscribers, was intemperate: 'Rome and her Priests' presided over peoples who often were 'degraded, ignorant and superstitious'. 'The whole of the Papal system' was 'a Blasphemous assumption of spiritual and Temporal Power and diametrically opposed to the simplicity of the Gospel of Christ'.[89] The worst of the tirades, during World War I, were hellishly close to being utterly demented.

In March 1915, under the heading 'Romanism', the publication carried a letter addressed to King George V by two evangelically charged Anglican churches in Johannesburg, and 'a letter of a similar tenor has also been sent by the Executive of the Grand Lodge of the Orange Institution [Order] of South Africa'. The signatories felt that their sovereign had been poorly advised by his ministers when he agreed to appoint a Minister Plenipotentiary to the Court of the Vatican. The letter was punctuated by seven numbered clauses, many of which roamed freely across the borders of credible evidence, if not sanity. 'The Papal Court' was 'the most dangerous enemy of British freedom' and had 'long been cognizant of the designs of the German Empire against Great Britain'. Predictably, the Jesuits were probably the worst of all. Their official documents revealed that they could 'command twenty-five million secret agents scattered about the world, a claim which we cannot help connecting with the extraordinary prevalence of German spies in all parts of the British Empire'.[90] English-speaking Protestants did not have a good war, and no dominee could trump their fear of *Die Roomse Gevaar*.

All was not lost, however. Protestant and Catholic missionaries could agree that their black congregants were being exploited by a third force, a religious adversary they shared – immigrant Jewish proprietors of the cheap eating-houses and general dealer stores that figured prominently in or around mine properties. *Africa's Golden Harvests* again led the way. The tithe should be paid without question because 'no Christian is worth the name who falls behind the Jew in that respect'. African miners earning a pittance needed no prompting to learn deeper lessons. As one 'native speaker' told his brothers: 'Jews in those days like Jews in our own days, used often to delight in selling rubbish to the heathen.'[91] Christians shopped carefully.

As in the children's game of 'broken telephone', biblical whisperings in the ears of migrants by missionaries, in the compounds or back home, could be appropriated, amplified and twisted for purposes other than simply spreading the Good News. There was no patent on the Ten Commandments or racist ideas. By the early 1890s, diviners in the Sul do Save had cottoned on to the idea of strict Sunday observance as 'a means of eradicating current misfortunes'.[92] It was an idea that ran contrary to the spirit of Catholicism and, as such, may also have sent a subliminal message of rejection to an oppressive Portuguese administration.

Antisemitic ideas harboured by Baker's compound missionaries were easily incorporated into the political repertoire of black Mozambicans when African mineworkers embarked on a boycott of mine stores in 1918, a year marked by inflation and rising prices. 'I beg of you people of Gaza', one pamphlet confiscated by the police read, 'that a person seen going to the Jew stores on Tuesday must be thrashed and the articles that they bought taken away from them and if a purse [is found on him] it must be thrown away, and if a blanket, it must be torn.'[93]

There was no easy way to predict how the transnational Protestant-Catholic divide across the region might become reflected in the lives of the working classes. In the case of the miners, by far the single largest cluster of male Mozambicans in South Africa, black workers could take elements of Protestantism and weave them into a low level of awareness that others, with more clearly thought-through objectives, could, decades later, build into forms of political consciousness that were more obviously anti-colonial and anti-Portuguese. It was a lesson that ran all the way from the diviners of the 1890s to Eduardo Mondlane and the persecuted Protestant elite of the 1960s.

But if black Mozambicans in the Sul do Save adopted and adapted selected elements of religious teachings in the compounds to further their struggles against Catholic oppressors, then white South African workers were more inclined to occupy the spaces that Catholicism opened across the region and to challenge the strictures that a largely Calvinist-inspired civil religion imposed on their social life this side of the border. In black communities in Mozambique, differences in Protestant and Catholic religious ideologies occasioned intermittent, weakly developed political short-circuiting. In South African white working-class suburbs, it led to significant resentment and consistent social short-circuiting.

Part of the unarticulated appeal that the more relaxed Catholic social regime in nearby Mozambique held for middle- and working-class whites in South Africa derived directly from the rigorous, unending campaign that mainly Calvinist ministers engaged in to enforce the Third Commandment , the injunction to keep the Sabbath holy. There was just no limit to the depth of their desire to impose on 20th-century cities a social restraint on Sundays of a sort matching that which Calvinism-of-the-countryside had inflicted on hamlets and small towns of the platteland throughout the 19th century.

From Union in 1910 until well into the 1950s, Anglican, Dutch Reformed, Methodist and Presbyterian ministers, and clergymen from several other denominations, objected separately, but often collectively, to the idea of organised sport on Sundays.[94] Team sports drained churches. You could play cricket or soccer on the Sabbath or you could be a good Christian; you could not be both. But if you thought you could slip away on your own or with a partner to engage in a little private recreation with friends, you were mistaken. The Control of Dancing Ordinance of 1957 put paid to Sunday dancing in the Orange Free State, while the Fish Preservation Ordinance of 1964 had the unintended outcome of rendering angling illegal from one bank of the Vaal but not the other.[95] Whether fish on the Free State side of the river grew larger because of the ban than did those on the Transvaal side was never recorded. Swimming or entering the waters of a health spa, singly or collectively, was also seen as a violation of a Mosaic law by the Protestant faithful across the country.[96]

Prompted by Calvinist zealots, laws intent on curtailing or eradicating amusements, such as playing billiards, attending a concert or a theatre, or viewing a film – even within the privacy of a club – as we have already noted, stretched all the way from the era of Kruger in the 1890s to John Vorster in the mid-1970s. For outsiders, unfamiliar with a country in the grip of enforced civil religion, the result was mystifying. Here was Johannesburg, a mining town in the industrial heartland of the country, locked into the richest economy on the continent, and yet, on Sundays, it was like a 'City of the Dead' – a white necropolis – while on the periphery, African and coloured townships pulsed with social energy.

A 'Trans-Atlantic' tourist approached the visitors bureau in March 1950 to see what he might do over a Sunday. 'All they could tell me was no movies, no drinks, no entertainments, no shows, no nighteries. In fact, nothing.' Disgusted, he wrote to the editor of the *Rand Daily Mail*, 'I am cutting my stay short and leaving tomorrow for a spell in Lourenço Marques as I simply have not the courage to face another Sunday in Johannesburg.'[97] For half a century Calvin lurked in the shadows of the city, threatening the social lives of white South Africans, and more especially those of the lower middle and working classes.

Not content with snuffing out any outbreak of collective cheerfulness in public spaces on Sundays, the Protestant police also set out to control the radio in a way calculated to avoid any spontaneous humming, singing along or foot-tapping in the kitchen, lounge or bedroom on the Sabbath. In 1934, the Hertzog government invited Lord Reith of BBC fame to visit the country and help frame the broadcasting act that would govern the South African Broadcasting Corporation (SABC). The son of a Scottish Presbyterian minister, John Reith was an ardent public advocate of virtue but a man whose private life fell somewhat short of his moral prescripts.

A Calvinist strongly opposed to commercial radio and jazz, and a staunch upholder of the Third Commandment, Reith did white South

Africa proud. Long bouts of dour classical music and no commercials on the Sabbath saw the SABC match, if not surpass, in two official languages, what the irreverent in England referred to as 'Reith Sundays'. The Reithian kiss of death, administered to the SABC at birth, had profound consequences for white listeners over four decades.

A significant number of white working-class listeners believed that the state broadcaster, under the spell of hardline theologians, limited their access to popular music, and its inability to cater to their preferences on Sundays – the only full day open to them for recreation – was especially restrictive.[98] In white society, for the most part as comfortable with social as it was with racial oppression, Protestant vigilantes popped up everywhere. Not long after the SABC reluctantly got around to launching its commercial service, Springbok Radio, in 1950, the Methodist Church requested that it drop all advertisements promoting the sale of alcohol. Shortly thereafter the Johannesburg Hospital Board stopped patients listening to Springbok Radio on what should be a day of peace and rest.[99] Presumably, there was no way of telling what the bedridden might get up to should they hear a snatch of Bill Haley & His Comets. In 1973, the SABC, where meetings of the Board of Governors were opened with a prayer, remained unwilling for the results of English soccer matches to be broadcast on Sundays.

At the SABC, and at Springbok Radio, Calvinist and commercial considerations were, like Siamese twins, joined at the hip in a way that appeared inoperable. From birth, the prognosis for financial mobility was unpromising. The state broadcaster could turn its back on the market for advertising, but it could not, simultaneously, scorn listeners who were reluctant to pay licence fees for radio with programmes that were sleep-inducing in the evenings or over weekends. By the mid-1930s Anglophone working-class families along the Witwatersrand, already shying away from Protestant churches inclined to evangelical social bullying, and unwilling to bow before the new masters of civil religion, were ready for something new and exciting. The heavens were open to opportunity and radio waves were contemptuous of national boundaries and nationalism alike.

One night in 1933, months before Reith had the chance to assemble his ball and chain for the dancing-averse SABC, the owner of a small Johannesburg printing works and a jazz enthusiast, GJ McHarry, chanced upon a broadcast from the Rádio Clube de Moçambique, and the idea of what, 36 months later, was to become Lourenço Marques Radio (LMR) was born. Relations between Lisbon and the Vatican had improved during the late 1920s, and in 1932 the mercantilist Salazar had been appointed prime minister in Portugal. The stars of an easy-going tolerance for late-night weekend entertainment and commercial possibility were in alignment above a Catholic but politically authoritarian Mozambique.

McHarry acquired the concession for a station that was to embed itself in the popular culture of southern Africa. From the 1940s, its signature programme, aired in open defiance of the Third Commandment on Sunday nights, was the 'LM Hit Parade' devoted exclusively to the modern pop music that the Protestant churches frowned upon and the SABC despised. By linking the radio's commercial potential to a smart marketing company in Johannesburg, McHarry ensured that the company became extraordinarily successful and he a remarkably wealthy man. The transfers of capital and black labour between the Rand and Lourenço Marques may have been skewed and grossly uneven, but by the 1960s – even as the rise of the police state in South Africa was underpinned by a booming economy and white affluence – the outflows were becoming significant enough to become a source of concern for the Pretoria government. Lourenço Marques Radio continued to flourish for another decade, until the station, by then secretly acquired by the SABC, was forced off the air by the Frelimo government in 1975.

The initial advance of LMR was built around a working-class audience that by the 1960s was shrinking, eventually giving way to a listenership that was more identifiably white and middle class in character. It was not by chance that LMR's success was attributable to a team of iconic disc jockeys drawing on the modern Western idiom and the pioneering market research undertaken by the company's commercial arm. The secret behind McHarry's transnational enterprise depended largely, but never solely, on the sullen resistance to Calvinist-infused civil religion by English-speaking listeners from across the class spectrum of the cities.

Resistance of that type may have come to the white middle classes relatively late, but there was nothing new about it for the mining communities and wider white working class of the Witwatersrand. They had been demonstrating spirited resistance to another Protestant injunction – to eschew the acquisition of wealth other than through the sweat of the brow and practice of thrift – for half a century. The struggle against gambling restrictions was directed by two creative entrepreneurs ready to challenge the Calvinists from beyond the nation's borders, from Catholic Mozambique. And, as with LMR, the demise of the lottery came after the Afrikaner nationalists had secured a republic and constructed their police state.

The seeds of state intervention were planted in the 19th century when Calvinists ventured out of the countryside, only to be confronted by the horror of lotteries and sweepstakes in the mining camps of the Witwatersrand. The Dopper faithful were having none of it. The Kruger administration responded with Law No. 7 of 1890, banning lotteries but leaving sweepstakes unregulated. Over the following three decades, different Transvaal administrations presided over an imprecise law with varying degrees of authority, enthusiasm and probity. It left an inviting space for wide boys wanting to cash in on a few determined gamblers, or the many hoping to buy a family home, or looking to escape the terrors of the mine.

The dream-hawkers arrived, in 1917, in the shape of an inspired Australian bookmaker, Rupert 'Rufe' Naylor, and a Catholic priest, an alumnus of the seminary at Cernache do Bonjardim but by then effectively defrocked – José Vicente do Sacramento. The former was based in Johannesburg and the latter in Lourenço Marques. A near-bankrupt Mozambican administration sold the pair the concession to run a lottery knowing full well, but always refusing to acknowledge so openly, that while the tickets would be legally authorised and printed in Lourenço Marques, they would be illegally distributed and sold throughout the Union of South Africa. The cheap indentured labour of the Sul do Save again sealed the lips of both governments.

For half a century, from 1910 to 1960, Protestant churches fought an unrelenting battle against gambling in various forms on the Witwatersrand. With the backing of successive governments led by Calvinist militants, the Protestant churches slowly gained the upper hand, achieving notable successes by eliminating or severely restricting dog and horse racing, pinball machines and football pools.

The one triumph that eluded them, however, was the lottery. The Lourenço Marques Lottery was so popular, so deeply embedded in working-class culture at a time when the Labour Party and trade unions were a powerful force in national politics, that police and prosecutors were reluctant to act against proprietors and punters alike. Indeed, so central was the lottery to the lives of many that, in 1930, the Labour Party, then in coalition with the National Party in government, briefly ran an illegal lottery of its own. It was the white working classes, in the decades before they slowly made way for the middle class in a racially constructed economy, who provided the biggest challenge to the successful imposition of what became a hegemonic civil religion in South Africa.

A silent covenant, attributable to the centrality of a functioning system of indentured mine labour, allowed the lottery to become the largest nominally illegal business in southern Africa between the two world wars. As a working misunderstanding between Protestant South Africa and Catholic Mozambique, the lottery enabled Rufe Naylor to amass – and lose – a fortune and for a while turned Father Vicente into a millionaire living the good life in far-off Estoril. A second generation of Naylors provided continuity in a transnational enterprise.

But by the early 1960s, the covenant was less secure. The South African economy was booming, and the mining industry was no longer as dependent on Mozambican mine labour as it had been for most of the century. From 1896 to 1956, men from the Sul do Save had, on average, constituted about 40 per cent of the complement of African mineworkers, but by the early 1960s the figure had dropped to 28 per cent.[100] A republic infused with a Calvinist-inspired civil religion was no longer willing to tolerate gambling that resulted in a noteworthy outflow of currency to a Catholic neighbour. The National Party, presiding over a cowed electorate and a powerful police state, had all the instruments it needed to hand.

Two strongmen in Verwoerd's cabinet, Albert Hertzog and John Vorster, led the attack against the Lourenço Marques Lottery and other foreign-based lotteries during 1963–1964. A subcommittee of six, chaired by the Commissioner of Police and flanked by two more leading securocrats, calculated that the country was being drained of approximately R135 million each year, or the equivalent of about

US$9 million today. A small army of lowly officials was deployed by the Post Office to intercept all incoming and outgoing mail and monies relating to the lottery, with devastating effect. In just 12 weeks, over a million items were intercepted, confiscated or trashed. The death knell for lotteries and other games of chance was sounded with the passage of the Gambling Act 51 of 1965, which rendered all forms of gambling in the country, other than horse racing, illegal.

Calvinists, ranging from Dutch Reformed Church dominees to Primitive Methodist ministers, had, after decades of public hectoring and private lobbying, successfully imposed God's will and their wishes on cities where the white working classes had long since given way to black workers in mining, manufacturing and the service industries. But the cross-border struggle of South Africa's Protestant militants against the comparative social tolerance displayed by Catholics, in Mozambique, was never confined to gambling or radio issues.

Extensive surveillance and rigorous enforcement of Sunday observance and other biblical strictures encouraged many white South Africans in the towns or on the platteland to seek temporary or permanent mental or physical reprieve from a socially oppressive state as the century unfolded. Trapped in a Calvinist cage of their own making, tens of thousands of South Africans sought to recover a measure of social balance, between discipline and order on the one hand and fun and freedom on the other, by escaping to southern Mozambique for their vacations. It cannot be 'proved', but the need for some social and psychological relief from Protestant excesses may have increased as South Africa, blessed by a comparatively strong currency even as it became increasingly socially repressive and internationally isolated, entered the decades of the police state from the 1960s to the 1970s. It was estimated that by 1970, over half a million tourists were visiting Mozambique every year – most of them middle-class South Africans.

It was, in part, an arrangement that was not without historical precedents and parallels. Did not Catholic Cuba, or Mexico, serve a similar function for many American Protestant visitors in the 1950s and 1960s? Or Catholic France and Italy for English Anglicans on vacation? Was it not Somerset Maugham who once, so memorably, suggested that Monaco was 'a sunny place for shady people'? Suitably tweaked for considerations of class, colour, culture, gender and sexual preference,

Lourenço Marques was a distant, poor relation of a family of resorts that included Havana and Cancún, Monte Carlo and San Remo.

The full or partial sanctuary that Mozambique afforded white South Africans was, however, perhaps better illustrated by examining the double standards applied to male and female experiences. For decades, white South African men visited Mozambique precisely because it offered them a more relaxed social environment in which to enjoy comparatively unrestricted access to the 'vices' most frequently decried by the Protestant police at home – alcohol, gambling and sex outside marriage. But the same moral exemptions never extended to white women.

The long-standing, startling disparity between the number of European males and females in Mozambique fuelled the perceptions, prejudices and reservations that the South African authorities entertained about Lourenço Marques and Portuguese men. From at least the turn of the 20th century, the east coast colony, and its principal city, were thought of as constituting a zone of great sexual danger, of moral hazard, for any visiting young white women. Calvinism and patriarchy locked arms and marched in unison when it came to controlling what were assumed to be Protestant women wishing to explore Catholic social freedoms. From the birth of the Union and well into the 1950s, the state was at pains to control, monitor and manage the real or imagined sexual proclivities of hundreds of white South African women vacationing or working in Mozambique.

In many parts of the world, World War I ushered in an era marked by the issuing of passports and greater monitoring of international travel. In South Africa, young women wishing to travel to Mozambique could apply for a 'permit' or 'tourist certificate', or a 'tourist passport' – all valid for three months. Acquiring a permit required a woman to present either a 'letter of permission' signed by a parent or a letter from any 'respectable citizen' that had been attested to by a commissioner of oaths. Since acquiring a tourist passport was less onerous, most women opted for the latter, but even then they were expected to present themselves to the commissioner of police in Lourenço Marques before they would be allowed to extend their stay, and they were not allowed to be employed in the coastal city.

But from at least the 1930s on, and more especially after the 1948 electoral triumph of the dominee-driven National Party, the Pretoria administration placed its Mozambican counterpart under consistent pressure to increase the control and policing of white South African women seeking refuge and/or work in the port.

Women fleeing financial exploitation or psychological and physical abuse from their spouses, or who had had a child out of wedlock, or who merely wished to explore their sexuality away from prying eyes on the platteland, often took up positions as casino assistants, dance hostesses or prostitutes in the port city's entertainment sector. But they were never secure. Throughout the 1930s, the South African consul made it difficult for women suspected of moral transgressions to acquire passports or to have them renewed. Other women, those who managed to slip the net and obtain employment illegally, were deported, at the state's expense, by the consulate, and by 1949 the police were circulating a list of the names of those South African women 'contemplating marriage to Portuguese nationals'. It is hard to imagine a clearer expression of the fears that Catholic social tolerance, born of a willingness of the Church of Rome to forgive human frailties, posed for a Protestant regime bent on controlling the morals of the elect.

Looking back, then, much of the historical relationship between South Africa and Mozambique was underwritten by the economic importance that cheap, indentured black mine labour and the resulting financial remittances held for both regimes. The South African gold-mining industry, and therefore much of the country's economy, was built on the backs of the men, women and children of the Sul do Save. That reality encouraged state-level exchanges that were, for the most part, conflict-free and, indeed, in the age of the African liberation struggles, gave rise to joint military operations.

Closer examination, however, reveals that while history and geography had herded the Protestant lion and Catholic lamb into a confined space from which there was no escape, they refused to lie down with each other. Against the backdrop of an industrial revolution, it was behind the lines and in the working-class strongholds across the wider southern African region – black and white – that many of the most important contradictions, conflicts and working misunderstandings attributable to religious differences played themselves out. In the mine compounds, Protestants and Catholics fought for the souls of black men in ways that missionaries and mine managers alike could approve of. In Lourenço Marques, white South Africans sought relief from Protestant prisons and explored some of the social freedoms that were a by-product of the Catholic world view. Back home, thanks to a Catholic regime in Mozambique, they could dream of escaping the working class by purchasing a lottery ticket or listen to modern popular music coming from a radio station unencumbered by the Third Commandment. Southern Africa was a place, part of a transactional zone in which borders, 'nations' and 'states' perhaps figured less prominently in the minds of ordinary men, women and teenage children than they did in the minds of their oppressive political elites.

––––––––––––

Historians are prisoners of the present when writing about the past in the hope of discovering connections between change and continuity in designated actual, or cognitive, spaces variously defined. Those interested in 'southern' Africa are no exception, and the passage of time itself would bring greater clarity to questions and answers alike. But those short of time do not have the luxury of waiting to offer answers, which is why the *Three Wise Monkeys* is a historiographical experiment, one conducted in the early 21st century, rather than a more definitive work of that nature that might be written, say, 50 years hence. It is what it is.

For those taking their cues from a new nationalist elite struggling to maintain control over its unruly constituents and shape its destiny, 'South Africa' exists. It is an entity with internationally recognised borders designated as a nation-state, and is recognised as such by the United Nations and other international bodies. Most historians tend to take these geographical, political and sociological parameters as given, and those who accept them uncritically proceed to write national, if not nationalist, accounts of the past in the hope that, in passing, they may also shed some light on what lies ahead in the hope of partially shaping it.

But upon closer examination the unit that 'South Africa' supposedly is struggles to cohere either as a longed-for, soul-bound, entity of the heart or as an empirically verifiable entity capable of persuading the head. It lies somewhere between the two; it is an idea for the future, one waiting to be born, one that may or not be realised depending on how its political elites will define and govern it.

'South Africa' does and does not have borders, barely a hundred years old. Their outlines emerged from a mess of Dutch, English, German and Portuguese imperial interests in the southern part of a continent where an entirely unremarkable plateau was discovered to be squatting squarely over the largest deposits of gold and diamonds the world has ever known. During the industrial revolution that followed, it developed borders, never fully demarcated or enforceable, that defined a zone of economic interest capable of protecting the 'national' interests of a white minority that denied the political existence of a black majority. As it enters a post-industrial era scarred by economic decline, the 'national' space as originally defined is almost as meaningless as it was prior to the discovery of an underground treasure trove. Border posts, manned by corrupt or incompetent officials, oversee the traffic of goods and people where the flow of stolen property forms an important part of a greater regional political economy.

The strongest roots for the word 'country' lie in the Latin *contra*, meaning 'against', or, in its medieval Latinate form, 'lying opposite'. It is now often used as a synonym for 'nation'. It may better to confine its use to the older form of the word. Within its porous borders, the country has, as the state is quite insistent about, four major racial groupings – Asian, black, coloured and white – that collectively make for a population of perhaps 60 million. Its inhabitants, including several million who hail from elsewhere on the continent, speak at least 30 different languages, but, in deference to difference, and out of respect, it has 11 official languages. Its believers are split between Christians, Jews, Muslims, Hindus and African traditionalists intent on venerating their ancestors. There are few familiar or strong links making for an identifiable 'nation'. As the Secretary-General of the South African Council of Churches recently conceded: 'We are not one nation at all. There is need for serious nation-building.'[101]

Such stark diversity contributes to centrifugal forces that are reflected in the constitution of the country and its formal political structures. It has a President who presides over a cabinet, and a parliament comprised of a lower House of Assembly and a National Council of Provinces. The country is divided into nine provinces, overseen by nine premiers, who marshal the political energies of the nine provincial assemblies. In the more remote traditional polities the government is supported by hundreds of traditional leaders, some of whom were once seen as chiefs or paramount chiefs. But in an age where inflation of titles is tightly coupled to deflation of administrative ability, the country now has at least ten state-subsidised 'kings' and 'queens', living in what are termed 'palaces'.

The state is the political organisation that enforces the will of the people, as expressed through its democratically elected representatives, over a defined territory. The rule of law rests on the efficiency, professionalism and probity of its prosecutorial and law enforcement agencies, ultimately sanctioned by a strong and independent judiciary, as represented by all from the lowest magistrate to the chief justice. Confronted by external threats to its sovereignty, the state is protected by the various arms of its defence force – the army, the air force and the navy.

A properly functioning modern state is also expected to preside over the development and maintenance of the country's economy. A continuous centrally or regionally generated power supply at competitive prices is expected to be distributed through a well-maintained national grid, which, along with other requisite factors of production, would ensure equitably distributed economic growth among cities and towns fit for purpose. In addition, the state – or some other authorised competent private operators – would, at competitive prices, in keeping with national objectives, develop and maintain the country's most basic transport infrastructure – its airports, harbours, roads and railway system.

There is little point in documenting here why contemporary South Africa does not now qualify readily as a nation-state underpinned by a functioning economy destined for growth and expansion. In 2022, much of the debate among analysts revolved around trying to arrive at a conclusion as to whether it was a 'failing' or a 'failed' state – optimists plumbing for the former and pessimists for the latter.

The point of all this is, as ever, to consider critically how it helps or hinders historians in their task of considering the past in the various ways capable of linking the past to the present in more imaginative and suggestive ways. If southern Africa lacked social, political and economic cohesion before the mineral revolution of the 19th century, and if the country, if not the region, is now destined for a long post-industrial decline in the 21st century, how is it best viewed and what are we to make of its wasted 20th century? Under such circumstances, how much profit is to be gained from writing a national or nationalist history?

There are, no doubt, as many ways of answering those questions as there are analysts, but, in this experiment, four things have been attempted. First, by casting the history of the region in the *longue durée* and seeing its emergence as being shaped most immediately by the differing economic trajectories of two imperial powers – Britain and Portugal – the historian can escape a few of the tyrannies imposed by considerations of time and space. Borders, colonies, administrations and governments, when viewed as being contingent, almost transient, allow for a deeper appreciation of long-term economic change.

Second, taking religious affiliation and civil religion seriously allows us to expose parts of the hidden, unarticulated grammar that informed several important transnational political, economic and social exchanges. Many of those exchanges, some at the point of production, as with black miners exposed to Protestant or Catholic missionaries, or in the suburbs of the cities, as when white workers bought lottery tickets or listened to Lourenço Marques Radio, took place not in elite circles but within spaces dominated by the working classes.

Third, by focusing working- and middle-class responses to different religious and secular promptings that came from across the region, it is possible to see how even though South Africa was largely Anglophone, Protestant, industrial and urban, and southern Mozambique largely Lusophone, Catholic, commercial and rural, the histories of the two could not always be easily, let alone fully, separated. The fate of South Africa and Mozambique, like the fates of several English- and Spanish-speaking countries around the Atlantic world, was bound up in entangled history. 'Entangled histories', some historians agree, are 'concerned with "mutual influencing," "reciprocal or asymmetric perceptions," and the intertwined "processes of constituting one another."'[102]

Fourth, by viewing the region's history over the *longue durée* we can see the industrial revolution on the Highveld and the rise of the South African state in a perspective that may enhance our understanding of where it arose from, where it found itself and where it may be headed. Seen over the *longue durée*, the white South African state barely constitutes a footnote in the history of the continent or in the histories of the Atlantic and Indian Ocean worlds that flank it. It lasted only from 1910 to 1994, less than a century, before it collapsed. It may have been a mere episode in a far wider continental and hemispheric history, yet in just 84 short years it managed to visit untold harm on most of the peoples of the region, attaining its most pernicious dimensions and reach two decades before its implosion, only to be replaced by yet another destructive nationalist regime.

The deeper roots of the repressive South African police state of the 1960s and 1970s can be traced to a strong tradition of Calvinist social surveillance, as well as political monitoring and intervention by its security forces. The police state drew on not only the state's intelligence services and willing civilian informers but on the beliefs and mindsets – embodied in civil religion – of its consuls, diplomats, magistrates, ministers of religion and politicians. It was a state that became willing to assassinate, murder and massacre blacks, to whom it steadfastly refused to grant the franchise or accord the rights of citizenship. Likewise, it was willing to assassinate or murder its exiled white political opponents, some of them in Mozambique.

If a relatively prosperous 'South Africa' has always lacked the necessary cohesion to designate it a state-nation, let alone a nation-state, then how much more so does that caveat apply to 'Mozambique', one of the ten poorest countries in the world? It, too, is more of a partially formed construct of the mind than a meaningfully integrated social, economic or political reality. Historically, its northern reaches, for many centuries, looked north and east, out over the Indian Ocean and the Arabian Sea – often in hope, frequently in terror. In the late 19th century, the mineral discoveries in South Africa forced a disjointed country to avert its gaze from the ocean and look south and west. Now, confronting an Islamist insurrection in the far north, 'Mozambique' may, once again, be forced to confront a future that lies more north and east, than it does south and west.

'Southern Africa' – however defined – predated colonialism and imperialism just as surely as it will postdate it. For those seeking to understand where the region came from, where it finds itself and where it is headed, ignoring its contemporary borders and looking at it over the *longue durée* may provide a few intriguing new perspectives.[103] There is a place for historians in a playground so rich in ideas.

THREE WISE MONKEYS

INTRODUCTION TO VOLUME 1

The diverse indigenous peoples of the world had been in Africa, Australasia, India, North and South America, and elsewhere since the birth of humanity. They were aware of what they had or had not achieved culturally and economically, who they were and where they found themselves in regional and continental, if not in global, terms. In the 15th and 16th centuries, it was the commercially advanced elites of Europe who, knowing little about geography or native populations spread across the globe but intent on expanding their trading networks, set out on 'voyages of discovery'. Their 'discoveries' changed, expanded and drew a world hitherto known imperfectly to Europeans, and very poorly to indigenous peoples, into a far more connected universe.

The detection of these new, far-flung sources of material gain and profit, sometimes obscured beneath an incoming fog of religious ideology that supported subsequent justifications for military occupation and cultural subjugation, was cast as a triumph for Europeans bent on 'civilising' the indigenous populations. The most notable imperial successes, in Africa, the Americas, India, the East and West Indies, and elsewhere, came in regions well-endowed in terms of human, mineral or natural resources that lent themselves to mining or plantation agriculture. The enslavement of the native populations, or the importation of chattels from Africa or elsewhere, helped ensure the economic viability of many of Europe's invasive trading enterprises.

Amid wealth-generating successes being turned into profit-hunting circuits dominated by northern hemisphere powers, Mozambique was a remote southern backwater, one lacking significant mineral and noteworthy natural, but not human, resources. An elongated territorial smudge on Africa's east coast, it was long viewed as a place fit only for supplying Arab traders with slaves for the predatory states to the north, or for providing way stations for Portuguese merchants and others en route to spice-rich India. Mozambique, for the most part, languished economically as the rest of the world made economic progress. For close on two and a half centuries – from the time that it conquered Goa, in 1510, until 1752 – Portugal administered its south-eastern African colony from the Asian subcontinent, from India.

Even after the first move south, the Portuguese saw little point in trying to govern their coastal wedge from the continental mainland of Africa, choosing instead to work from Ilha de Moçambique, an island fortress at the northern extremity of the colony, straddling the route to and from India. In terms of cartographic realities, as much as the Lusitanian imagination, Mozambique was part of a liminal experience, more of an extension of routes to and from India than a destination or a desirable place of settlement for Europeans. The colony's extensive coastline was overseen with a mixture of imperial insouciance and tropical lassitude, the interior viewed largely as a repository of African slaves and taxes.

From the early 17th and well into the mid-19th century, millions of slaves, forcibly removed from the African littoral, not excluding Mozambique, helped underwrite the growing prosperity of the Americas. On a planet where the oceans flowed seamlessly, one into the other, the Atlantic drew many vital nutrients out of the Indian. Fed with black bodies, those parts of the Americas that bordered the Atlantic steadily put on white economic muscle, while southeastern Africa, deprived of most resources, remained financially undernourished. In the first half of the 19th century, Brazil alone imported 2.5 million slaves, most of them plucked out of Mozambique as the slaving frontier moved down the coast towards the south of the colony.

If the Mozambican coast marked exit points for those sold into slavery and transported across seas unknown to them, then the familiar riverine interior of the colony, too, failed to provide millions of other Africans with any guarantee of lives free of a slave, or slave-like, existence. *Prazos*, sprawling feudal-like estates, recognisably African in cultural terms, saw Portuguese titleholders farm humans for taxes as readily as they did for paltry agricultural outputs lacking markets.

This seemingly endless and immutable Conradian existence, between slavery and the *prazos* in the northern and central reaches of a colony always hopefully tied to India by seasonal monsoon winds, endured for centuries. The tectonic plates of profitability underlying the always emaciated Mozambican economy appeared unmoving – relics of a distant past firmly centred on the Arabian Sea.

But then, quite unexpectedly, the plates *did* shift – dramatically and swiftly. Mozambique underwent a geo-economic inversion of profound proportions. It started with the discovery of diamonds in central South Africa, in the 1870s, and gained additional, unstoppable momentum when gold was discovered on the Witwatersrand in the mid-1880s.

The African continent's youthful southwestern economic plate slid effortlessly over the older, northeastern Asian plate beneath the Indian Ocean, pushing the frontier of largely unchallenged Arab and Indian coastal commerce back northwards from where it had come in the 8th and 9th centuries. An enormous tectonic shift saw the influence of industrial capitalism extending into an adjacent agricultural backwater, sucking black men once bound to a subsistence existence on the land into seasonal migrancy and dark, underground labour as mineworkers.

Frequently retarded when it came to initiating industrial programmes, but often commercially nimble and tax-hungry, the Portuguese colonial administration felt the earth move and voted with its feet. Whereas the hop and a skip that had taken it from India to Ilha de Moçambique had taken centuries to execute, the jump from the island to Delagoa Bay on the continental mainland was, by comparison, almost instantaneous. It landed, feet splayed, hundreds of miles south, at Lourenço Marques.

Founded as a trading settlement in 1544, tiny, miasmic Lourenço Marques responded almost instantly to the change in the financial gravitational fields of southern Africa. Indeed, it was designated a town in 1876, two years before the diamond city of Kimberley was accorded equivalent status. In 1887, 12 months after the discovery of gold on the Rand and the founding of Johannesburg, Lourenço Marques became a city, and was declared the capital of Mozambique in 1898.

The modern port, capital of a Cinderella colony managed by a second-tier imperial power with a third-tier bureaucracy, Lourenço Marques was the by-product, a mere extension, of a remote inland industrial revolution over which it had little control. Born dependent and of lowly status, it was seen as such not only by bullying British imperialists intent on dominating the continent from Cape to Cairo but also by their South African allies – capitalists, forwarding agents, importers, industrialists, merchants, strategists, politicians, statesmen – and much of the English-speaking public of the interior. By referring to the place only as 'Delagoa Bay' rather than Lourenço

Marques – much to the annoyance of its Portuguese denizens – the South Africans sought to appropriate the city and its labour-rich hinterland psychologically. The annual exodus of tens of thousands of African indentured workers to the Witwatersrand mines, which had secured the exclusive right to 'recruit' mine labourers in Mozambique, underscored that dependency.

Southern Mozambique, then, had the misfortune of being colonised twice over – first, formally and ineffectually by Portugal, and second, informally and indirectly by South Africa, backed by Britain. Unable to acquire the province of Sul do Save and the port through military occupation in an age that struggled to balance European bellicosity with international diplomacy, it was left to industrial capital to capture and subjugate Delagoa Bay ideologically, politically and psychologically.

Unsurprisingly, the South Africans concentrated first on acquiring and managing the physical infrastructure of the harbour and the railways serving the port. Indeed, it was this cluster of considerations that informed the Portuguese administration's position when it sought to tie a guaranteed flow of black labour westward, to the gold mines, to the ongoing development of their port. But even then it took three decades, and it was only in the mid-1920s that the most vital parts of the harbour infrastructure were secured by the colonial administration.

The coastal shipping trade, too, fell to interests locked into South Africa and, indirectly, the mining industry. By the late 1920s, only eight per cent of the shipping tonnage entering Mozambique's two principal ports was in the hands of Portuguese shipping lines – that is, from the seafaring nation that had pioneered the oceanic links to India. Forwarding agencies, too, were firmly in the grip of the Witwatersrand mining houses that dominated their ownership. 'Nearly the whole of the shipping and forwarding business of the port', the Chairman of the Lourenço Marques Forwarding Agency informed Prime Minister JBM Hertzog in 1925, 'is in the hands of Union firms or companies.'

In addition, at the Matola end of the port, the Witwatersrand companies acquired large timber yards used for the curing, storing and processing of imported lumber destined for use as underground props in the mines. Timber secured in Australia, Scandinavia and the

United States connected Lourenço Marques to global trade but only as an entrepôt, servicing a remote industry that did little for its long-term development.

Between the wars, this dominance of the port and the Sul do Save's economic hard muscle was complemented by the consciously directed invasion of Mozambique's soft financial tissue by South Africa. Prior to the tectonic shift, the venerable Indian Ocean trade ensured that the rupee dominated coastal currency, but after the mineral discoveries in the interior, it was gradually displaced by British sterling. The colony was particularly vulnerable to monetary assault not only because it lacked substantial financial backing but also because it was governed largely from afar, from Lisbon, while in Lourenço Marques, it was sub-ject to the policies of the ineffectual, self-enriching Banco Nacional Ultramarino (BNU) – 'a private bank controlled by the government'. The Mozambican administration was unable to directly influence the minting or distributing of whatever passed muster as its own specie. Portugal's always parlous financial situation and the dividend-seeking policies of the BNU gave rise to prolonged periods of rampant infla-tion, which further strengthened the South African currency.

World War I whetted South Africa's appetite for territorial expan-sion as it sought to become the pre-eminent regional force in both de jure and de facto terms. But imperial caution in London combined with local white settler sentiments to thwart such hopes, and South Africa then embarked upon war by other means. In 14 months, between December 1921 and January 1923, the twins – the Chamber of Mines and the South African government – working closely together, assem-bled three formidable pieces of heavy financial artillery: the Rand Refinery, the South African Reserve Bank and a branch of the Royal Mint. Although designed primarily to accommodate domestic objec-tives, these weapons were mounted on swivel turrets and were thus perfectly capable of being trained on South Africa's economically vul-nerable eastern neighbour.

Pushing downward on the growth of real wages of black migrant workers for much of the 20th century, the Chamber of Mines, sup-ported by the South African government, determined how, where and when east coast African miners would be paid. The decisions whether to pay wages directly, on site, in South Africa or through deferred pay in their home districts in Mozambique, in gold sovereigns or in notes, to the workers or via administrations in Lisbon or Lourenço Marques, all impacted heavily on the fortunes of the colony and many small traders.

But so marked was the South African government's desire to see Mozambique's financial muscle atrophy and to increase its dependency that, between the wars, it intervened aggressively and successfully in international capital markets to retard the colony's development by ensuring that it was denied loans that might help restore its economic stability. By 1950, so overriding was South African financial hegemony in southern Mozambique that Lourenço Marques and its hinterland in the Sul do Save were effectively the dependencies of the mineral revolution that had taken place in the adjacent interior.

The underdevelopment of Mozambique, now one of the ten poorest countries on earth, has deep and diverse roots. Many of these, including the taking of slaves, dated back several centuries, and can be linked to the rise of merchant capitalism in the northern and western hemispheres. Condemned to an exceptionally sad entry into the modern world, the fate of the southern part of Mozambique was rapidly sealed as tragedy when Mozambique was colonised, for a second time, as mining capitalists unleashed an industrial revolution with an insatiable appetite for cheap black male labour on the southern African Highveld. The story of Mozambique is, in good measure, the painful journey from global slavery to one of regional industrial servitude.

PART I

FROM INDIAN OCEAN SLAVERY TO BLACK INDUSTRIAL SERVITUDE IN SOUTH AFRICA, CIRCA 1500–1939

Just as none of us is outside or beyond geography, none of us is completely free from the struggle over geography. That struggle is complex and interesting because it is not only about soldiers and cannons but also about ideas, about forms, about images and imaginings.

EDWARD W SAID

For an African terrain to be informally and later formally colonised, at a great distance, by a politically weak European power during the centuries-long evolution of the international trade in black slaves and spices, was a misfortune. To then be partly recolonised, informally, for a second time, by a neighbouring European settler-dominated state drawing on the economic power derived from gold in an era characterised by the globalisation of Western finance capital and black industrial servitude in the far south of the continent, was a disaster. The tragedy of modern Mozambique, then, was to have been subjected to colonisation twice over: first, by remote Portugal, capable of pursuing only commercial pathways to the accumulation of capital from the 15th century, and, second, from the late 19th century onwards, by an omnipresent South Africa set on securing vast supplies of cheap black labour that rendered 20th-century industrial capitalism profitable for investors spread around the northern Atlantic world.

It was this double colonisation – under distantly related economic regimes that were briefly overlapping, partially reinforcing and consistently in predatory mode, the one nominally Catholic and the other nominally Protestant but sharing racist ideologies that differed in degree only – that was primarily responsible for the human calamity that came to extend over a third of the African continent's eastern

seaboard and its hinterland in the 20th century. The pernicious misery occasioned by this double colonisation was compounded by the
covert actions of Portugal's long-standing 'ally', imperial Britain,
which, along with South Africa, connived repeatedly to ensure that
southern Mozambique remained economically dependent and vulnerable. Mozambique's misfortunes stemmed as much from its 'friends'
as it ever did from its adversaries.

Sequential assaults, differing in duration and intensity, subjugated
Mozambique. The first, was a centuries-long pounding up and down
the coastline, powered in part by monsoon winds and sail. The second
was a shorter and sharper set of body blows delivered to the solar
plexus, the Sul do Save, during the shift from sail to steam and from
road to rail. Between them, they radically changed the economic
profile and stance of Mozambique. For centuries, the spine of the
country remained relatively intact, with its head tilted slightly north
and east, towards the Arabian Sea, India and Zanzibar, from whence
emanated the despair and hope of its inhabitants in unequal measures.
The relatively late powerful blows to the belly, however, caused the
continent's eastern coast to slump to its knees, leaving Mozambique's
imagined economic spine bent, head turned inland to the south and
west. The change in posture of the coastal expanse, from an ill-defined
terrain with a predatory slave economy once loosely constructed
around Mozambique Island in the north, to a wage labour-exporting
colony focused around the greater Lourenço Marques and Inhambane
region in the far south, has not always been either fully appreciated or
understood. Indeed, in many ways the northern, central and southern
parts of Mozambique have been, and are, worlds apart. Our story is
focused largely on the south.

A large part of sub-Saharan Africa's eastern seaboard was never a
country fully colonised, one subjected to crisply defined, uncontested
vectors of control and power, be they economic, political or social.
Nor did it comprise an overwhelming number of indigenous people recognisable by a single distinctive culture, language or religion.
Mozambique, always more 'country' than 'nation', was – perhaps
still is – more than a thousand miles of coastal confusion split into
a southern part aspiring to coherence and an amorphous middle that
gives way to a distant northern part. All countries and societies have

explicit and implicit lines of fracture and are constantly in the throes of being made or remade, but nowhere has Fernand Braudel's warning ever been more apposite: 'To draw a boundary around anything is to ... adopt ... a philosophy of history.' In southeastern Africa, history has faux real and imagined borders alike, and when Mozambique one day splits, as it will, it will be along those poorly defined lines.

Janus-faced 'Mozambique' – looking both inland and seaward – was an illusory 'colony', one that could be sensed but not easily seen. It was an aspirant entity that could be experienced, sometimes delightfully so, but not readily understood. It was, and still is, better appreciated as a place where there are few fixed cognitive, physical or temporal signposts to tell you where you have come from or where precisely you are headed. Like frontier badlands, Mozambique stretches out endlessly, an environment in which everything tangible or intangible is seemingly metamorphosing and then vaporising before the eyes, only to reappear a little later in yet another guise, as something completely different, leaving one only with a mystified sense of undefined loss, occasionally imagined, often painfully real.

Even allowing for the nature and pace of social change in southern Mozambique after the mid-19th century, the sandy Sul do Save was never locked into time or space in ways that allowed its indigenous peoples to understand easily where all the disturbances they were being subjected to were coming from. Initially, it seemed like it was a slowly encroaching commercial order, blowing in off the sea as mists of misery, with limited opportunities, later as wind howling in from the continent's mineralised interior. The region always presented itself as an unstable economic, political and social environment, one barely comprehensible to the subject, the indigenous majority or its rulers. It was mostly an imperial illusion where continuities, other than human suffering, were at a premium. Little appeared to settle or take on a recognisable form for any length of time. It was a volatile place where people and practices could change unpredictably, where nothing existed in a steady state, where everything seemed to be forever in the throes of becoming.

The Sul do Save, more so after the discoveries of diamonds and gold in southern Africa between 1867 and 1886, was constantly on the doorstep of something fictional – historically, more on the threshold of hazard than of hope, a point of departure rather than an attainable or desirable destination. It was part of a space characterised by its liminality, a zone halfway between the centuries-old feudal-like institutions or structures of subsistence or peasant agriculture on marginal land and, later, a new and largely cannibalistic industrial order that spirited away and then consumed young black men.[1] Southern Mozambique was almost always a deceptive place, and its most distant aspect, some of its modern state of flux, its hesitancy and tentative grasp of reality, can be traced to the sometimes paradoxical economic misfortunes of Portugal and its allies over five centuries.

Portugal's Seaborne Empire and the Limits to Primary Colonisation in Mozambique, circa 1500–1900

One of the first and more significant imperial powers of the modern age (and among the last to shed that tortured legacy), Portugal – unlike its Iberian neighbour, Spain – entered the era of global expansion in the late 15th century by making the most of an otherwise unpromising dowry. Anchored in an archaic dispensation dominated by agriculture on estates where quantity often took precedence over quality of output or an expansive repertoire of products, it lacked extensive reserves of capital or great domestic markets. Offsetting that, over the centuries, came an ability to export wine, a modest textile industry and the fact that it overlooked and fished the northeastern Atlantic, which provided it with relatively easy access to continental Europe and the wider Mediterranean world.[2]

These formative economic and political realities did much to constrain and shape the world view of the Portuguese agrarian elite, nobility and court. Although hardly a stranger to the strengths deriving from trade and great port cities such as Lisbon, most notables derived their status and wealth from the countryside. It gave rise to a state with a largely commercial outlook, one where income was derived from concessions, customs duties, estates, handling charges, interest, licences, property, rent, taxes or tariffs. Such income was more highly valued than that derived from nascent craft and manufacturing skills. The state lacked the underlying bedrock of the economic revolution that later engulfed England, France and Germany, which were all blessed with far greater natural resources than Portugal.

The rapid ascent of Portuguese imperialism in the 16th century, its subsequent faltering successes and its gradual demise in the 20th century can be partly attributed to the dominance of notions of rentier capitalism. Its strengths derived from an ancient agricultural universe rather than early industrial capitalism. It got a head start in a globalising world because the voyages of discovery were underpinned by trade, not manufacturing. Commerce, trade and rent-seeking might have facilitated Portugal's entry into the modern world, but they were insufficient to sustain its advance. In the 19th and 20th centuries, Portugal struggled to compete with English, French and German imperialism, powered by industrial capitalism and intent on creating chains of added value by employing cheap semi-skilled labour, operating machine-driven forms of mass production and utilising powerful combinations of coal, iron and steam. Portugal's seaborne empire, born of sail and trade, blown along by sluggish mercantile motives, struggled to compete with faster-evolving forms of European imperialism, which, driven by manufacturing and trade, came to overtake it, and it then expired amid the steam and industry of its rivals. How this came to materialise and express itself in southern Mozambique is our principal focus.

It was the explorers Bartolomeu Dias and Vasco da Gama, the naval successors of Henry the Navigator (1394–1460), who, successively, pioneered the rounding of the Cape of Good Hope (1488), the finding of a sea route to the Asian subcontinent (1497–1498) and the 'opening up' of the greater Indian Ocean world to Europeans intent on establishing a global trading empire.[3] But while this coastal universe was entirely new to the Portuguese, its northern reaches, in the Arabian Sea and around the Horn of Africa, were well known to Muslim traders in much of the Middle East, who had been trading spices and capturing slaves along the east African coast since at least the 8th century.[4]

For most of the 16th century the Portuguese, despite losing some traction during the short-lived Iberian Union with Spain (1580–1640), held the upper hand in the new European trade built around cotton, gold, ivory, sugar and spices, drawn largely from southwestern India, and, of course, slaves from eastern Africa. Calling in at Mozambique Island for fresh supplies and water on the outward journey, before catching the summer monsoon winds (June–September) that pushed their caravels to the Asian subcontinent, the Portuguese based the capital of their 'Estado da India' at Goa, from where they aspired to enforce a monopoly over all ocean-going traffic working the western Indian Ocean. The homeward journey, also via Mozambique, relied on the winter monsoon winds (October–December), which lost their puff around the port of Inhambane, in the Sul do Save.

Portugal's early dominance of the western Indian Ocean trade proved difficult, and eventually impossible, to sustain. The principal focal points of the spice trade had, for centuries, been known to be located on the Asian subcontinent. European shipyards continuously extruded bigger and better ocean-going vessels and the seasonal monsoon winds to and from India hardly lent themselves to a monopoly. More importantly, Portugal's inherently limited financial resources could never match the expansion of European merchant capitalism in the 17th century, facilitated by the development of joint-stock companies that limited the risk of the far more numerous individual urban English, French and Dutch investors.

The monopolistic advantages acquired by the English East India (1600), Dutch East India (1602) and French East India (1664) companies forced open trade not only in the western Indian Ocean but also in the Bay of Bengal and well beyond that, into southeastern Asia, thereby providing steadily widening west European markets with access to competitively priced supplies of silk, other textiles and spices. Of the three companies, however, it was the English East India Company that mutated most rapidly into a global-corporate, company-state monster that eventually accounted for half of the world's trade. Backed up by a standing army that, by 1803, comprised a quarter of a million men, the company effectively gobbled up most of the Asian subcontinent. Confronted by a tsunami of North Sea capital sweeping all before it as it swamped the fringes of the Indian Ocean, Portugal's early promise of securing wealth by enforcing a pioneering monopoly was progressively eroded. Incapable of asserting itself fully in bountiful India, it

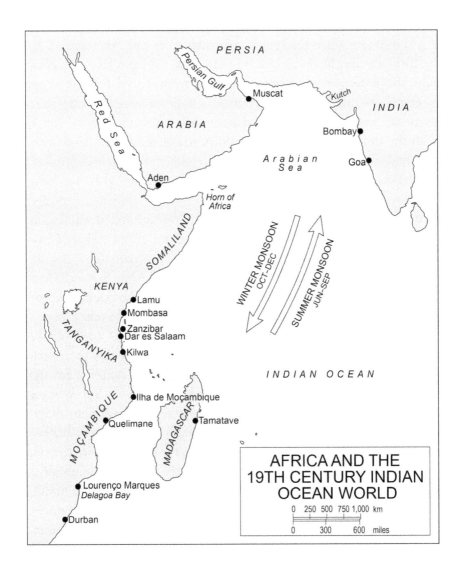

PERSIA

Persian Gulf

Muscat

Kutch

INDIA

Red Sea

ARABIA

Bombay

Arabian Sea

Goa

Aden

Horn of Africa

SOMALILAND

WINTER MONSOON OCT-DEC

SUMMER MONSOON JUN-SEP

KENYA

Lamu

Mombasa

Zanzibar
Dar es Salaam

TANGANYIKA

Kilwa

INDIAN OCEAN

Ilha de Moçambique

MOÇAMBIQUE

Quelimane

MADAGASCAR

Tamatave

Lourenço Marques
Delagoa Bay

Durban

**AFRICA AND THE
19TH CENTURY INDIAN
OCEAN WORLD**

0 250 500 750 1,000 km

0   300   600   miles

gradually retreated to eastern Africa, to Mozambique and the unpromising Sul do Save – places where slaves were often more easily procured
than gold and ivory.

The signs of Portugal's gradual decline in influence over the greater
Indian Ocean world and the realignment of its economic priorities in
eastern Africa – long before they were overtaken for a second time by
the mineral revolution in southern Africa – can be tracked via the changing circuits it employed in administering one of the least promising

of its colonies. When the grand Lusitanian fairy tale commenced, in the 16th century, Mozambique was administered from the Estado da India, the better part of a hemisphere away from the Sul do Save; when the empire eventually ended as a horror story, four hundred years later, it was still being controlled from Lisbon, half a world away.

By the 18th century, the grip that Portugal exercised on the trade with India had slipped to the point where it no longer effectively controlled Mombasa, an east coast harbour particularly well-suited to working the monsoons. In 1752, the administration of Mozambique, formally uncoupled from Goa in the far north, shifted south, to Mozambique Island, not far from the border with modern-day Tanzania, where a fortified deep-water port had, half a century earlier, successfully seen off two attacks by the Dutch.[5] There, a familiar mix of Arab dhows, Indian merchants and a trade in gold, spices, textiles and slaves underwrote the financial fortunes of the modest island-capital for a hundred years.

But the discovery of diamonds near Kimberley, in the Cape Colony, in the late 1860s and the opening of the Suez Canal shortly thereafter set off a further subterranean slippage of the economic centre of gravity in the western Indian Ocean. It moved south, towards the Sul do Save, a shift already under way through the opening of an emerging labour market for African men in the sugar-cane fields of the adjacent British colony of Natal.[6] When, in late 1886, the largest gold reefs known to man were discovered around what was to become the city of Johannesburg, the financial rumblings emerging from a new industrial Deep South could be felt around much of the dividend-seeking world. The emergence of the greater Witwatersrand and its insatiable demand for cheap, docile black labour, which collectively enjoyed substantial purchasing power, was serviced, at a distance, from the Atlantic and Indian oceans. The advent of the industrial revolution on the Highveld caused the already weak magnetic field of the economy in the Portuguese colony of Mozambique to reverse its polarity. The industrial south and the west became what the commercial north and east had once been.

The economy of the Ilha de Moçambique – already in decline for several decades as the demand for slaves in the Atlantic world and Indian Ocean islands eased off noticeably – was left high and dry. Lourenço Marques, the tiny port settlement founded by the Portuguese on Delagoa Bay in 1544, began to prosper. Located just beyond direct reach of the monsoon winds proper but with the finest natural harbour on the African east coast, and with relatively easy access to the emerging markets of the interior, from the moment gold was discovered in the Zuid-Afrikaansche Republiek (ZAR), or South African Republic, Lourenço Marques did more trade than did the northerly island capital of the province, and Mozambique Island was reduced to an economic 'backwater'.[7] Within a matter of a few decades, the capital of the ocean-centred colony, once based, in part, on the sale and shipment of African chattel slaves for plantation labour, gave way to the new southerly port city of Lourenço Marques. The latter was buoyed by the contracted sale of indentured black male labourers transported by rail, at first in sealed coaches, to work underground on the Witwatersrand mines.[8] As the emerging administrative and financial centre of the country and pulsed overwhelmingly from the heart of the South African mining industry, the hamlet of Lourenço Marques mutated into a town in 1876, became a city in 1887, and in 1898 was declared the capital of Mozambique.[9]

The centuries-long southerly shift in administration of the Portuguese province into southeastern Africa, along with the relatively swift emergence of Lourenço Marques as an entrepôt, spoke to the commercial-financial fixations and limitations of a metropolitan elite. Most of that, in turn, derived from Portugal's deep agricultural roots, but it also spoke of ideologies and practices, and a profound unwillingness to try and systematically broaden and diversify the economic foundations of the empire. The effects of these inherent weaknesses were evident not only in the western Indian Ocean but in Portugal itself, which, since the 12th century, had been so economically shaky and militarily vulnerable that it relied heavily on an alliance first with England and then Britain.

Imperial Britain's strategic priorities in the southwestern Indian Ocean

From the time of the Crusades, when England was still Catholic and its forces had once relieved the citizens of Lisbon from the unwanted attention of the Moors, Portugal and the island kingdom had enjoyed a relationship of trust that was cemented, in 1386, with the signing of the Treaty of Windsor. But, in the modern era, Portugal's greatest moment of need came in 1808, when Napoleon invaded the Iberian Peninsula. Britain came to the aid of its ally, which, rather ambitiously, had dared to challenge the French naval blockade of the British Isles. A further consolidation and refinement of naval strategies, and an understanding among the allies about the future of the slave trade, came with the signing of the Anglo-Portuguese Treaty of Friendship and Alliance, in 1810.[10]

But the Anglo-Portuguese Treaty, along with subsequent agreements, was not entered into by countries of equal standing. On the contrary, there were gross disparities in the military and naval strengths of the two nations, and when it comes to agreeing to hunt together in times of need, a hound and a hare might differ in their understanding of what might ultimately take place. Growing inequality failed to foster mutual respect, and as the 19th century unfolded, England became more industrial and imperial and Portugal weaker and impoverished, with harsh consequences that dragged on into the early 20th century.

In the early 1820s, barely a decade after the Treaty of Friendship and almost half a century before the discovery of diamonds in the Cape Colony, the British Admiralty, assisted by the East India Company, began charting and surveying the southeast African coast in aggressive fashion, including taking soundings in Delagoa Bay. With little of value in the hinterland at stake at the time, Lisbon's objections were easy enough to accommodate. Britain's burgeoning contempt for Portugal, however, remained in full view, fuelled by its electorate's growing outrage at the slave trade. In 1839, the British parliament 'unilaterally voted to allow its warships to stop and search Portuguese vessels for slaves', heralding three years of a 'state of almost undeclared war' between the friends.[11] The political tensions this aroused gradually subsided, and in 1847 Britain, largely unconcerned about the volume of legitimate commercial trade in the southwestern Indian Ocean, agreed not to question any of Portugal's territorial claims along the continent's apparently unpromising extended eastern coastline.[12]

But in 1869, when the Suez Canal was opened and the first diamond claim was pegged in Kimberley, a streak of economic lightning lit up the African interior and everything changed. Faced with a Boer republic north of the Vaal actively seeking access to the Indian Ocean to circumvent British control, Britain suddenly took a different, far more ambitious view of what it considered to be its entitlement throughout the subcontinent. Within months of the opening of the diamond fields, Whitehall laid claim to Delagoa Bay and some adjacent territory, basing its case on the assertiveness that it had displayed in the 1820s. The dispute between two friendly nations was referred to the President of France, Marshal MacMahon, for arbitration, and in 1875 he awarded Delagoa Bay to Portugal.[13]

Arbitration was a mistake that Britain, whose appetite for African colonies was by now well stimulated, was not keen to repeat. But, as we will note below, it did do so in another matter that was related less directly to territorial claims. About fifteen years later, Britain – in partnership with the United States, and with both parties looking to protect the interests of shareholders – again lost when it and Portugal went to arbitration. In 1900, the earlier Portuguese decision to nationalise the Lourenço Marques–Komatipoort railway, in 1889, was upheld in Berne. In arbitration, as opposed to arms races, conducted openly and before independent judges, outcomes were harder to rig and sometimes a hare might well outrun a hound.[14]

Britain's and its European rivals' hunger for colonies was far from being satiated, however. Even gluttons can only choose from the *menu du jour*. Seen from that perspective, when Britain and her other friends set about carving up Africa, at the Berlin Conference, in 1884–1885, they did so not knowing what the chef was keeping in reserve for the next day. Within 12 months of the conference's ending, the continent's greatest mineral prize, the Witwatersrand goldfields, was suddenly on offer. Could Britain only have seen what was coming – the MacMahon award notwithstanding – it may well have been even more vigorous in queue-jumping Portugal, the weakling at Bismarck's buffet. Delagoa Bay and the Sul do Save had both increased exponentially in value. In the end, it took Britain another decade and a half and an infamous colonial war to secure control of the world's greatest-ever supplies of diamonds and gold.

As things stood, however, Britain and other imperial powers simply elbowed the weakling aside and a good time was had in Berlin

– but not by all. Fired up by the ambitious cartographic daydreams of the Lisbon Geographical Society and sections of its political elite, Portugal had gone to the conference hankering after the Congo basin, hoping for a transcontinental linkage between Angola in the west and Mozambique in the east. The morning after the feast was a sobering experience. The Portuguese delegation left Berlin thinner and trimmer, with only half of what they had aspired to secure at the time that they and their friend and ally, Britain, had agreed to the international conference carve-up.[15]

For Britain, the timing of the discovery of gold on the Highveld, and the long-term implications that it held for Delagoa Bay and the Sul do Save, removed some of the gloss from the recent delights of Berlin. In theory, the settlement reached at the carve-up tempered the crass imperial jostling and shoving in southeastern Africa. But, in practice, Britain's view was often at odds with that of Portugal.

London was broadly in sympathy with Cecil Rhodes's Cape-to-Cairo aspirations – a north–south dream – while Lisbon entertained an east–west imperial vision for the African continent. Britain came to employ a vigorous stick-and-carrot approach when dealing with Portugal, which, while ailing financially, remained in legal, albeit nominal, control and possession of real estate and potential labour resources in southern Mozambique that were appreciating rapidly in value. So when the Portuguese nationalised the railway concession that they had granted an American, Edward McMurdo, to link Lourenço Marques to Komatipoort, on the ZAR border, in 1889 the British sent a gunboat into Delagoa Bay. The carrot was a bit slow in following the stick. In the early 1890s, amid increasing financial woes in Lisbon, Rhodes appealed to the rentier capitalist notions that dominated much of the thinking in the Iberian metropolis by attempting to purchase outright, or to lease, Delagoa Bay from the Portuguese government.[16]

By then, however, Rhodes was restricted to playing catch-up politics in Lourenço Marques largely because of a great British-Portuguese train smash, a diplomatic disaster. Ironically, some of the mess could be attributed to Rhodes's constantly activating the imperial alarm system about developments in central Africa. In 1889, a pivotal year, Portugal, hoping to curb British northward expansion, laid claim to a huge swathe of territory encompassing much of what is now Malawi, Zambia and Zimbabwe. These claims were contested, and the request by Portugal to go to arbitration was dismissed by an 'ally' smarting from the smack administered to it when Marshal MacMahon had awarded Delagoa Bay and environs to Lisbon.

In January 1890, Britain issued an ultimatum to Portugal to withdraw its claims in central Africa, and showed its determination by sending warships into Mozambican waters. Portugal backed down and, angered and humiliated by the treatment meted out to it from an ostensibly friendly ally, the Lisbon government collapsed. Many Portuguese notables were left with a legacy of bitterness and the nondescript east coast colony with a new set of northern and western borders that have, in large part, endured to the present day.[17] As one of the first graduates of the late-19th-century no-nonsense school of diplomacy, Britain frequently drove home its advantage in southern Africa with gunboat diplomacy.

In June 1894, the US consul on Mozambique Island, Stanley Hollis, reported on a strong British naval presence up and down the length of the southeastern African coast and on 'four "men o' war" currently lying at anchor in the harbour channel'.[18] With Joseph Chamberlain, Secretary of State for the Colonies, aware that political tensions on the Witwatersrand were rising and that Rhodes and his sidekick, Dr Jameson, were planning a raid aimed at unseating President SJP Kruger of the ZAR, British interest in Lourenço Marques remained high throughout the 1890s.[19] Germany's hope of extending its interests in east Africa through the acquisition of a northerly part of Mozambique, coupled with its expression of support for the Kruger government during the Jameson Raid, only served to further heighten Whitehall's ongoing interest in Delagoa Bay. At various moments through 1897, the port authorities in Lourenço Marques hosted 17 different British warships.[20] As late as 1926, the Foreign Office official in charge of Portuguese affairs, irritated by the persistence of problems with Lisbon, suggested that 'The real solution would be British cruisers in the Tagus and off Lourenço Marques.'[21]

In 1898, with Albion's eyes focused firmly on the main prize – the acquisition and control of the Witwatersrand gold mines – Britain set about preparing for its coming war in southern Africa mindful of the need to keep Germany content and out of any conflict by pandering to her territorial aspirations in northern Mozambique. In secret negotiations so scandalously devoid of ethical considerations that even some in the British political elite were outraged, Britain and Germany agreed that should the financially teetering government in Lisbon reach a point where it could no longer effectively administer or control its east African colony, they would split Mozambique between them, the northern part falling to Germany and the southern to Great Britain.[22] Not content with that betrayal, in 1912, Edward Grey, the Foreign Secretary, revisited the odious agreement with Germany for the British acquisition of southern Mozambique, only for the drawn-out negotiations to be overtaken by the outbreak of World War I.[23]

'The attitude of England towards Portugal in the nineteenth century', suggests one authority, opting for understatement, 'was frequently characterized by pious cant and on occasions by hypocrisy'.[24] In Delagoa Bay, Britain's arrogance and bullying behaviour, if not always a proclivity for perfidy, was on open display during the South African War (1899–1902). The commanders of British warships assumed control of the approaches to, and the harbour at, Lourenço Marques, boarding foreign vessels at will. As Hollis, by then based at the southern end of the province, noted, 'the British treat Delagoa Bay as if it was an enemy's port' and, 'as no blockade of this port has been proclaimed and as Portugal is at peace with Britain' these practices were perceived as being 'arbitrary and unfriendly'.[25]

British displays of political and military muscle along the coast of Mozambique were not indulged in isolation. They reflected and translated back into the contempt, discrimination and prejudice found elsewhere in Anglophone society. It is worth noting how, just as Britain's imperial thrust into southern Africa became ever more manifest, important parts of the English-speaking world, including banking and business, literature and later film, came to portray growing prejudice as regarded Portugal and the Portuguese. Afrikaners and English-speaking white Protestants on the Highveld, too, had long been exposed to a religiously cultivated dislike of their Catholic neighbours, who were cast as idle, much given to racial mixing and sexually permissive.[26]

Britain led the way. Even before the Anglo-Boer War ended in a British victory, the Sul do Save fell into the lap of Lord Milner's

administration as a source of cheap labour for the gold-mining industry. A plea from the Portuguese for a guaranteed percentage of rail
traffic to be routed through their port at Delagoa Bay turned on their
being willing to sell off the African labour of southern Mozambique
in a monopolistic agreement. The modus vivendi of 1902 was followed in 1909 by the signing of the binding Mozambique Convention,
which, through serial renewals, served industrialising South Africa for
half a century.[27]

When Britain eventually withdrew its musclemen from the region,
it left southern Africa in safe colonial hands, with the local notables
well on their way to establishing the Union of South Africa in 1910.
The small, squabbling political elites of the new would-be white
'nation' – the one largely urban, English-speaking and imperialist, and
the other mainly rural, Afrikaner and nationalist – were well placed
to continue the British tradition of bullying Portugal and pursuing an
unending quest for cheap black labour that predated the South African
War.[28] Fattened on a generous financial diet of gold and maize, it was
not long before South African governments – dominated for decades
by three forceful elderly military men – felt that they, too, were in a
position to demonstrate their prowess along the Lourenço Marques
waterfront. This they did, for the most part under the watchful eye of
an imperialist big brother in Whitehall.

After the advent of the Union, Britain became preoccupied with
matters closer to home, leaving it in danger of becoming overextended
in Europe and marginally more inclined to lend an ear to its increasingly demanding and sometimes troublesome proxy in southern
Africa. The generals – Louis Botha, Jan Smuts and JBM Hertzog –
transformed into prime ministers were presented with the opportunity to advance their ambition to see primary and secondary industry
on the Highveld served by the most economical of the east coast ports
– Lourenço Marques. Smuts had a 'predatory eye' on Delagoa Bay
from as early as 1908.[29]

The outbreak of World War I, Portugal's belated, politically divided
and reluctant entry into the conflict and South Africa's ready participa-
tion in the East African campaign opened new political space in southern Africa. It reminded Britain and Portugal that the Union was a growing regional force that had to be reckoned with, even if Whitehall was

unwilling to indulge its ambition to appropriate Lourenco Marques.[30] When an angry Portuguese monarchist faction threatened the safety of British and South African residents in Lourenço Marques in 1919, the South African government ensured that HMS *Minerva* was dispatched to Delagoa Bay, where it lay at anchor until it returned to the Royal Navy base at Simonstown.[31]

War debts added to Portugal's economic enfeeblement and financial woes, further limiting its ability to negotiate better terms whenever it came to renewing the Mozambique Convention or providing more modern and efficient rail and harbour facilities at Lourenço Marques. Smuts the general, still mutating into the 'great statesman' that he was lauded to be by the end of his career, did not hesitate to use strong-arm tactics rather than diplomacy to force the Portuguese to the negotiating table. What could no longer be realistically aspired to through the anchoring of men-o'-war in Delagoa Bay, or by reaping the spoils of an imperial war, the South Africans, with the help of their ever-reliable older brother in Westminster, now set about achieving by starving Mozambique financially.

In 1923, when Portuguese administrators in the east coast colony sought to raise funds via a loan in London, Smuts 'put pressure on his friends in the City and persuaded the Colonial Office to reinforce such pressure semi-officially', which it promptly did. The Foreign Office was as blunt as it was cogent in its assessment of the latest betrayal, which it described as 'blackmail at the behest of General Smuts, whose avowed object is to prevent British capital being invested in Portuguese colonies, lest any development should enable the Portuguese Government to resist General Smuts's imperialistic designs on his neighbours'.[32] Nor did this conscious South African desire to keep southern Mozambique impoverished, and to benefit from its seemingly endless supply of cheap black labour, end when Smuts was voted out of office the following year. The next general in the production line, JBM Hertzog, leader of the Labour-Nationalist 'Pact' government that held office until 1933, stepped into the breach and continued to block loans to an ailing Mozambique in 1925, 1926 and 1927.[33]

The consequences were largely predictable. The three generals, products of the great era of modern imperialism, gunboat diplomacy and two major wars, may not have resorted to using the crudest instrument of all to try and overrun the Sul do Save and gain control of Delagoa Bay on behalf of the Witwatersrand mining houses and their subsidiaries, but they had nevertheless triumphed using other financial and political means. In 1980, two leading authorities on Mozambican history suggested that '[w]ith the advent to power of Salazar in 1928, it was conceded that South Africa had won the stakes and that the colony would remain dominated by South Africa – a situation that still exists today.'[34]

The centuries-long neglect and systematic undermining of the larger part of Mozambique, and more latterly that of the Sul do Save, can then, stated crudely, be traced back to three fundamental overlapping causes. The first was Portugal's early entry into the age of modern imperialism lacking significant capital and subject to the limitations of the dominant mercantilist and rentier ideologies that became ever more apparent as the 19th and early 20th centuries unfolded.[35] Indeed, in the Portuguese countryside, parts of the ancient order and privilege, the target of reforming liberals, were still evident as late as the 1830s.[36] Second, and linked to the first, was Portugal's inability to see off Britain and other imperial rivals in coastal southeastern Africa after the discoveries of diamonds and gold in the interior. Third was the consequent formation and rapid economic development of a capital-rich industrialising state in South Africa, which, after Union in 1910, echoed and reinforced Britain's desire to treat Mozambique as a client.

But the outer workings of European and regional imperialism that determined the profile and limited the growth of the Mozambican economy had another, less obvious and partly contradictory outcome. It allowed British and South African entrepreneurs to latch on to the soft inner workings of the colony's commercial and financial systems, and to serve the interests of local and metropolitan capital. Britain and South Africa had a vested interest in keeping the existing economic infrastructure of Delagoa Bay from imploding totally – a possibility that, seen from Lisbon, London and Pretoria, often seemed imminent. But, to understand fully how these later interwar 'successes' transpired, it is necessary first to explore how a few of the older and more prominent institutions in northern and central Mozambique endured and adapted when the colony's geo-economic centre shifted to the south and west.

Mozambique and the Pull of the South,
circa 1600–1914

The underlying forces causing the Mozambican field of economic gravity to switch from a centuries-long north–east polar alignment to a new south–west orientation were at their most powerful between about 1870 and 1918, and were inextricably bound up with the discovery of diamonds and gold in southern Africa.[37] But, even then, the intensity of the forces behind the flipping of the poles over just five decades was never of constant strength, nor were those forces distributed evenly along the east coast. Indeed, the clearest and primary manifestation of the flip lay firmly in the south, in the Sul do Save. The 'power' behind the forces of gravitational inversion has, therefore, to be assessed not only in terms of the gathering strength of the new invasive industrial capitalism emanating from southern Africa but also against the inherent weaknesses of the principal economic institutions of the much older would-be colonial polity.

The spectre of a hoped-for Mozambican 'state', forever in the making rather than made, quivered on ramshackle economic foundations. Especially in the north, the country's wealth – such as it was, and to the extent that it was visible to the naked eye – was based, in large part, on the *prazos*. These ill-defined extensive domains, estates and plantations were within relatively easy reach of rivers flowing east, including the Rovuma, the Zambezi and, in the south, the Save. The most substantial rivers and their tributaries were like arteries in the system. At many, if not most, coastal ports and at some inland sites that marked branches leading from important junctions on river and track alike were to be found Arab or Asian traders. These trading networks served as capillary tubes or tumours in the system, extracting value from men and materials in the hinterland via goods that were sold at a premium once pumped downstream for profit. The profits were then repatriated back into the Indian Ocean littoral and global economy.

But a careful look beyond the arteries and capillaries hinted at the logic behind, and inner workings of, the system when viewed over two centuries. For much of the 19th century, Mozambique figured largely as a robber economy, not unlike King Leopold's Congo Free State, depleting its human and material resources over vast swathes

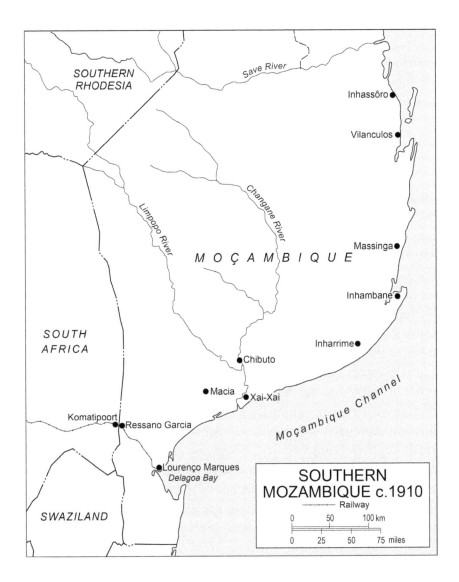

SOUTHERN
MOZAMBIQUE c.1910
———— Railway

of the interior, including the capturing and auctioning-off of African men, women and children into slavery. In the south, and for much of the 20th century, those predations were partially matched by selling off indentured black peasants to the Witwatersrand mine owners. From within the mists of process and time, spread over thousands of square miles, it is difficult to determine precisely where and when the weaknesses of the rentier capitalist mentality ended and the strength of invasive industrial capitalism began. The *prazos* offer one, albeit imperfect, way of charting the glacially paced change in the economic orientation of Mozambique that culminated in the polar realignment caused by the southern African mining revolution.

Prazos and pressures from the south

The *prazo* system – derived from ancient Roman and civil law rootstock – was an offshoot of feudal notions of land grants transplanted from 17th-century Portugal and locked into an Indian Ocean economy underwritten by seasonal monsoon winds. The system took root slowly, albeit often in unintended ways, and over two centuries mutated into a complex Afro-Luso hybrid. It proved resistant to attempts at change and reform emanating from a remote imperial power intent on preserving rentier capitalism, and was transformed largely in the mid-20th century when it was subjected to the forces of industrial capital advancing from the Deep South.[38]

After 1629, among the first *prazeros* – titleholders benefiting from grants of what nominally was 'crown land' – were the *prazos da coroa*. Among such beneficiaries were single males, women and female orphans from Portugal, people of mixed descent (*mestiços*) from Goa, some Indians and a few criminals drawn from a penal colony opened in the middle reaches of the Zambezi.[39] The diverse cultural, economic, social and geographical origins of grant-holders encouraged a few of the more successful *prazeros* to become absentee landlords, presiding at a distance over African tenants, residents and refugees.[40]

It was not the only fuzzy logic to be found in a scheme designed partly to deepen Portugal's shallow political footprint on the African continent. To attract single male colonists from the metropole who, upon marrying, would become settlers with families of their own, title was granted to female orphans and women. Over three generations or lifetimes their daughters, in turn, would be expected to pay only a modest quitrent in the hope that their presence would help to consolidate a firmer Portuguese presence in the remote central and northern parts of the country. But the longed-for Lusitanian bachelors never materialised in meaningful numbers. So the spinsters and most of their female offspring tended to marry locally, adding to the thickening cultural, ethnic and racial mix in the country and to the development of ever more complex identities.[41]

As important – no, *more* so – as the founding weaknesses of estates that beggared belief in terms of their size was the absence of a long-term economic logic centred on renewable resources. How were the *prazos* to yield the returns and investment necessary to hold together, let alone develop, domains governed by imprecise mutating arrangements entered into between the *prazeros* and a state lacking in administrative ability and clout? Thus, to suggest that the *prazos* constituted a 'system' is slightly misleading. Neither the settlement scheme nor the way in which the land might subsequently be exploited was ever 'clearly thought through', and throughout the 18th and 19th centuries, 'an administrative custom developed without ever being incorporated into a single code or finding clear expression in the terms of the land grants themselves'.[42]

With the arguable exception of those *prazos* along the central coastal strip, which served as the region's breadbasket through the cultivation of maize and rice, there was no sign of a sustainable, marketable food surplus worth noting. For the *colono*, or 'free' Africans, living on the large estates spread along the Zambezi between Sena and Tete, and locked into predatory economic arrangement with their landlords, it was thus a saving grace as well as a weakness that they were not expected to cultivate cash crops for the export market in a universe where there was little incentive or capital to modernise techniques of agricultural production. There were a few commodities that were in demand for export: gold dust drawn from the far interior along ancient routes, ivory from elephant hunting along retreating frontiers and wax collected from the hives of wild bees. These may have enjoyed the benefit of a relatively high value-to-weight ratio when hauled over terrain that, beyond the rivers, had no transport infrastructure, but they were derived from sources that were not always readily accessible or renewable.[43]

In an unpromising setting, where the difficulty of raising commercially viable crops was trumped by the presence of an apparently fertile black population, European landlords and the state preferred farming people to plants. For the *prazeros*, harvesting *mussoco*, the annual tax that crown grants entitled them to, required less effort and risk than cultivating crops in a taxing climate. Extracting modest but reasonably certain tax returns from Africans spread across an estate was often preferable to trying to wrest marginally higher returns by gambling on intensive crop cultivation over a smaller area that lacked access to significant markets. On the *prazos*, medieval contractual arrangements resulted in a low-order, self-replicating economic logic that ensured that the number of people on the estate mattered more than agricultural progress through innovation.

Few, if any, in the indigenous African population embraced, let alone welcomed, the idea of being cultivated or grudgingly tolerated for an annual counting that culminated in a demand for *mussoco*. In addition to the annual levy, they were taxed further by colonial invasions, famine brought about by the vicissitudes of nature and inter-tribal warfare, which gave rise to incoming and outgoing refugees. Landlords, in turn, lacked the power to be derived from an overarching economic rationale that might benefit most of their hard-pressed tenants, thereby bolstering their frequently contested political legitimacy.

The net result was that, in the remote inland locations of a weak 'state', *prazeros* often relied heavily on force to ensure their independence and keep their estates intact. *Achikunda* (soldier-slaves) defended or extended the borders of the *prazos*, ensured 'law enforcement' locally and oversaw the smooth functioning of domestic and other slaves operating in and around the inner core of estates. *Prazos* were often marked by formidable, strategically positioned stockades, or *arringas* – small administrative centres of local fiefdoms, in would-be polities.[44]

The need for *achikunda* on domains that abutted or extended beyond the south bank of the Zambezi acquired an additional logic after the 1820s as the Zulu kingdom, further south, began shedding predatory militaristic offshoots that spread out over an arc that covered much of the proximate north and west. Half a century *before* the demands for cheap black labour came from the southern African diamond and gold mines, Nguni invaders were already extracting tribute and softening up indigenous polities in south-central Mozambique even as Portugal sought to reform the archaic *prazos*. Raids from the south coincided with attempts at reform. In 1833, 'a Zulu warrior led the governor of Delagoa Bay, Dion'isio Antònio Ribeiro, naked into a cattle kraal' where a series of charges were put to the prisoner. 'A slave shot and killed the governor', and then 'a warrior opened his chest with an *assegai* and cut out the dead man's heart.'[45]

But nothing, not even attempted reform, moved along meaningfully, let alone with administrative coordination, precision or speed, in coastal or inland Lusophone east Africa. The front door, facing the Indian Ocean, where new thinking about the weak *prazo* economies was most likely to enter, remained firmly closed. Resident *prazeros*, clinging to the land they occupied, were largely devoid of significant start-up or other capital, lacking in entrepreneurial skills and so few in number that their presence was often as difficult to discern as was their behaviour to change. But the back door, the one with the creaking hinges in Portugal itself, the one facing Europe and revolutionary challenges, was marginally less secure.

Napoleon's invasion of Iberia, in 1808, and the loss of Brazil eased open the back door to liberal thinking by Portuguese merchants about problems arising from the old order and then – but with a focus hopelessly blurred by distance – the *prazos*. Two decades later, in 1832, with the liberals in control of the northern part of the mother country, the crown lost any remaining rights to private property in Portugal and, at the stroke of a pen, the *prazo* system in Zambezia was abolished. Except it wasn't. Half a decade later still, there was yet more administrative fumbling when it was decreed that there were to be no more grants of land – only there were, albeit much less frequently. Long-standing political uncertainties in the metropole did nothing to encourage the reconstruction of dated agricultural production in Mozambique. When it came to reforming the *prazo* 'system', Portugal attempted, intermittently and almost always unsuccessfully, to forge new economic keys capable of opening old, rusted, unyielding African locks.[46]

It is noteworthy how such limited economic responses as there were from some of the Mozambican estates, which had assumed cultural practices more African than Lusitanian, were driven and paced by external forces, other than those coming from Lisbon and playing out locally. These included modest increases in the export of gold, ivory and wax once the plundering of slaves destined for the Americas and the Caribbean – including from *prazos* – eased gradually and unevenly between 1860 and 1880, and once the demand for black labour in the southern African mining industry picked up.[47] Likewise, it is perhaps significant that it was just three years after the discovery of gold on the Witwatersrand – between 1889 and 1892 and a huge inflow of capital into the new southern African investment market – that Portugal set up a commission to re-examine and modernise the *prazos*. The modest resulting reforms attempted to realign the estates with the emerging regional economic realities by making provision, on paper at least, for 25- or 30-year leases, and for the more productive use of land by 'free' Africans residing on the properties, but all the while retaining the right to levy *mussoco*.[48]

Not even the emergence of an increasingly prominent industrial giant in South Africa, and a regional offshoot in Rhodesia that shared an aspiration to develop a capitalist economy for the sole benefit of Europeans, could shake off fully the lethargy of semi-autonomous isolated Mozambican estates, some dominated by African cultures. The *prazos*, their roots embedded in the soils of a mediaeval twilight zone, lacked the ability and resources to send out shoots capable of reaching the light of economic 'progress'. Their 'potential' lay largely in providing some of the growing demand for black labour in the region south of the Congo. This labour-providing function, as we will note below, gained impetus in the late 19th century when Portugal, again responding to ideas entering through the Iberian back door, authorised a few chartered companies with concessionary rights and coastal frontages to gobble up many of the *prazos*. But, even then, the *prazos* 'survived into the twentieth century as units of fiscal and administrative policy'.[49]

For more than three centuries, the *prazeros* and a faux colonial administration with a feeble presence moving slowly south, sought to extract as much value as possible through the exploitation of African men and women by levying taxes. In essence, the resented poll tax was payable to ghost-like, sometimes entirely invisible, absentee landlords who controlled armies of slaves to enforce their will. But Lisbon's gift of the right to levy *mussoco* was a mixed blessing. While Africans generally presented themselves as one of the few readily renewable economic resources in an unpromising environment, black hands and taxed heads did not always willingly render unto Caesar that which the *prazero* considered to be his or her due in cash or kind. In remote inland settings, where black bodies were sometimes more readily acquired and rendered submissive for sale at coastal ports than were heads for tax purposes, slaving could be as attractive and profitable an enterprise for *prazeros* as was the farming of people for *mussoco*.

Slaving and a shuffle south

It was the advanced Islamic civilisations of the 8th and 9th centuries, focused on Baghdad, that first developed a well-documented appetite for African slaves. Favoured sources of supply included the Horn of Africa and the coastline stretching as far down as the equator and beyond. For centuries, the mouth of the trade, the Arabian Sea, took in substantial numbers of black male and female captives before funnelling them into the twinned, elongated throats of the Persian Gulf and Red Sea. From there, slaves were fed into the digestive system of the more advanced economies of the wider region, which revelled in ostentatious displays of palatial wealth. By the 15th century, when the Portuguese 'opened up' the Indian Ocean to Western traders, the slaving frontier had long been shifting south. Slaving was part of a robber economy creeping down the Indian Ocean coast and therefore increasingly avoided by coastal-dwelling Africans. It took only a few decades before the Portuguese were riding the monsoon, shipping African slaves back east, across the Arabian Sea, to Goa, Daman and Diu in India.[50]

The slave trade around the Arabian Sea caused Africans to view the Indian Ocean and Middle East with considerable apprehension and distrust. But, when the east coast trafficking of humans is seen in broader perspective, over the *longue durée*, then it was the Atlantic rather than the Indian Ocean they perhaps needed to fear most. It was the industrial revolution, along with wholesale and retail merchants serving the emerging working classes of Europe, that drove the growing demand for the cotton, coffee and sugar cultivated by slave labour spread through much of the Atlantic world and the Indian Ocean islands of Mauritius and Réunion.[51]

With the coastal regions north of the equator in danger of becoming 'slaved out' by the early 19th century, the frontier of the trade in human beings dispatched around the Cape of Good Hope and into the western hemisphere picked up and crept south.[52] Slaves from the lower east African coast were closer to their Atlantic end-destinations and therefore cheaper to transport than those captured in more northerly African outlets. Mozambican slaves – as culturally adaptable, mentally able and physically robust as any of their counterparts – were soon in considerable demand in North and South America, as well as in the Caribbean, including Cuba.[53] Human trafficking on so extensive a scale, including that by God-fearing Portuguese Catholic traders, helped ensure that the DNA of east coast Africans – long since threaded into the populations of India and the Middle East – became ever more widely dispersed throughout the Atlantic world. But a death rate of around 20 per cent from disease and malnutrition in the Middle Passage saw the flesh of Mozambican men, women and children being fed to the fishes of two oceans.[54]

The racially profiled plundering and physical transplantation of millions of Mozambique's indigenous population for the benefit of plantation owners, European industrialists and merchants of products destined for the white working classes of the Atlantic world, reached its apex during the closing decades of the 18th century but continued, at elevated levels, until at least 1850. While it is impossible to retrieve precise numbers, it seems that between about 1770 and 1840, slaves constituted the single most important 'export' from Portugal's east coast colony, easily eclipsing the older and more modest trade in gold, ivory and wax.[55]

Some idea of the magnitude of this part of the global trade in slaves can be gauged from surviving fragmentary evidence. In 24 months, between 1789 and 1790, 'about 46 ships carrying well over 16 000 slaves, circumnavigated the Cape, almost all bound for the sugar and coffee plantations of northern St Domingue'. In 1822, sixteen vessels 'left Quelimane [in northern Mozambique] for Brazil carrying an estimated 10 000 slaves'.[56] In the three decades between 1821 and 1852, '15 per cent of *all* slave exports to the Americas came from the east coast of Africa including the section to the north of Mozambique under Omani Arab control'.[57] In the first half of the 19th century, before the legal trade in slaves was halted in Brazil, in 1851, it imported about 2.5 million slaves 'most of whom came from Portuguese ports in eastern Africa from Ibo in the north to Delagoa Bay' in the south – a nursery for economic progress around the Atlantic.[58]

Quelimane, on the Cuácua River in the northern part of the colony, had a reputation as a centre for the trade in slaves and, later, indentured labour. The port drew on the hunting-heads-for-tax experience of the *prazeros* along the Zambezi to help provide shipments of enslaved black muscle power and female reproductive organs.[59] And, in the southernmost reaches of the Zambezi, Nguni invasions triggered by the demographic and political upheavals that accompanied the rise of the Zulu state in the 1820s gave rise to additional social turbulence.

Local black populations became increasingly vulnerable to slave-taking, not only by coastal traders but also by some inland African polities, including the formidable Ndebele.[60] Pre-capitalist upheavals emanating from African societies may not have been the determinative factor in facilitating the disasters of slavery and indentured labour that befell many Sul do Save inhabitants in the latter half of the 19th century, but they helped pave the way for the industrial servitude of black men pushed and pulled into the South African gold mines in the 20th century.[61]

But, as David Livingstone knew only too well, the slave-raiding frontier along the lower African east coast was best developed and most difficult to disrupt, let alone eliminate, in areas north of the Zambezi.[62] Slavery there persisted into the early 20th century and then mutated into its near relative – indentured labour, often destined for the sugar-producing islands of the Indian Ocean. New euphemisms provided legal post-abolitionary disguises for the continued ultra-exploitative demands of African workers in return for predetermined low wages. Yet, for all the longevity of slavery in the northern reaches of the colony and beyond, a slow southerly movement in the slave-raiding frontier is discernible in Mozambique.

Mozambique Island in the far north, within comfortable reach of dhows coming down from the Arabian Sea on monsoon winds, was for centuries not only the administrative capital but also the slaving capital of the colony. The port reflected many aspects of a culture richly endowed by Islam that was equally visible among the 'people of the coast', the Swahili. The far southern end of the colony lay beyond easy reach of monsoon-driven dhows, and around Inhambane and Delagoa Bay the influence of Arab slave traders, Islamic culture and the echo of Swahili did not loom large, if at all.[63] How and why, then, did the slave-raiding frontier shift, almost imperceptibly, south from the late 18th to the mid-19th century?

The tentative answers to those questions lie in a mess of inter-twined factors that are inherently difficult to sequence and unravel. As already noted, in passing, the depredations occasioned by the earliest Arab and Indian traders and the 'slaving out' of the northeast coast of the continent provided some of the impetus for moving into north-ern Mozambique. Inland slave-raiding excursions, for self-evident reasons, were not only more difficult and dangerous to conduct than coastal operations but also more expensive. Part of the attraction of Mozambican slaves was the fact that they were cheaper than those from further inland. But, to remain competitive, slave raiders needed to keep their prices under control. To ensure access to new supplies that lay beyond those areas already stripped of their human capital, raiders were inclined to move south down the coastline.

This same age-old economic logic acquired additional and increased momentum once the primary market for Mozambican slaves switched from the Indian Ocean to the Atlantic in the 17th century. While there is, again, no hard statistical data to support the suggestion, it appears that the sheer scale of the new trade links to North America, Brazil and the Caribbean encouraged these more southerly, cost-containing coastal predations. By the same token, it became increasingly cost-effective to take slaves on board at points further south along the coast – ports closer to their ultimate Atlantic destinations – than in the northern ports of Ilha da Moçambique and Quelimane.[64] Further savings were made possible using faster ocean-going clippers that reduced the number of days spent at sea and thus the number of deaths in the notorious Middle Passage. And, of course, again as noted, the post-1820 Nguni invasions helped disorganise and sap the resistance of local black communities, making slave-taking in the far south a more attractive proposition.[65]

There are no surviving accounts of Delagoa Bay or even Inhambane –
at the outer edge of the monsoon winds – serving as major slave-
collecting points in the early 18th century, as the Indian Ocean trade in
slaves shifted south and then deepened, as demand from the new markets in the Atlantic world increased. In 1804, an American schooner
transporting slaves to Argentina found it profitable to weigh anchor
at Inhambane, as did several others in the years that followed.[66] But
it was the official opening of the southern Mozambican ports to the
Brazilian trade, in 1811 – a decade before the Nguni-induced disturbances even further south – that kick-started the trade in slaves in the
southernmost reaches of the colony.

By the 1820s, at which time the force of the explosions in the Zulu
kingdom were beginning to be felt further afield, there was a slave station at Lourenço Marques. It lay at the centre of a regional monopoly
dominated by Lisbon merchants, whose business flourished, albeit
under different direction, well into the 1840s.[67] By then, Delagoa
Bay and Inhambane were both 'notorious centres' of the supposedly
banned trade in slaves. In 1857, when the British consul made his way
up the coast, he saw 'shore beacons being lit to warn [slave traders]
of the presence of a British warship' all the way from Delagoa Bay to
Mozambique Island in the north. In 1863, 3 000 slaves laboured on
the plantations around Inhambane, while in Lourenço Marques one
in every three of the inhabitants was a slave.[68]

But, as we have seen, despite this southerly extension of the slaving frontier after 1820, it was slowly being replaced in the north by
slave labour, often masquerading as indentured labour. The demand
for slave-cum-indentured labour from the French-controlled sugar-
producing Indian Ocean islands meant that slave-taking probably
remained deep-seated and persistent north of the Zambezi.[69] This late
seaborne human trafficking in 'indentured' workers – often indistinguishable from slave labour – picked up after the formal abolition of
slavery in French territories in 1848. It persisted into the 1860s, only
to be revived in the 1880s, when the demand for slaves drawn from
Madagascar ensured that the long-illegal slaving frontier in Mozambique
was pushed back further into the remote interior.[70] Trying to eliminate
the shifting slave-raiding frontier in the western Indian Ocean was
always somewhat akin to a game of musical chairs.

When the trade in slaves was officially outlawed in Zanzibar, in 1876, many affected Arab and Swahili slavers moved south into northern Mozambique. And, as we will have occasion to note in due course, the psycho-social scarring occasioned by ongoing slave raids was long-lived up and down the entire length of the coastline. As late as 1894, reporting from Mozambique Island, then in its twilight years, US consul Hollis noted that when a Portuguese navy transport put in to the harbour, 'the cry of "slave ship" goes around the natives and there is a regular exodus of natives from the island to the continent'.[71]

Black Mozambicans in the 19th century were often unwilling to draw meaningful distinctions between slavery, forced labour without wages on public works, compulsory military service and low-wage indentured labour on the Indian Ocean islands, backed by criminal rather than civil sanctions. Nor could their objections always be conveniently, or convincingly, divorced from the way Mozambican labour was recruited for the South African gold mines before World War I.

In 1906, agents of the Witwatersrand Native Labour Association (WNLA) – the recruiting arm of the Chamber of Mines – were gathering indentured labour drawn from the former heartland of slavery south of the Rovuma River. Four years later, in 1910, after a quarter of a century of gold mining along the Reef, the Johannesburg-based *Rand Daily Mail* was still having to actively question 'A Slavery Lie' being carried by rival newspapers reporting on black mine-labour 'recruiting' practices around the old port of Quelimane.[72] And right up to World War I, if not well into the 1920s, indentured labourers from the Sul do Save, many of whom had been forcibly 'recruited', were being transported to Johannesburg in WNLA trains with barred windows and locked doors.[73] The origins of modern South African primary industrialisation – in mining and agriculture – cannot be divorced from an understanding of Mozambican slavery, which fed into the greater southern region in various quasi-legal disguises well into the 20th century.

The deeper significance of this chronological and structurally important overlap in the emerging labour markets of a new Deep South, between the formal abolition of slavery in coastal Mozambique, on the one hand, and the emergence of industrial South Africa on the adjacent Highveld plateau, on the other, has been largely overlooked by both

Anglophone and Lusophone historians. The economic viability of the diamond- and gold-mining industries was initially underwritten – in good measure – by two generations of cheap, foreign black Mozambican labour drawn from a slave or immediate post-slavery economy.

The South African reliance on 'free' Mozambican labour persisted until well into the 1920s. It was only in the interwar years that South Africa's evolving, racially discriminatory land and tax policies started delivering a stream of migrant labour drawn from within its own borders in the quantities necessary to satisfy the industrialising state's near-insatiable demand for cheap labour. Black South Africans, like their Mozambican forerunners, were denied residential rights at their place of employment, as was customarily associated with emerging industrial proletariats in the northern hemisphere. And, as with British foreign policy in the 18th and 19th centuries, the formal unravelling of slavery in Portugal, as experienced in Mozambique, needs to be understood against the wider, changing patterns of economic self-interest in southern Africa. Indeed, in some respects, much of the southern African region needs to be seen as a zone of conflict at the intersection between two unequal empires – the British and the Portuguese – giving rise to marginal contestations and political turbulence.[74] If Britain's foreign policy towards Portugal during much of that period was filled with 'pious cant' and 'hypocrisy', then so too was its policy regarding the abolition of slavery, which was often punctuated by considerations of financial self-interest and global trade.

A veritable chasm separated the reach and nature of economic development in Britain from that in Portugal. Given that, it may have been inevitable that, despite being joined at the hip through bilateral treaties, the struggle to abolish the slave trade would proceed at a different pace, and follow differing trajectories, in the two countries. In Britain, the initial challenge to the slave trade, in 1788–1792, came from upon high, from divine inspiration as experienced by wealthy Anglicans and other patrons. Their agitation culminated in the passing of the Slave Trade Act of 1807. But, in the sugar-rich islands of the Caribbean, the trade persisted until 1811. It took a further quarter of a century for the Slavery Abolition Act of 1833 to halt human trafficking in the wider British Empire.

Operating in the shadow of the United Kingdom meant that

abolition came to Portugal more slowly. Lisbon's stuttering attempts at abolishing slavery, modernising agricultural practices and advancing constitutional democracy came via a largely secular route after the Napoleonic upheavals. The six-year civil war of 1828–1834, between the church and conservative landowners on the one hand and liberal constitutionalists on the other, opened new political space. But, even then, reforms were slow to gather momentum. The effective outlawing of the slave trade in near-bankrupt Mozambique took a lifetime, perhaps three or four. In Lisbon, as in London, politicians took to the parliamentary dancefloor only when the noise from the brass bands in the street guaranteed them easier access to new electoral partners.

The music was often loudest along the Thames. In 1810, the Treaty of Amity and Friendship bound Portugal 'to move towards the gradual abolition of the slave trade', an intention underscored in a second treaty five years later. Two decades later, little had happened and the trade was flourishing in Mozambique. By the mid-1830s, under pressure from missionaries, who like most imperialists thought that all global horizons were potentially British and Christian, Westminster was becoming impatient with the tempo along the Tagus. In 1839, Lord Palmerston unilaterally declared that any seaborne trade in slaves was to be construed as an act of piracy. Members of the Cortes Gerais, the Portuguese parliament, sighed, and for four years thereafter, the Royal Navy patrolled the Mozambique Channel with the support of Lisbon, and British seamen boarded any vessel suspected of furthering the slave trade.[75]

It was not as if Portugal's political elite, struggling to keep up with a guide intent on leading Lisbon into the modern world at a pace that did not threaten its own interests, was wholly wanting in effort. The Cortes showed some intent when it came to limiting or abolishing slavery. The problem was that it did so – repeatedly – to little practical end. For two decades in the mid-19th century, Bernardo de Sá Nogueira de Figueiredo (Sá da Bandeira, five times prime minister of Portugal between 1836 and 1870) sought to have slavery abolished in the Portuguese Empire. In 1854, he got so far as to have a bill passed, backed by a decree in 1858, confirming that, within 20 years, slavery would be a thing of the past. In 1878, slavery was eventually abolished in Portugal's African colonies.

By comparison, the slave-like *shibalo* (forced labour) conditions that followed – in the shape of legislation governing everything from five-year contracts of indenture and military conscription to public works fed by ill-defined 'vagrancy' laws – came to Mozambique in double-quick time, between just 1878 and 1899. A finely meshed set of new laws was designed to facilitate the economic transition from slavery to an ostensibly 'freer' market for black labour.[76] It engineered an intermediate stage of impoverishment by creating a coercive racist order scarred by forced labour for ultra-cheap or sub-subsistence wages – or no wages at all. In chronological terms, the emerging low-wage order overlapped perfectly with the industrial dispensation engulfing the southern interior. It was a domestic labour regime moving between slavery, formally abandoned, and a supposedly new 'free' labour market that attracted the late-19th-century South African mining industry and then drew in transnational migrant Mozambican black miners.[77]

The post-1878 labour dispensation in Mozambique, then, lay somewhere along a spectrum between classic chattel slavery and an allegedly 'free' market for bonded black workers. But the emerging order was never poised equidistantly from the market extremities. The binding of African labour by 'contracts' that seldom manifested themselves in tangible documented form was, in practice, little more than 'slavery by any other name'. The primary institutions for the renewed, partially modernised racial oppression and exploitation of black workers in central and northern Mozambique were the chartered companies. These drew African labourers into a regional industrial revolution that, in turn, was locked into the global economy.[78]

Chartered companies and the Witwatersrand Native Labour Association

In the late 1870s, shortly after the discovery of diamonds in the south and before the Scramble for Africa formally got under way, the Lisbon government began granting concessions to Portuguese nationals. It was nothing new, and 'outsourcing had a long history within the Portuguese empire'.[79] The hope was that they would attract capital and encourage economic development in the soporific east African colony. In 1888, with the Berlin template for the imperial carve-up by then superimposed on the map of Africa, and, significantly, just months after the discovery of the imposing new gold deposits on the Witwatersrand, Portugal ratified the first of two chartered companies, the Companhia de Moçambique, which lasted from 1892 to 1942.

In less than three years, in February 1891, proceeding at what for Lisbon was almost a breakneck pace, the charter of the Mozambique Company underwent some tweaking. The Portugal-based resident directors of the new joint-stock company were granted sovereign rights over a vast centrally located territory straddling the provinces of Manica in the west – hard against the domain newly claimed by Rhodes's British South Africa Company (chartered in 1889) – and Sofala in the east, which twisted south down to the Save River. The Mozambique Company was, in effect, a state within a state, with rights to pass regulations, enforce laws, man borders, control movements, settle colonists, raise taxes and, after 1899, extract forced labour from all Africans within its reach.[80]

The smelling salts of new economic opportunity in southern Africa, mixed with a few old European imperial political intrigues, were still working their magic along the Tagus when, six months later, in September 1891, the financially stretched Lisbon government ratified a second charter, for 25 years, in the far north of the colony. Although the poorer and uglier of the two sisters, the Companhia de Niassa (1891–1929) had a familiar corporate architecture. Like the Mozambique Company, it too had the right to make laws, issue currency, establish a police force and dispense favours through the granting of sub-concessions. As with its sibling, the vast domain of the new company, which straddled the districts of Cabo Delgado and Niassa, pressed up against an international boundary in the shape of the Rovuma River – the mouth of which had already been appropriated by Germany – represented a state within a state.[81]

Yet more evidence of haste and the desire to exploit the mounting enthusiasm for capital investment in southern Africa followed within months. In 1892, the Zambesi Company acquired a huge concession in central Mozambique, in the heartland of the old *prazo* system, concentrated in the Tete and Zambezia districts. As with the other chartered entitlements, the Zambesi Company soon spawned a set of sub-concessions; among the more important were those going to corporate estate and plantation owners in the shape of the Boror, Lubo and Sena Sugar Estates companies. Born in the mists of an African speculative frenzy, the Zambesi Company, working in areas until recently loved by Arab slavers, soon began sending conscripted labourers to the South African mines.[82]

As distinctive as the chartered and other companies were, with their public share listings, they were not the only important corporate entries into Mozambique as the 19th century gave way to the 20th. In 1900, the Witwatersrand Chamber of Mines formed an unlisted subsidiary – the WNLA – to control the regional recruitment of cheap black labour for the South African gold mines. It was a company within an association, part of a cartel. Twelve months later, even before the Anglo-Boer War was concluded, Milner's reconstruction administration entered into the modus vivendi with their Portuguese counterparts in Lourenço Marques. In return for the WNLA being granted exclusive recruiting rights for black miners throughout the Sul do Save, the British – acting on behalf of the South African mine owners – would ensure that a little more than half of all the rail traffic destined for the goldfields would be routed through Mozambique's capital and port city. It was, as one historian remarked, a 'naked exchange of rail service for human service', without the people being trafficked – African peasants – being asked or consenting to a most oppressive arrangement.[83]

In theory, the weak colonial administration in Lourenço Marques retained exclusive responsibility for the governance and adminis-tration of the Sul do Save. But, in practice, the notoriously corrupt Portuguese bureaucracy formed little more than an additional layer of local management of the powerful WNLA. An official Portuguese cap could not disguise a pointy South African head. The WNLA soon had more officers and recruiters on the ground than the colonial administration had staff on its books. As a company within a com-pany, the WNLA functioned as another quasi-state within a state, often operating much like one of the chartered companies.

The WNLA was part of a temporal and structural bridge linking southern Mozambique to South Africa. It led the way from a 'state' in which African chattel slavery had barely been formally abandoned to another perfecting a form of low-wage mass industrial servitude. On the Rand, African contracted labourers were housed in compounds under prison-like conditions, subjected to criminal sanctions and denied all political rights or the right to form trade unions. Under slavery, northern Mozambique supplied African male and female bodies, along with their children, to the plantations of the Atlantic world from where they were destined never to return. Under the WNLA, southern Mozambique sent healthy black men to the mineralised continental plateau, where, as contracted labourers, they were worked to near-death on poor diets for cheap wages, and their shattered bodies returned in 'Red Cross' train coaches unattended by doctors or nurses.[84]

After chattel slavery in the Portuguese colony made way for its domesticated cousins – contract labour for the chartered companies or *shibalo* labour for the state – approximately three out of every four black Mozambicans in the Sul do Save opted 'voluntarily' for indentures with the WNLA. They were 'up from slavery' but nowhere near a free market for their labour. Before World War I, about one in every four Mozambicans was forcibly channelled into mine labour and transported to the Witwatersrand goldfields in sealed trains that amounted to little more than mobile prisons. Hoisting the flag of 'voluntary' enlistment above a regionally rigged 'free' labour market, the WNLA was a long-lived success, serving the South African coal- and gold-mining industries with 'recruits' into the 1970s.[85]

The WNLA was the heir to, and immediate beneficiary of, a centuries-old east coast slaving regime and the slave-like labour regimes that followed. It was the WNLA and black Mozambicans that lifted the Rand gold-mining industry from its knees after it lost access to its British-gifted contingent of Chinese indentured labour (1902–1910). In so doing, the workers helped ensure the economic success of the wider South African economy during the interwar years. Not once between 1903 and the mid-1950s was there a time on the South African mines that Mozambicans did not constitute most of a labour force that increased from about 77 000 in its earlier years to around 300 000.[86] Like the chartered companies, the WNLA was a creature that emerged from the economic and political swamps of southeastern

Africa between 1870 and 1900. Imperial rivalries, nationalist pride and the need to demonstrate effective occupation of a regional backwater all combined to ensure that Mozambique could breathe life into the primary industries that shaped modern South Africa.

The WNLA, in many ways the ugliest of the corporate sisters operating in colonial Mozambique, was born of an economic need and revolved unequivocally around an economic logic. Its overriding purpose was to provide a continuous stream of black muscle power to help drive the industrial machinery that churned out profits for mainly northern-hemisphere investors. The chartered companies, by contrast, entered the world primarily as the political rather than the economic offspring of nationalists in Lisbon. Members of the Cortes were intent on finding ways of keeping other European imperialists from snaffling an otherwise unappetising lunch rotting away slowly on a neglected Indian Ocean shoreline.

But no joint-stock company with shares listed on a European bourse, let alone one based in capital-starved Portugal – on the brink of bankruptcy, which arrived soon enough, in 1891 – could attract investors by promising dividends payable only in national-anthem song sheets and paper flags. Chartered companies, coaxed into life by political midwives without meaningful bank balances, were forced to invent rudimentary economic programmes and attract some shifty financial nurses if they were to survive their birth trauma. But, in an age characterised by gross market manipulation through speculative activities, encouraged by prospectuses puffed with misleading, if not downright deceitful information about the fast-evolving markets for capital in central and southern Africa, these demands only spawned other, more serious problems.[87]

The chartered entities may have aspired to economic viability, but the lingering desire by rival imperial powers to expand their spheres of influence were difficult to fend off while stock markets remained open to all. British, French or German investors – often enjoying the covert political support of their governments – could bustle into the bourse whenever they chose to do so and buy a controlling interest in the companies by acquiring the majority of shares on offer. The northern rivals did not, however, have things entirely their own way.

After 1906, those vying to shape the destiny of the Niassa Company felt the sharp elbows of an aggressive adolescent in the shape of Lewis & Marks, South African mining capitalists whose search for black mine labour trumped the desire for meaningful dividends. A decade later, in 1916, Lewis & Marks, with the support of the British Foreign Office, were supplanted by Sir Owen Philipps (later Lord Kylsant), chairman of the Union-Castle shipping company, to protect the labour supplies of Robert Williams's mines in Katanga. The net result was that, during the early years, the 'national identity' of the boards of both the Mozambique and Niassa companies frequently changed hands, which did little to sharpen their supposed pursuit of purely economic objectives. Unrealistic promises, bullish rumours strategically planted and cynical market manipulations arising from all of them helped boards keep the laws of financial gravity largely at bay. British shareholders fought off the French and Germans, or the French and Germans tried to see off the British, while the echoes of age-old or new imperial battle cries rang out in hollow battles for companies offering largely contrived dividends.[88]

There was, in truth, little hard economic data to call on while beating the east coast bush in the hope of flushing a few fledgling profits. As the slave traders of yore had discovered over the centuries, in Mozambique the vastness of the terrain was in inverse proportion to the richness of its potential natural resources. The wealth of the place lay not in what was in, on or under the soil but in the labour of the African families who struggled to wrest a living from it. In the west, in Manica province and Chimoio, the Mozambique Company had early access to some revenue from a few small-scale gold mines and from some marginal, settler-managed farms producing maize. But, even then, these produced only modest revenues when compared with those in neighbouring white Rhodesia. Up north, the Niassa Company pondered its even poorer natural dowry and then fell back on the old robber-economy stalwarts – copal, cotton, beeswax and wild rubber.

In the 16th century, the silver mines of Potosí had set Spanish imaginations aflame, and the smoke had drifted across Iberia. Early Portuguese explorers had sailed south and east rather than west, hoping that the fabled central African kingdom of Monomatapa – Mozambique, or Prester John's backyard – might one day deliver to them gold in quantities that matched Spain's silver. But beeswax and copal, the essence of candles and incense, the stuff of cathedrals and chapels, were poor substitutes for precious metals. The chartered companies, too, lived largely on a hope and a prayer until they, like the *prazeros* and slave traders before them, came to terms with reality. They had to squeeze cash out of bush villages located on what had once been the commonweal but which, at the stroke of a Lisbon pen, had been privatised and become the possession of foreign shareholders. Hut tax on company properties was paid for by forced labour on the estate or from the sluggish low- or no-wage regimes on the mines, public works and settler farms. On the fringes of the integrating regional economic system, tax became the financial mainstay of the two chartered companies, dovetailing with the interests of the WNLA.

In the far north, the terrain was nominally under the control of the Niassa Company. In its various guises, it manifested features that the age-old Arab east-coast slave traders recognised all too easily, and that the modern agents of Leopold's Congo had already embraced with alacrity and surpassed. Indeed, so poor was the company's control of the vast expanse it presided over that it connived readily at an ongoing Arab slave trade that persisted right up to World War I.[89]

The persistence of a slave-taking core during the early industrialisation of the subcontinent was not without benefit for the chartered company, its South African mine-owning shareholders or the WNLA – a close ally in the hunt for cheap black labour. Active slaving at remote sites, when it did not make for the flight of entire African families across national borders, drove many of the remaining displaced persons towards the periphery and into the waiting arms of those in search of indentured labour. For refugees, indentured labour was preferable to slavery; it was a way station en route to the allegedly 'free' labour market developing to the south, while for employers it provided a fig leaf of voluntarism and wages that might be paraded before foreign governments and shareholders.

After 1903, encouraged by the presence of Lewis & Marks's footprint in the ancient bloodied soils by then controlled by the Niassa Company, the WNLA set about 'recruiting' the scatterings of slavery and others with gusto. Indeed, it did so with so much energy and focus that it precipitated a series of African uprisings that culminated in the defeat of the weak company forces in 1906. Recruiting faltered while the company underwent financial restructuring, recommencing with renewed vigour three years later, only to be abandoned in 1913 when the death rate of 'tropicals' recruited by the WNLA in regions north of 22 degrees south reached such appalling levels on the Witwatersrand gold mines that even the South African government felt that it had become indefensible.[90]

In the west, the Mozambique Company, benefiting from the transit trade into Rhodesia facilitated by the emergence, in 1903, of the Beira & Mashonaland Railway Company and the relative proximity of its holdings to the emerging labour markets of South Africa, did slightly better than did the Niassa Company. But not much. In essence, it too was a financial failure. The only dividends it ever paid were not derived from solid performance-based earnings but from loose change employed for share market manipulations. The Niassa Company went one better and never once declared a dividend during its 30-year existence.

The Mozambique Company, like its northern sister, came to rely more on the mining of African bodies than of ore bodies. It farmed hut taxes, the *mussoco*, delivering cheap coerced labour to its sub-concessionaries, small mine owners, miners and maize producers who then squeezed the workers for the modest profits that they shared with the company. In Mossurize and Alto Save, the southwestern districts closest to the emerging 'free' market for black labour in South Africa, company agents extracted hut taxes from the repatriated earnings of miners employed on the Witwatersrand mines. There, too, in the southernmost parts, WNLA agents, supposedly restricted to the Sul do Save, ignored the provincial boundary and used a familiar stick-and-carrot repertoire to maintain a steady flow of 'recruited', 'voluntary' black labour to the Witwatersrand mines.[91]

From 1902 to 1914, from the Rovuma River in the north to the Incomati River in the south, the Niassa and Mozambique companies, operating slave or slave-like systems for the collection of hut taxes – directly and indirectly – helped to underwrite the earliest phases of industrialisation on the South African Highveld. They extruded cheap black labour into a wider, regionally integrating economy that included the new settler-state of Rhodesia. Aided by the WNLA, the bodysnatching, body-peddling companies helped Portugal sustain a plausible presence in its east coast colony at the high point of imperial contestation in Africa but did next to nothing, or very little, to develop the territories they occupied.[92]

After World War I, once the threats of direct imperial territorial expansion in southern Africa by outside powers had been stayed for the moment, the political logic that had originally informed the establishment of the two Mozambican chartered companies was dramatically reduced, but Portugal, saddled with a huge war debt, remained as financially compromised as ever. Under changed circumstances, new questions about the purpose of the chartered companies, now focusing more on their economic as opposed to their political viability, began to emerge in Lisbon.

The days of the chartered companies were numbered. Disillusionment with liberalism, along with prolonged post-war political and economic chaos in the metropole, led to the 1926 coup in Lisbon. It ushered in the rise of the economist António de Oliveira Salazar, first as a reforming Minister of Finance in 1928, and then, in 1932, as prime minister of a new state, the quasi-fascist Estado Novo.

Under Salazar, public finances in Portugal were restored with remarkable rapidity and the colonies saddled with demanding new neo-mercantilist economic policies. The first to fall, predictably, was the corrupt, bankrupt Niassa Company, which had, in effect, been placed on terms as far back as 1917 for failing to meet its chartered obligations. On the eve of the Great Depression, in October 1929, Portugal resumed administrative responsibility for the northern territory. In the west, the sister Mozambique Company, propped up by the spindly legs of sub-concessionaries and coerced labour, did not keel over after an initial push back by the markets. Then, in 1930, the company got a long, lingering goodbye kiss from Salazar, who allowed it to operate until the charter expired, in 1941, by which time South African hegemony in the region was long established.[93]

Over the four centuries that separated the 15th-century 'voyages of discovery' by the Portuguese explorers and the eventual incorporation of the Sul do Save into an industrialising regional economy dominated by South Africa, in the late 19th century, the focal point of the political economy of Mozambique, along with its administrative capital, gradually shifted south. In the age of sail and spice, the elongated east coast colony looked steadfastly north and east, towards Arabia and India. But by the time steam and industry commanded the world more fully, Mozambique's eyes had swung around, and it was looking inland, to the west and south, for its fortunes. Although this glacially paced shift southward began in the late 18th century and gathered momentum during the first half of the 19th century as the global trade in slaves increased, it reached maximum momentum after the mineral discoveries in southern Africa in the 1860s and 1880s.

The most important reasons for this slow incorporation of the east coast colony into an emerging global economy that came to take an increasing interest in southern Africa lay in Europe. First, Portugal's lack of mineral resources and significant quantities of capital alike meant that the relics of an archaic agrarian economy lingered longer there than they did elsewhere on the continent. Lacking financial resources and dominated by notions of mercantile capitalism, the Portuguese political elite was largely incapable of adjusting and developing its economic muscle in southeast Africa. Instead, for centuries it relied on vast, agriculturally moribund estates, the *prazos*, and later on slave trading to signal its presence and occupation of Mozambique. When these ancient institutions, whose practices centred on the gross exploitation and/or buying and selling of Africans for labour, either domestically or abroad, were no longer politically viable, they were supplanted by chartered companies with new political roles.

The chartered companies raised capital on European share markets at the high point of imperial rivalries, supposedly demonstrating Portugal's meaningful occupation of territories that it never commanded convincingly. After the turn of the century, and in the far south of Mozambique, the chartered companies' performances were easily eclipsed by an association that had a genuine economic function, supported by mining capital that came directly from South Africa. The WNLA, a corporate child of the Chamber of the Mines, was granted the sole 'recruiting' rights to African indentured labour in the Sul do Save. Portugal had the wherewithal to enter the age of imperialism, but its east coast colony lacked the resources to sustain meaningful progress.

Second, Portugal's economic and political vulnerability during the

Napoleonic Wars rendered it acutely and progressively more vulnerable to the rising industrial power, imperial ambitions and diplomatic reach of Britain. The results were especially visible on the southeastern coast of Africa. As the 18th century gave way to the 19th, and the 19th to the 20th, Mozambique's misfortunes could be located, ever more readily, within a nexus of three forces: first, the unerringly strong and duplicitous changes in the way the foreign policies of imperial rivals played out in the region; second, Portugal's weak and vacillating administration of a colony, acquired initially in a fit of absent-mindedness during a passage to India; and third, the gathering strength and sub-imperial motives of Britain, Portugal and South Africa in the 20th century. It is only through the transcending logic of triangulation that we can start to make sense of how it was that Mozambique entered the modern world so vulnerable.

But it was not only the rural Sul do Save that South African capital had captured by World War I. The countryside, prepared for centuries by rentier capitalism, slavery and quasi-slave practices, might have been the most vulnerable and the first to fall, but it was not on its own. By the mid-1920s, Lourenço Marques, along with small towns and the retail trade up and down the clientelist countryside, was also in the hands of South African mining capital, who, with the help of comprador trading allies, had the colony locked into industrial servitude. It is to the latter that we will turn our attention in Part II.

PART II

SOUTH AFRICAN PREDATIONS: LOURENÇO MARQUES AND THE SUL DO SAVE, CIRCA 1875–1950

Imperialism was born when the ruling class in capitalist production came up against national limits to its economic expansion.

HANNAH ARENDT

Like their northern-hemisphere counterparts, southern African capitalists aspired to controlling a black working class in the making not only at the point of production, through the repressive compound system, but in its residential domain, in Mozambique. Ideally, migrants needed to be drawn into the emerging centre of the regional economy both as proletarians – when they presented as wage workers on the Witwatersrand – and as peasant-consumers when back home, in their villages of origin on the periphery. It was this underlying impetus, the need to promote the tie-in of migrants as proletarians and peasants, to align as far as possible the economic centre with its geographical periphery, that provided South African mining capitalists with the incentive to control as much of the weakly developed financial muscle and tissue of the greater Sul do Save as was possible.

The quest to develop chains of value when importing machinery and timber destined for the Witwatersrand, along with that of ensuring the circulation and retention of migrant labour, helped protect profit margins in the South African gold- and coal-mining industries. Similar considerations encouraged the informal conquest of Lourenço Marques and parts of the Sul do Save. These objectives could not have been achieved, however, without the direct or indirect assistance of the administrative-political, financial and commercial sectors of an emaciated local economy staffed by resentful Portuguese nationalists and colonial subjects who, simultaneously, aspired to lessening their dependence on South Africa.

Iron Horse turned Trojan Horse:
The Pretoria–Delagoa Bay Railway

Founded amid deep suspicions about British imperial ambitions and racial policies in southern Africa, and particularly following the abolition of slavery in the Cape in the 1830s, the Zuid-Afrikaansche Republiek was established in 1852. It entrenched the rights of an aspirant agrarian elite – 'Boers', of European descent – over African ethnic communities across a vast inland area. Far from being an agricultural or a pastoral paradise, the trans-Vaal functioned in near splendid isolation for close on two decades. A nascent 'national' economy was underwritten by semi-literate subsistence farmers practising summer farming and winter hunting with the assistance of nominally free or indentured black, often seasonal, labourers resident on vast estates. But, in 1867, this somnambulant agrarian order, not unduly distressed at the prospect of dreaming its way into a future devoid of outside influence, was subjected to a series of unwelcome, industrially induced shocks. The new focus of the ZAR's discomfort once again lay to the south, where the discovery of diamonds had eased the sub-continent's economic centre northwards.

Calvinist and conservative to the core in all matters religious and social, the Transvaal Boers were not indifferent to the lure of the markets for their produce, nor to the prospect of the making of money that came with the rural and urban transformation of the diamond fields around Kimberley. Indeed, in 1872, months after the first major gemstone discoveries, they showed just how open they were to new economic and political possibilities. The Boers' newly elected president was TF Burgers, once an NGK minister in the Cape Colony. An improbable choice, Burgers had, a few years earlier, seen a charge of heresy overturned by the Privy Council in London. A man of ideas who sensed radical change in the air, Burgers lacked the financial resources to see most of his projects to completion. He drafted several innovative policies and initiatives that, he sincerely believed, might enhance the economic prospects of his constituents without drawing them into the expanding ambit of British influence.

To avoid being encircled by regional political strongholds in the thrall of empire and to bolster the fragile independence of the republic,

Burgers looked east rather than south for a solution. The objective was for the Transvaal to benefit from the growing demand for fuel, grain and livestock on the diamond fields without compromising the essentially agrarian identity of constituents who had severe reservations about the supposed benefits of modernity and industrialisation. Thus, a decade before the discovery of gold on the Witwatersrand, the landlocked Calvinist ZAR linked up with the coastal, commercially minded Catholic administration of Mozambique in a search for profit free of British meddling.

Burgers's attempt to transform ideas into realities, based on changing market opportunities and increasing property values in the ZAR, peaked three years into his presidency. In 1875, the ZAR and Portugal signed a Treaty of Commerce allowing for the duty-free exchange of goods between the Transvaal and Mozambique. It was an agreement entered into at a time when both partners were, at best, sluggards insofar as international trade was concerned, largely devoid of financial reserves and much richer in potential than in practice, and was set to expire in 1902. But it was overtaken by events. The discovery of gold at what was to become Johannesburg, a decade or so after the treaty was signed, radically changed the economic status of the partners. The Witwatersrand and adjacent coal-producing areas – centred on Witbank in the eastern Transvaal – were transformed by primary industrialisation and urbanisation while Portuguese Mozambique barely stirred from its centuries-long, feudal-like slumber.[1]

But, back in 1875, President Burgers's desire for access to a port capable of supporting the economic development of the republic was boosted by the discovery of a few modest gold deposits in the eastern Transvaal, which he promptly fed into an ambitious plan – a rail link between Lourenço Marques and Pretoria. So, in the same year that saw the signing of the Treaty of Commerce, Burgers embarked on a tour of Europe to raise the capital necessary to underwrite his new project. But his imaginative, debenture-driven initiative was stillborn. Some rails were shipped to Mozambique, where they lay waiting for construction crews, but most never left Holland, rusting in the Zeeland port of Vlissingen (Flushing).[2]

Burgers's political eclipse, for reasons that had little to do with the failure of the railway to materialise, or the imminent bankruptcy of the Boer state, saw the republican dream of an east coast rail link deferred rather than destroyed. Indeed, when the British annexed the Transvaal three years later, only to be defeated by the Boers in the First War of Independence (1881) that followed, the objective behind the original scheme acquired greater importance in the eyes of the ZAR political elite. In 1884, still months before the epoch-changing discovery of the Rand gold deposits, President SJP Kruger's administration awarded a concession to a Dutch-German consortium for the construction of the Transvaal section of the Pretoria–Delagoa Bay line. But matters continued to drag until the Rand goldfields were thrown open. Within 12 months of the discovery of the reef, in 1886, the concession was transformed with the flotation of the new railway company, the Nederlandse Zuid-Afrikaansche Spoorweg-Maatschappij (NZASM).[3]

In that same year, 1886, with the subcontinent's economic pulse visibly primed and pumping like a vein on a bald man's head, Lisbon, too, was spurred into uncharacteristically swift action. A concession was granted to an American, Colonel Edward McMurdo, to build a railway from Lourenço Marques to Ressano Garcia on the ZAR border, where it would link up with the NZASM. But McMurdo was more interested in speculative profits than railway construction. So half-hearted were his efforts that he alienated the Mozambican administration, which was hoping to steal a march on other southern African ports in the race for a lucrative inland connection. Thirty-six months after granting McMurdo the concession, the Portuguese nationalised the railway, naming the new company the Caminhos de Ferro de Lourenço Marques (CFLM). By 1890, with the Rand goldfields in their infancy, the CFLM line had reached Ressano Garcia, where it waited on a longed-for connection to the NZASM. But it was only in January 1895 that the Pretoria–Delagoa Bay line eventually opened to east–west traffic.[4]

By then, much of the economic logic underlying Burgers's original scheme had undergone a profound change. An agrarian elite that had once aspired to industrialisation only insofar as it might add value to the farm products of its constituents – as when it turned its fruit and grain surplus into alcohol – found its world turned upside down. Anything that it had hitherto produced from its principal asset, the

TOP Ressano Garcia station, on the South Africa–Mozambique border, c. 1898.

ABOVE View of industry on the Inkomati River, Ressano Garcia, c. 1902.

land, was eclipsed in value by the proceeds of mining.[5] The founding idea behind a railway linking the ZAR and Mozambique – two regimes hoping to boost commercial ties by fostering the distribution, exchange and sale of goods and products of their own making – had been overtaken by industry. Wealth no longer derived only from what was on the land but from what lay hidden beneath it.

In short, the politics of the ZAR was no longer in alignment with the economy. A venerable Boer governing class, agrarian-industrial in outlook, was presiding over an effervescing industrial-agrarian state. While politicians drawing on the old order in the countryside were governing from the God-fearing bucolic capital, Pretoria, the mining centres were already shaping a younger, industry-oriented elite for the stock exchange-worshippers of Johannesburg – a government in waiting. The resulting tensions, couched in the political rhetoric of nationalism and imperialism, assumed proportions that could not be dissolved through debate.

In December 1895, the bottle popped its cork, releasing the pressure but without neutralising an explosive mixture that continued to bubble away within it. The Jameson Raid, an abortive coup d'état led by the mine owners, ushered in a short interval of readjustment. The agrarian elite attempted to accommodate the most pressing needs of the captains of industry as best they could, but to no lasting effect. The Randlords and their British allies by then believed – even if they did not say so openly – that what was needed was not compromised piecemeal reform but a full-scale revolution. The mine owners aspired to control the politics *and* the economics of a new state, one that would prioritise finance over farming, bullion over beef. It was not just the cork, but the bottle itself, that would have to go if they were get meaningful change. To achieve this, however, would require Britain to wage war against the Boers, and Albion was not long in delivering.[6]

The Anglo-Boer War of 1899–1902 presented the victorious British and their mine-owning partners in reconstruction with the opportunity to shape the future. They presided over an industrial-agrarian state that would dominate the fortunes of the entire subcontinent, Anglophone core and Lusophone periphery alike. It was a troubling prospect, one that held potentially disastrous consequences for Lourenço Marques and what had once been the financial hope of chronically underfunded Mozambique – the success of the Delagoa Bay–Pretoria line. Fearing that British hegemony in the region would see preference being given to other southern African ports to the exclusion of their own promising east coast outlet on the Bay, the Portuguese administration scrambled to put together a deal.

After the advent of deep-level gold mining, in the mid-1890s, the Mozambican administration became ever more aware of how dependent the new industry was on a steady supply of east coast black labour if it were to guarantee northern-hemisphere investors sound returns on their investments. In the Sul do Save, with an African population only recently freed from chattel slavery but still powerfully locked into a state-sanctioned system of forced labour, Portugal had access to a priceless resource.[7] Indeed, in many ways black workers were more prized by Lord Milner's reconstruction regime and the mining industry than was the Pretoria–Delagoa Bay railway, which had lost much of its original *raison d'être*.

Moreover, for black Mozambicans who had within living memory experienced the horrors of slavery and indentured labour, waged work on the mines, paid for in a strong currency, seemed like a step up rather than sideways in the struggle to meet the never-ending tax demands coming from Lourenço Marques. What the Mozambican administration needed was to find a way of linking the mines' demand for cheap black labour to its own need for a steady flow of rail traffic between Delagoa Bay and the Witwatersrand. Only by so doing could it ensure the continued development and expansion of its lower east coast port and ensure that a proletariat in the making could help it grow its modest tax base.

The modus vivendi entered into by Portugal and the appointed, unelected Milner administration, in 1902, secured the interests of the Mozambican administration and the Rand mine owners. But it did so at the expense of a third party who had never been consulted about, let alone agreed to, the arrangement – the trafficked black miners. Lourenço Marques would be guaranteed 50 to 55 per cent of all rail traffic destined for the core Witwatersrand zone. In return, the Chamber of Mines, through its subsidiary, the Witwatersrand Native Labour Association, would be guaranteed exclusive recruiting rights in the Sul do Save. But the modus vivendi did more than assign the descendants of black Mozambicans to generations of industrial servitude at low wages. It also cemented into place the changed logic behind the Pretoria–Delagoa Bay railway line, with far-reaching consequences for nearly all the inhabitants of the Sul do Save and well beyond.

The 1875 Treaty of Commerce between Portugal and the ZAR rested on the dream of facilitating commercial exchange between two colonial states, both then facing the prospect of bankruptcy. The modus vivendi, by way of contrast, entrenched an unequal exchange between an emerging industrial state and a weak commercial, port-based authority reliant on the east coast railway to keep it financially viable. The signing of the modus vivendi entrenched Mozambique's status as a dependent, supplicating enclave for most of the 20th century. The iron horse, the Pretoria–Delagoa Bay line, was meant to encourage economic development among equals. The modus vivendi turned it into a Trojan Horse, carrying within it the forces for the impoverishment of Mozambique.[8]

The British victory in the war had, simultaneously, secured the future economic progress of southern Africa and Mozambique's growing dependency on it. The modus vivendi, a short-term post-war arrangement, was followed, in 1909, shortly before the advent of the Union of South Africa, by its longer-term successor, the Mozambique Convention. This, in turn, was successfully renegotiated in 1928 and renewed in 1934 and 1939, only to linger on, in phantom form, into the 1960s.[9]

From around World War I and well into the 1950s, the South African mines employed between 200 000 and 300 000 black miners annually, and there was never a year over the entire period that Mozambicans did not constitute most of that labour force. Not only did the Sul do Save continuously bleed black migrant manpower into the South African mining industry, with all the attendant mental, physical and social costs, but it did so at wages that, over the longer term, were declining continuously in value and purchasing power. As has been noted: 'In real terms, using 1938 as the base year, black cash earnings [of miners] in 1969 were no higher and possibly even lower than they had been in 1911.'[10]

The systemic danger that slavery had posed for black Mozambican families in the 19th century was mainly for the benefit of plantation owners around the Atlantic Ocean. By the early 20th century, that danger had been largely replaced by a low-wage indentured labour regime closer to home. The new male-only system was largely for the benefit of financiers in Europe, mine owners on the Witwatersrand and ordinary white South Africans benefiting from a system of racist exploitation and segregation that culminated in apartheid. Many of those destined for waged slavery during the first quarter of the 20th century, including those who had been forcibly 'recruited' by WNLA agents in the Sul do Save and forwarded to the Transvaal coal and gold mines in sealed train compartments, were transported along that old Delagoa Bay railway line.[11]

The insertion of a railway syringe into the fleshier parts of southern Mozambique failed to vaccinate black households against impoverishment. African men, and more especially their wives, struggled to raise crops of maize or legumes for the market from sandy soils, in a region prone to alternating periods of drought and flooding, in an attempt to supplement declining cash remittances.[12] Before World War I, when real wages on the mines were at their highest and exchange rates more favourable, peasant investments in draught animals and ploughs saw an uptick in otherwise weak local markets for food products in the Sul do Save.

Reporting from Lourenço Marques, in 1904, a bank inspector noted the buoyancy of the city's market for peasant produce. 'In good years', he wrote, 'the country produces large quantities of mealies', 'the surplus over local consumption being forwarded to the Transvaal.' The regional market held up reasonably well for several seasons but then showed signs of strain. Staples brought into the country, in bulk, by rail from South Africa often undercut African production costs. During the 1906–1908 recession it was noted that '[t]here has been no outlet of late for the produce (chiefly maize and beans grown by natives) of the territory, the good crops grown elsewhere having put the local produce out of the market.'[13]

By World War I, the South African market was largely lost to peasants. A decade later, in the mid-1920s, with the mines drawing in ever-increasing numbers of contracted workers, African families were still producing maize, but for 'local consumption' only.[14] Investment

African market, six kilometres northwest of central Lourenço Marques, c. 1929.

in South African-manufactured single-furrow ploughs and improved methods of cultivation propped up black agricultural production. Families continued to produce staples to the point where, in good seasons, into the 1940s and 1950s, occasional maize surpluses were recorded in the Sul do Save.[15] In most peasant households, to slow the rate at which their standard of living was declining, African women were called upon to invest more in agriculture and to work harder. Thus, mine owners benefited from female labour, and a growth in peasant maize production helped offset the decline in black wages.[16]

Nor did the few European agriculturalists in the colony producing basic foodstuffs benefit greatly from the east coast rail link. True, Delagoa Bay and the proximity of South African commercial farmers in the fertile, well-watered eastern Transvaal could not account fully for the inability of the Mozambican administration to attract a class of economically viable settler-farmers to the southern part of the colony for more than half a century. But it did not help. The railway was more of an economic problem than a solution when it came to supplying Lourenço Marques with fresh foodstuffs. Mother nature, too, was not on the side of small would-be commercial farmers.[17]

In 1895, the year that the rail link inland became a reality, there were only two commercial 'farms' in the province of Lourenço Marques, which gave 'no sign of their existence by supplying the town with vegetables or any other form of farm produce'. Fresh vegetables were, for the moment, still being imported by steamer from Durban, but, in an ominous sign of things to come, 'fresh butter is ordered from Pretoria, 350 miles away, small quantities by mail train, on which, of course, a high carriage rate is charged'. The result was, as the British consul reported, the 'cost of living is exceptionally high and for a sea-port Lourenço Marques can claim to sell the necessaries of life dearer than any other town in the world'. The situation later improved slightly when some hard-working entrepreneurial Chinese market gardeners set about supplying inhabitants with everyday essentials.[18]

Four decades later, when José Santos Rufino surveyed the nature and extent of commercial agriculture in the Lourenço Marques district, the situation was hardly transformed. African households, increasingly short of manpower, showed a growing preference for crops – other than maize – that required 'little or no labour', such as manioc and groundnuts. Around the Umbeluzi River, west of the port, and at Xinavane, north of the city, small-scale Portuguese farmers cultivated sugar, but noteworthy commercial success depended on large-scale capital investment, such as that on the Inkomati Sugar Estates. Likewise, it was only one or two wealthier farmers, such as those at Shibaza and Xinavane, who were able to supply the port city with some, but not all, of the milk and butter it required.[19]

There were daunting environmental reasons behind the city's protracted dependence on outside supplies. As noted, the local climate swung wildly and unpredictably between prolonged droughts and bouts of flooding. Bushy scrubland required extensive clearing and de-stumping before reluctantly granting access to soils of indifferent quality. Remote areas, devoid of reliable transport links, held little appeal for even the most hard-working and poorest of peasants drawn from Portugal.[20] Most immigrants, let alone the few destined to settle, entered the colony lacking capital and local knowledge in equal

Sugar factory on the Inkomati Sugar
Estates (ABOVE) and manager's
residence (LEFT), c. 1929.

proportions. The east coast railway never presented itself as a modern
marvel to settler farmers. Incoming trains pumped cheaper imports
into their largest market; outgoing ones dragged off what they saw as
'their' black labour to the mines.[21]

The cries of the settlers could be heard above the screech of steel
as the trains rattled westward to South Africa. And, as the number of
miners bound for the Rand mushroomed, leaching the coastal colony
of black labour, the Mozambican administration came to share some
of the settlers' frustrations. After World War I, and especially in the

mid-1920s, the voice of the farmers was increasingly audible whenever the Mozambique Convention was renegotiated. The administration sought to curb the outflow of African workers to ensure agricultural development in the Sul do Save. It was part of a very old Portuguese dream, to redirect a 'flow of peasant emigrants to villages of sturdy yeoman farmers in the colonies'.[22]

But pouring undercapitalised settlers into a colony draining most of its cheap or forced labour into a neighbouring economy was a fool's errand.[23] European immigrant numbers were dwarfed by the scale of black emigration – legally and temporarily via the railway, or illegally and permanently when black families walked into South Africa across an unguarded border in what the authorities characterised as 'clandestine emigration'.[24] Few of the whites arriving in Mozambique, overwhelmingly male until the 1930s, were moved by the prospect of trying to wrest a living from the land. Farmers and settlers formed part of a small class, one always more in the breaking than in the making. Many abandoned the countryside for the nearest town, took up lowly positions in the civil service, made their way back to Lourenço Marques or gave up and returned to Portugal.[25]

The number of new arrivals in Mozambique before World War I was barely worth recording, as was the number of residents in a colony hoping, in vain, to become a country. The interwar years saw no qualitative improvement in demographic terms. The European population remained embarrassingly small, increasing from about 18 000 in 1932 to around 50 000 by 1950, and improving significantly to about 95 000 only by end of that decade.[26] The advent of Salazar's Estado Novo and an austere, restrictive immigration policy after 1929 did nothing to help.

It was not only the number of immigrants that proved problematic for a local administration struggling to construct a population with a recognisably European demographic profile but its composition by gender. A wafer-thin class of settlers in the making was almost wholly incapable of reproducing itself entirely from within its own ranks. Beyond a small corps of cosmopolitan adventurers, barmaids and prostitutes in the ports, the colony long wanted for a sizeable contingent of European women who were both eligible for marriage and in search of husbands. In 1912, there were 105 white women in Lourenço Marques, barely four per cent of the city's population. In rural areas the discrepancy was, if anything, much greater. It was only in the 1930s that the number of female immigrants in the city exceeded males, but even then the number was derisory.[27]

The imbalance between the number of European men and women in the colony encouraged miscegenation. The descendants of mixed marriages, some formal but for the most part informal, formed part of a small but very significant population that the administration and settlers alike found as difficult to categorise as they were to pigeon-hole in social, economic or political terms. Known variously as *mestiços*, *mulattos* or *pardos* ('leopard-coloured' folk), they formed part of a liminal population in a country that was itself seldom one thing or another, but both.[28]

Insufficient European immigrants and the perceived lack of suitable female social cement contributed to the notoriously slow development of commercial agriculture throughout the Sul do Save. So small, scattered and precariously poised were the pockets of commercial farming that bank inspectors could seldom bring themselves to devote a dedicated heading to the subject of 'agriculture' in their reports. When they did do so, their observations swung between gloom and resignation. The country was incapable of attracting a 'desirable class of farmer', or 'agriculture in this country [is] in its infancy'.[29] Not even the meat-eating proclivities of a few thousand Europeans, or a potentially far larger number of African consumers, encouraged large-scale cattle ranching in one of the few parts of the colony suited to the production of dairy or beef products.[30]

The potential for successful cattle-raising in the southern part of the colony was noted repeatedly by outsiders. Newly developed techniques of refrigeration added to the attraction of a chilled-meat business for export and gained the interest of South African investors. A cold storage company was eventually established at Matola, upstream from the main part of the port, shortly before the Great Depression.[31] But, for various reasons, including an outbreak of foot-and-mouth disease, the enterprise seemed jinxed and 'the whole project was abandoned, and the extensive building and plant left to decay without once having been in operation'. The business was resurrected after World War II but was not a great success.[32]

A similar story, that of an inability to compete with cheaper produce

The Victoria Cold Storage and Ice Factory, Lourenço Marques, shown c. 1929, was partly owned by the Central Mining and Investment Corporation of Johannesburg.

coming down the line to Delagoa Bay, was to be found in regard in fruit exports. In the decade after World War I, South African citrus exports to Europe nearly doubled, from around half a million to a million cases of oranges by 1929. Fruit growers in the Sul do Save, lacking capital and skills, were unable to compete with Zebediela (in what is today Limpopo province), at one time the largest citrus estate in the world.[33]

In the 1950s, the Portuguese administration directed settler farmers to new and more fertile lands that African families had been forced to forfeit in the Limpopo Valley. But the Sul do Save remained as incapable as ever of providing Lourenço Marques with the basic foodstuffs needed by a city then growing at a reasonable clip.[34] For some everyday necessities, this had been the case for half a century. In 1890, a consular official reported that life in the port 'is sustained entirely on imported tinned goods', and in 1950 it was noted that 'fresh milk supplies are still inadequate and imported [tinned] condensed milk largely used'. Butter and cheese, too, remained at a premium, as they were in many countries after World War II, but surprisingly so did tomatoes and onions, which were brought to market in large quantities from South Africa. 'Both vegetables grow splendidly in the immediate environs of the town', an observer noted, 'but local growers are chary of over-producing for a limited market'. In other words, they were unable to compete with cheaper imports railed into the country in substantial quantities via the old east coast railway line. Older Boers would have smiled.[35]

With the growth and productivity of both African peasant and settler agriculture in Mozambique often constrained by South African imports, the cost of living in Lourenço Marques remained notoriously high throughout the colonial period. The railway was not the only factor in determining the price of food in the port, but its effects were never negligible. Importing expensive basic foodstuffs while simultaneously exporting vast quantities of migrant labour did nothing to improve the prospects for food security in a colony long short of start-up capital at competitive prices.

LOURENÇO MARQUES: THE CAPTURE OF AND STRUGGLE FOR THE PORT, 1895–1950

We should be reminded that the emergence of the 20th-century port took place at the tail end of a change to the centuries-old pattern of slaving and trading in the Indian Ocean, triggered by the discoveries of diamonds and gold on the southern African Highveld in the 1860s and 1880s. An industrial revolution in the proximate interior inverted the field of gravity of the Mozambican economy from its ancient north–east alignment to an inland south–west orientation. The shift, coinciding with the demise of dhows and sailing vessels and their replacement by coal- and oil-fired steamers, had global consequences. In southern Mozambique it facilitated the move from the trade in import-export commodities, by many small merchants of heterogeneous origin, to a growing reliance on a transit trade dominated by a few British capitalists on the Highveld. After the mineral discoveries, Delagoa Bay became a classic entrepôt, whipped into modernity at a pace set by industrial capitalism and the railways, and by the turnaround speeds demanded by the new, larger cargo vessels.

Old trading patterns along the Bay, easing in and out of view like ships on the distant horizon, lingered for a while before being ousted by the forces of the new south–west economy. In the early 1890s, steamers began the first direct runs from Bombay and Calcutta and down the long African east coast, calling at ports as far south as Durban. In mid-ocean they would still have encountered a hundred or more monsoon-driven dhows still making the annual crossings from western India to Mozambique Island. A dwindling number of dhows then worked the coastline down to Inhambane, where a mere handful, hoping for favourable winds, occasionally pushed even farther south. In 1891, barely half a decade after the opening of the Rand goldfields, the British consul at Lourenço Marques used his annual report to record their presence, perhaps for the last time. 'There were also five dhows from the East Coast and India to this port this year', he recorded.[36]

In analogous fashion, the opening of the Witwatersrand goldfields and the railway hollowed out a few of the better-established trading establishments on the Bay. Traders found it increasingly difficult to compete effectively with Rand retailers and wholesalers who, benefiting from a larger, cash-flush market, imported tinned foods and other goods at substantial discounts from leading English suppliers. Several merchants abandoned the swampy coastal enclave, bought themselves one-way tickets west and headed for the new promised land.

The mid-1890s boom on the Highveld proved to be a turning point. By 1896, the change in commerce in the port was all too apparent to Stanley Hollis: 'Lourenço Marques has degenerated into a mere forwarding station', he remarked, 'many of its leading merchants having moved their headquarters to Johannesburg.' 'At this time', he continued, its 'transit trade is very considerable but its local trade is practically nil.'[37] Although the retail and wholesale trade around the Bay undoubtedly improved subsequently to become increasingly vibrant during the interwar years, the substance of Hollis's observation about the dominance of the transit trade remained true into the 1950s.

The port's infrastructure, rail complex and larger properties were central to the emerging dominance of the transit trade. This shift was the outcome of a protracted struggle for the ownership and control

A coal train crossing the Inkomati Bridge, on the Great Eastern Line linking South Africa and Mozambique, c. 1929.

of the port facilities, between the Mozambican administration and Witwatersrand mining capital, that took place from the early 1890s until well into the 1920s. The origins and trajectory of that conflict can be traced back to the collapse of the London merchant bank Baring Brothers in 1890, Portugal's near bankruptcy in 1892 and the unprecedented speculative boom on the Witwatersrand in 1893–1895. The earliest development of the port and rail complex occurred when Portugal was at its most financially vulnerable and European capital – as invested in the Rand mines – never stronger, with access to an enormous speculative war chest.[38]

The precocious interest of the Witwatersrand mining houses in the potential of Delagoa Bay was, as to be expected, based solidly on financial considerations. The transition from outcrop to deep-level mining, accelerating rapidly after 1893, necessitated the importation of machinery. Much of it came from the United States and was most cheaply transported inland from the nearest port, Lourenço Marques. But, almost as importantly, as we will see, deep-level mines had a near-insatiable appetite for sturdy mine props, timber that was in short supply in South Africa and more especially so on the treeless grasslands of the Highveld.[39]

The need to secure the responsible handling and forwarding of heavy machinery and lumber to the Rand via the recently opened rail link paved the way for 'hard' investment in the port in the 1890s. It also provided plausible cover in the market for other, softer ventures – such as the Delagoa Bay Development Corporation and Delagoa Bay Lands Syndicate – that had links to British mining capital but were more focused on short-term speculative gains.[40] From as early as 1895, the development of the port was also underwritten by the coal-mining companies around Middleburg and Witbank, in the eastern Transvaal, which first attracted speculative capital and then began exporting large quantities of bunker coal for the growing number of steamers and warships docking in Lourenço Marques.[41]

The port

When President Burgers of the ZAR attempted to facilitate commercial ties with Mozambique via a rail link to the east coast, in 1875, the British government, alert to the danger the initiative might pose to its dominance in the region, took immediate steps to protect its interests. Even as Burgers busied himself with signing railway contracts in Europe, Portugal was forced to pledge 'to make no concessions in Mozambique to any third power without Britain having been given the first opportunity to acquire whatever rights were on offer'.[42] These 'pre-emptive rights', reconfirmed when the ultimatum was issued in 1890, effectively allowed Whitehall a veto when it came to the development of the port, the railway and the foreshore. Lourenço Marques was a port merely aspiring to autonomy.

Extensive and well-sheltered, Delagoa Bay made for a fine harbour at a point where three rivers debouched, but its sandy, shallow approaches meant that it was not a natural deep-water port. Given Portugal's parlous financial position in the early 1890s, the first (and only) wooden pier was erected with private capital routed through the NZASM and not via the CFLM, its Mozambican counterpart, or a shadowy port authority. Confusion and tension between the partners was evident within months of the rail link's opening, in 1895.

The Netherlands company, intent on maximising its revenue by turning around and carrying as many goods inland as swiftly as possible, wanted all incoming cargo to be unloaded at its pier. The Portuguese, steeped in commerce, wanted to maximise their income by insisting that any goods *not* clearly designated for carriage by the NZASM be unloaded onto lighters piloted by African women, thus providing the administration with additional tax and handling revenue.[43] The problem appeared insoluble, and the company then attempted to force the Mozambican administration to purchase the pier, offering it a ten-year lease at £3 000 per annum. It was a sum beyond the reach of Lisbon, let alone Lourenço Marques, and a standoff crippled the inland service for several weeks.[44]

The impasse was resolved only when the Mozambican administration and the British forwarding agencies and shipping companies – the latter acting as the hidden hand of UK foreign policy – established a commission to guide improvements in the port.[45] But, in truth, the betterments were confined to bureaucratic and handling procedures. No additional fixed direct investment in the port's infrastructure was forthcoming, and for good reason. An enhanced interest in southern Africa by Germany and France prompted Whitehall to curb any commercial development in the port and to thwart the ZAR's growing independence. Amid the growing political tensions of mine owners in the Transvaal, and aware that Rhodes might attempt to unseat the Kruger government, the British were content to maintain a strong defensive naval hold on Lourenço Marques. With the Colonial Office's conscious 'policy of blocking the Bay's development', the port not only missed out on the 1893–1895 boom on the Rand but did so right up to the outbreak of the Anglo-Boer War. The result was that the port 'lacked any permanent piers, substantial repair and coaling facilities or adequate warehouses' for either commercial vessels or modern men o' war. Delagoa Bay constituted a crucial regional node in British imperial expansion.[46]

The Anglo-Boer War saw Britain behaving as an occupying force in Lourenço Marques; only an imperial victory eased Whitehall's fears of a 'foreign' takeover in Delagoa Bay. The Mozambican administration was quick to take up the slack and claw back some of the authority ceded during the pre-war imperial rivalries. In 1900, making liberal use of forced black labour to underwrite 'free enterprise' and reclaim the adjacent swamps with massive earthworks, the administration began constructing the Gorjão wharf and several warehouses. A new wharf, on the Espírito Santo River, put 30 feet of water beneath ships even at low tide. It was funded exclusively by the state and calculated to provide the administration with revenue over and beyond the cost of servicing its debts. It ended the practice of African women working launches and lighters and reduced handling charges on equipment and goods destined for the Rand.[47]

Five years later, in 1905, with the British focused on reconstructing the Transvaal with the assistance of cheap east-coast labour – not excluding *shibalo* workers 'recruited' for the mines – the Portuguese administration tightened its grip on the harbour facilities. The port and railway authorities were refashioned into a single entity and the opportunity taken to free the administration of its reliance on private capital for new developments.[48] The coming of the Union of South Africa and the threat that newly incorporated southern ports posed to Delagoa Bay spurred the cash-strapped administration into yet more pre-emptive action. By 1910, all key infrastructural installations in the harbour previously dominated by foreign investors were under Mozambican control. A new 60-ton hydraulic crane capable of unloading the heaviest of mining machinery, along with new facilities for handling goods trains, provided the port with an essential competitive edge. Despite occasional muttering on the Rand, most suppliers agreed that the new infrastructure at Lourenço Marques was functioning reasonably well.[49]

The Mozambican administration's two-decade-long struggle to regain control of the port infrastructure as it related to the importation of capital goods for the Rand gold mines was partly matched by its determination not to be excluded from new export opportunities. There was a time when the Transvaal exported coal to Mozambique for local use only, but, after 1905, producers grew in ambition.

Eastern Transvaal coal producers, heavily reliant on WNLA *shibalo* labour, became more export-oriented and, over the subsequent two decades, the movement of bunker coal to Lourenço Marques grew rapidly in significance.[50]

The earliest opportunity for a share in the coal-exporting business fell to a long-standing port entrepreneur who also compiled one of the earliest dictionaries in the vernacular for the colony – Ernesto Torre do Valle. A customs broker and railways agent, Do Valle was a classic middleman who by 1904 had a well-established business focused on the shipping, landing and forwarding of goods. More importantly, Messrs Torre do Valle & Co became the local agent for the Transvaal Coal Owners' Association and by the outbreak of World War I dominated the coal bunkering and export business, which expanded dramatically after 1918.[51]

But Portugal's continued support of efforts at modernising the port facilities in the face of its post-war financial constraints failed to win the approval of Mozambique's aggressively industrialising neighbour. Wartime military success in Africa had whetted the South African government and mining industry's desire to control, if not acquire, the port and rail complex at Lourenço Marques. That, and the desire to extract as much 'voluntary' black labour from the colony as possible under the terms of a Convention in need of renegotiation, fuelled complaints about how the allegedly inefficient functioning of the port and rail complex retarded industrialisation.[52] But with half of South Africa's imports entering the country through Durban, and other port authorities alleging bottlenecks to economic development on the Highveld, the complaints rang hollow in Portugal.

A debate about how the Convention frustrated development in Mozambique followed in the Cortes Gerais. It succeeded in raising the hackles of the Lisbon Geographical Society, the leading ginger group championing Portuguese colonialism. The Society countered allegations of mismanagement and neglect at Lourenço Marques with a factual description of the infrastructure at the port and rail complex, which it described as 'excellent'. A 1 500-metre reinforced-concrete pier, able to accommodate 12 ocean-going vessels, had been erected at a cost of half a million pounds sterling, and was flanked by 12 warehouses and the largest electrically lit customs area in southern Africa.

Main wharf, Lourenço Marques harbour, c. 1919.

A dry dock was under construction at a cost of £30 000, along with two others offering shelter to smaller vessels. The port was served by 15 electric cranes, including the largest one operating in southern Africa.

But pride of place, at a cost of about £100 000, went to a new coal-tipping plant with an enormous capacity, devoted exclusively to serving the Transvaal coal-exporting industry. The modern McMyler coal-tippler, similar to one recently installed in the port of New Jersey, was capable of inverting rail trucks to deposit coal directly into a ship's hold.[53] Moreover, the functioning of the port complex was overseen by an autonomous board on which two 'foreign' merchants – that is, British or South African – served for two years at a time. All of this, critics were reminded, 'had been done with Portuguese money only'.[54]

It was an impressive set of achievements that had been two decades in the making. The harbour infrastructure had, with the ongoing assistance of tens of thousands of *shibalo* labourers, underwritten the cost of importing heavy machinery and materials for the Witwatersrand mining and other industries at competitive prices. South Africa's core Highveld industrial development owed much to Portugal's willingness to provide the greater region with crucial supplies of forced labour. The ownership of the harbour facilities was, after a lengthy struggle, out of the hands of private capital, but there could be little doubt as to who benefited most from a port that remained admirably modern and competitive into the 1950s.[55]

Shipping

The grip of foreign capital on the port's infrastructure after the mineral discoveries, and the role of aggressive South African-based interests, were matched in shipping. Ships berthing in Delagoa Bay, especially after the shift to deep-level mining on the Rand in 1893, came from many countries, but vessels belonging to Portugal, notable for its historic seafaring feats, especially in the Indian Ocean, were predictably few in number.[56]

The primary competition for control of shipping interests along the Mozambican coast, and for command of Lourenço Marques, took place between two legendary Scottish magnates, William Mackinnon and Donald Currie, between 1883 and 1910, and was carried on by their immediate successors. The contest was at its height during the formative years of the industrial revolution on the subcontinent and offers a further illustration of the way the weakly developed Mozambican field of economic gravity 'flipped' in the latter half of the 19th century

– ensuring the triumph of the new south–west alignment over the old north–east one. It also contributed to the fact that Currie, most of whose money was made in the ascendant new south, eventually gained the upper hand over his rival, Mackinnon, whose wealth derived from the much older, declining north Indian Ocean locus.

Mackinnon (1823–1893) started his career working for a Glaswegian merchant with Asian interests and moved to India, in 1847, where he began his shipping operations in coastal ports around the Bay of Bengal. Buoyed by early success, he went on, in 1862, to form the British India Steam Navigation Company (BISNC). It soon became one of the most prominent lines serving Burma and the Persian Gulf before pushing down the ancient east African trade routes from Aden, initially as far south as Zanzibar. After the discovery of diamonds, however, British interest and imperial rivalries in the region heightened, as did the impetus to follow new patterns of global investment in the 1880s. With the blessing of a Foreign Office increasingly wary of the German East Africa Line (established in 1890) in the years leading up to the Anglo-Boer War, Mackinnon's BISNC was encouraged to push ever farther south.[57]

If the Indian Ocean made Mackinnon, then the Atlantic made Currie. At the age of 19, he joined Cunard, gaining experience of the transatlantic trade before being put in charge of cargo moving between European ports around the North Sea. Currie also made valuable contacts in Lisbon, which he cultivated assiduously. In 1862, he began operating a vessel between Liverpool and Calcutta, via the Cape, before the opening of the Suez Canal, in 1869, revitalised economic life on the African east coast.[58] But it was the opening of the Kimberley diamond fields and the lucrative mail contracts between the United Kingdom and South Africa that, in 1872, prompted his introduction of the Castle Mail Packets Company Ltd, a highly successful steamship service to and from Cape Town. In 1887–1888, a visit to southern Africa, which fortuitously came at a critical juncture in the corporate histories of both Kimberley and Johannesburg, led to meetings with several of the most important figures in the emerging economic and political elites. More importantly, it exposed Currie directly to the diamond fields and the new goldfields on the Rand, where canny early investments underwrote his shipping business.[59]

When Currie secured a mail subsidy from Portugal, in 1883, he extended Castle Mail Packets' operations up the African east coast, where they soon collided with Mackinnon's BISNC moving down the continent. In the anti-competitive, price-fixing 'ring' mode that southern African shipping firms were notorious for, Currie and Mackinnon soon struck a deal. The Castle Line would refrain from pushing up as far north as Zanzibar – a Mackinnon stronghold – while the BISNC, in turn, would not probe as far south as Delagoa Bay, a Currie outpost. The rest of the Mozambican coastal trade the 'rivals' carved up between them. This cosy arrangement between two Scottish legends persisted until 1888, when the Castle Line's Portuguese subsidy lapsed. The Highveld gold discoveries triggered a new round of slightly more competitive behaviour from the companies in the early 1890s, with Currie – personally invested in a leading West Rand mine – taking an ever-greater interest in the Lourenço Marques–Pretoria corridor.[60]

Despite excellent connections in Lisbon, it was not the Castle Line that won a new mail contract from virtually bankrupt Portugal in 1893. The contract went to one of Currie's future corporate partners, the Union Steam Ship Company, which at once pushed its operations up the east coast as far as Zanzibar. Mackinnon, for his part, hankered after a London–Zanzibar–Lourenço Marques route, but his hopes ran aground on the shoals of Whitehall as the Foreign Office attempted to steer a course between the interests of British capital and German ambitions in southern Africa. Currie also developed a working arrangement with Adolph Woermann and his expanding German East Africa Line in the early 1890s. The end of the Anglo-Boer War saw renewed company skirmishing for east coast traffic, but by 1909, with Mackinnon gone, the balance of power had shifted to Currie's amalgamated Union-Castle Line. His position was further strengthened the following year when the coming of Union ended old colonial port rivalries.[61]

The triumph of Currie's 'southern' capital pushing north, backed by investments in diamond and gold mining, over Mackinnon's 'northern' capital, supported by the Foreign Office, offered a further example of how Mozambique's field of economic gravity was inverted by South Africa's industrial revolution. In the interwar years, Union-Castle commanded the pre-eminent position in commercial shipping around southern Africa.[62] Industrial capitalism laid siege to Mozambique from land and sea alike.

Perhaps it was because Lisbon, in 1913, was the fifth-largest port in the world by volume of trade handled that Portugal managed to gradually reclaim the harbour infrastructure in Lourenço Marques from the grip of South African capital. But, if so, it was a success that was not to be repeated in shipping. Without significant domestic reserves of coal and iron, let alone capital, Portugal found making the transition from sail to steam difficult, even though it was at pains to protect its colonial routes, including that to Lourenço Marques. Lisbon's merchant navy did reasonably well with ships seized from enemies during World War I, but when Portugal attempted to ensure that only ships flying its flag carried goods to Mozambique, in 1922, it sailed slap-bang straight into its oldest 'ally', in the form of the Foreign Office, which soon put paid to the idea. In 1929, on the eve of the Great Depression, 'only 8% of the shipping tonnage entering Lourenço Marques and Beira flew the Portuguese flag'.[63] And such cargoes as did enter Delagoa Bay, destined for the mines, passed first through the hands of foreigners.

Forwarding agencies

Between 1901 and 1918, a third of all Mozambican revenue derived from customs and transshipment charges, with most of that coming from Delagoa Bay, while another third derived from the repatriated wages of indentured black workers.[64] The regional dominance of first British and later South African financial interests ensured that Lourenço Marques remained a largely hollowed-out, one-dimensional port and its unpromising hinterland a backwater, an emaciated peasant-proletarian reserve for cheap labour directed to the Witwatersrand. In theory, given the success of the port of Lisbon, Portugal had access to the experience and expertise, if not the capital, to make more of opportunities in Lourenço Marques. It might have taken ownership not only of the harbour infrastructure but also of a more meaningful share of the revenue derived from essential cargo-loading and moving operations in the port. But in that respect, too, it had almost from the outset to bend the knee to British or South African capital.

It is one of the ironies of economic history that the collapse of Baring Brothers, followed by the virtual bankruptcy of Portugal, in 1890–1892, overlapped in good part with the beginnings of the transition from outcrop to deep-level mining in South Africa. The transition heralded massive new investments in genuine and speculative ventures on the Rand. By the time the boom reached its apex, in 1895, the larger mining houses knew which of their many ventures were probably going to be sound, long-term paying propositions, requiring yet more investment in machinery and mining timber, and which of them were marginal operations lending themselves more to gross market manipulation. Indeed, for the smartest mine owners, the skill lay in mixing their propositions in ways that underwrote short-term profits.[65] Jameson's raid checked some of the excesses.

By the mid-1890s, with Portugal reduced largely to concession-peddling in Mozambique, a number of far-sighted and cash-flush mining finance houses on the Rand found investments in the port and surrounding areas of Lourenço Marques increasingly attractive. Not only did new investments in property make for possible speculative windfall profits but, more importantly, they helped grow the South African footprint in the area around the harbour, further facilitating the importation and short-term storage of capital and other goods. The Delagoa Bay Development Corporation and Delagoa Bay Lands Syndicate – both riding in on the coat-tails of mining capital – were at the forefront of these speculative forays. The opportunistically named 'Development Corporation' acquired several vital utility concessions within the city. Other mining houses floated subsidiaries with a direct interest in port infrastructure, unloading cargo, customs clearance and the handling of capital goods destined for upcountry industries.

Given the relatively slow development of the harbour infrastructure as it shifted from private to state ownership, the earliest problems in the port related more to the landing of goods than to their forwarding. A lack of deep-water berthing facilities meant that cargo had to be unloaded in the shallows of the bay and then transported into the port proper by tug or lighter. Unsurprisingly, landing agents – of which there were about half a dozen – figured as prominently in the commercial listings of Lourenco Marques as did forwarding agents. At the height of the Rand's 'Kaffir Boom', in 1895, there was a shortage of lighters. Ships were rerouted to Cape ports; in one instance, a cargo of timber was simply tossed overboard and then rafted or towed ashore. Costly inefficiencies ensured that the earliest mining-house interests came from landing cargo rather than its forwarding by rail to the Witwatersrand.[66]

In 1894, Leál (Leon) Cohen, a resident Sephardic Jew, as imbued with entrepreneurial ideas and political influence in Lisbon and Lourenço Marques as he was unable to render projects financially viable, acquired the concession for the urgently needed deep-water pier in Delagoa Bay. A rising tide lifts all boats, as they say, and in the following boom year, making use of a London agent, Cohen floated the Rand-Delagoa Bay Landing Company. The company, focused on shifting coal and providing lighterage services, was later retained by Rhodes's Consolidated Gold Fields. But, in keeping with Cohen's reputation as an irresponsible speculator, the company declared its only dividend, in 1895, and was soon in deep trouble.[67]

Infrastructural improvements to the port and a more stable regional political environment after the Anglo-Boer War encouraged many Rand mining houses to shift their interest from landing operations to the forwarding business, the hallmark of any successful entrepôt. With ownership of harbour facilities shifting to Portuguese control, the most important mining houses and other importers of capital goods saw in forwarding agencies profitable opportunities for cutting out unwanted middlemen – and for extending and safeguarding control of a chain of value that ran all the way from customs house to the shaft head on the Rand.

Present from the dawn of deep-level gold mining, Wernher, Beit & Co and its two most important investment arms – the Central Mining and Investment Corporation (CMIC) and Rand Mines (1893) – went on to become the dominant finance and mining houses on the Witwatersrand. By the eve of World War I, CMIC companies controlled 11 per cent of the world's gold output and had long since diversified their holdings across the Americas and into other non-mining operations, including cotton plantations, oil production and railways.[68] The floating of a subsidiary, during the 1906–1908 recession, to take care of important east coast interests might have been mildly surprising but was not out of character.

The Lourenço Marques Forwarding Company (LMFC) acquired the property of the troubled Lourenço Marques Wharf Company in late 1905. The company was floated the following year with share capital of £30 000. Investors included Lewis & Marks, Johannesburg Consolidated Investments (JCI) and Parker, Wood & Co, who were later joined by another major importer of mining machinery, WF Johnstone & Co.[69] Predatory by nature, CMIC and the LMFC took over the Delagoa Bay Lands Syndicate from JCI and obtained a share in the Victoria Cold Storage Company during the interwar years. By the mid-1920s the LMFC had investments in agriculture and mining not only in Mozambique but also in the adjacent eastern and northern Transvaal. Within months of first commencing operations, the LMFC set up a sawmill on the Bay to provide mining companies with props cut from timber acquired from across the world.[70]

Almost from the outset, the LMFC operated so profitably that its success surprised not only its local management but the delighted mine owners too. It was hardly a flash in the pan. The lumber yards feeding the sawmill expanded steadily, as did the handling of bulk goods and materials along the wharf for other Rand-based companies, including importers of candle wax, tyres and newsprint for *The Star* newspaper. Expanded operations saw the acquisition of a crane and a pier upriver at Matola that required increasing quantities of manual labour. As ever, the Mozambican administration was happy to oblige by providing contract-bound, coerced *shibalo* labour for a company that also fed its customs-house revenue.

Before World War II, the LMFC, like the Rand mining industry itself, made extensive use of indentured 'contract boys'. There was no free market when it came to African labour; the system was rigged. In early 1939, an LMFC agent informed the owners: 'By now you will certainly be informed of the favourable development both in Lisbon and here of the position with regard to the additional 10 000 natives, and for that reason I am not going further into this matter.'[71] Nor was there a 'free' or 'open' market determining competition within the sector as a whole. The British and South African forwarding agencies set up an informal association that set prices to ensure that 'competition is limited and fair'.[72] With prices fixed and labour costs contained, it was colonial capitalism of a special kind, much like the way that the Chamber of Mines and the WNLA operated as a cartel on the Witwatersrand, and that halted unfettered economic development in Portugal's colony. It also guaranteed respectable profits and returns on investment. Between 1908 and 1918, the LMFC failed narrowly to make a profit in but one year, 1912, and declared annual dividends that were almost invariably between eight and ten per cent.[73]

The Mozambique Convention and Trojan Horse remained key to the structured backwardness of the Sul do Save, and by the 1920s, South Africa – like Britain and Rhodes before it – longed to appropriate it with money rather than Maxim guns. Some of the confidence, if not arrogance, that this engendered in the LMFC was on display when, in 1925, the Convention was up for renegotiation. The chairman of the LMFC informed Prime Minister JBM Hertzog: 'I think that I am correct in saying that very nearly the whole of the shipping and forwarding business of the port is in the hand of Union firms or companies such as our own, and the amount of Union capital invested is very considerable.'[74] Quite so, and, in familiar fashion, the capital of one of the most powerful gold-mining companies in the world became, with the aid of a single rhetorical flourish, 'Union capital'.

The Convention was renegotiated on terms acceptable to 'Union capital' in 1928, and on 1 January 1929 the Mozambican administration, hoping to gain full control of a harbour long dominated by outside interests, took over 'all waterfront cargo handling'. The forwarding agencies had ensured that cargo handling was the single most powerful business in the city for close on half a century. The LMFC and other agencies retained their importance long after the Great Depression, but thereafter the transit trade was slowly offset by the commercial development of other sectors in Lourenço Marques's growing urban economy.[75]

Timber yards: The South African mines' warehouses-by-the-sea

Some of the creative genius and persistence of capitalism as a system lies in its unparalleled ability to mobilise, organise and sequence disparate factors of production into chains of added value, resulting in competitively priced and desirable products. The emergence of the innovative finance- and mining-house systems on the Witwatersrand bore testimony to an ability to raise capital from across the Western world, and to spread risks and reward investors, in an industry that was recession-proof and that declared solid dividends throughout the 20th century.

All industries have a real or potential Achilles heel. The South African mining industry had two limitations to its development and sustainability that might have been crippling and that required transnational solutions. The first was a reliance on indentured, legally entrapped African male labour drawn from a neighbouring domain only recently weaned off full-scale chattel slavery. The second was a dependence on imported lumber worked up into timber props, without which safe deep-level mining operations were clearly impossible. The solutions to both problems came via impoverished Mozambique – one directly, the other indirectly.

If certain of the advanced and more 'civilised' countries around the northern reaches of the Atlantic profited from Mozambican slaves in the 19th century, then many of the same economies and societies, and others, benefited financially from dividends drawn from South Africa's cartelised mining industry in the 20th. Widespread northern-hemisphere (European) involvement in the construction and refinement of the centralised, labour-repressive, racist gold-mining industry went further than the receipt of dividends. It also profited indirectly – and handsomely – by supplying, in unimaginable quantities, the lumber that supported ethically questionable businesses in a country intent on extending a system of racial segregation. Europe first helped South Africa reduce Mozambique to a client state, and then, very belatedly, discovered modern racism.

Well into the 1950s, the Mozambican administration, mindful of the lessons of history when it came to the port infrastructure, expanded its handling facilities for imported petroleum and timber six miles upriver at Matola. Lourenço Marques at that time was still forwarding to the Union a quarter of all its lumber requirements – between 100 000 and 150 000 tons annually – much of which went to the Witwatersrand, which was heavily dependent on the port for petroleum and timber imports. A fraction of the business came via Bay entrepreneurs, including Santos Gil, but most of it was routed through long-established forwarding agencies.[76]

Imported timber, for mine props, drying in the yard of R Santos Gil, Lourenço Marques, for shipment to the Transvaal coal and gold mines, c. 1929.

Historically, the proportion of cut and lopped forest that entered Delagoa Bay to be forwarded, and then shoved down the dank underground workings of the Highveld, would have been far higher than 25 per cent. Lumber arrived at Lourenço Marques as large tree trunks from all around the world – Australia, Burma, India, the Philippines and New Zealand to the east, and Scandinavia and the United States to the west – to be sliced into stocky little mine props. In 1928–1929, the Rand gold mines constituted the most important wood-consuming industry in southern Africa, with the trade running to between US$3 million and $4 million annually. And, as with the forwarding agencies, the timber importing business functioned via 'a gentlemen's agreement' that protected and maintained prices.[77]

It was part of a 'free enterprise' capitalist system that appealed to the Australians and Americans in the 1890s and, as the 20th century unfolded, proved as attractive to the Scandinavians. Sweden, Norway and Finland, in order of importance, provided most of the timber imports. In Finland's case, lumber destined for South African mines accounted for 1.5 per cent of all exports between 1929 and 1935. So lucrative and vitally important was this bulk trade with the mines that the Mozambican administration, true to character, imposed a hefty tariff on all imported lumber. For lumber arriving at Lourenço Marques from the US west coast, tariffs accounted for fully half the cost of transporting all mine timber.[78]

The origins of this worldwide trade lay at the point, around 1892– 1894, when outcrop mines on the Witwatersrand, tracing the reef as it dipped ever deeper and further south, were forced into supporting adits, shafts and tunnels, with the first makeshift wooden poles sig- nalling the arrival of much deeper-level mining. The need for enor- mous quantities of robust timber – a decade and a half before a limited amount of second-choice, home-grown eucalypts became available from South African plantations – was seized upon by two remarkable entrepreneurs who had grown up amid indigenous forests, albeit at opposite ends of the world.

The first to think globally, act locally and organise the importation of lumber via Delagoa Bay was, by his own telling, Walter D 'Karri' Davies. In truth, however, the original inspiration probably came from his father, proprietor of MC Davies Co Ltd in Western Australia. Karri Davies (1861–1926), Anglophile and imperialist, was a political diehard during – and long after – the Jameson Raid and served as a major during the Anglo-Boer War. He hailed from a family steeped in the timber industry. The Davies family owned part of the huge Karridale forest, about 300 kilometres south of Perth, and had laid rail tracks into its most remote corners to harvest the indigenous jarrah and karri trees that, as West Australians already knew, were admirably suited to propping up mine excavations. It was MC Davies who sent his son to South Africa to look for promising new business.[79]

Walter did the family proud. By 1893, the firm had built a large private jetty for exporting timber, in Hamelin Bay, about 25 miles from Karridale, the company township housing around 300 employ- ees. By the mid-1890s, the firm commanded a fleet of a dozen sailing ships – the 'Karri Line' – transporting mine timber across the Indian Ocean. When port traffic in Lourenço Marques ground to a halt in

1895 because of the dispute between the Mozambican administration and the NZASM pier owners, several Rand mines came to a standstill. Karri Davies, making the shift of the decade, hired a tramp steamer, the *Indianapolis*, to ship mine timber from Hamelin Bay to Durban, circumventing Delagoa Bay. Earlier in that boom year, the Davies Company was delivering eucalypt props to the Nigel Deep and Nigel Central Deep Mines, east of Johannesburg, within six weeks of vessels – under sail – leaving Hamelin Bay.

Davies established the reputations of both jarrah and karri on the Rand and, even though the family firm in Karridale lapsed shortly before World War I, the export of Western Australian timber to Delagoa Bay continued unabated until World War II.[80]

The other noteworthy pioneer in the imported timber industry, Frederick R Lingham, hailed from the other end of the world but shared some of Davies' political pedigree. Born in Ontario, Canada, in 1854, Lingham liked to refer to himself as a British Canadian and, like Davies, was a dyed-in-the-wool imperialist and member of the Johannesburg Reform Committee, which provided the Jameson Raid with its ideological *raison d'être*.[81] By the mid-1890s, however, Lingham appears to have been content to be considered an 'American' – hardly a disadvantage in a mining town dominated by American mining engineers most partial to using North American timber. As a young man, Lingham made his way to the forested west coast of the continent, first to British Columbia and later to Tacoma on Puget Sound, in Washington State. It is not clear when – possibly in the early 1880s – or why he moved to southern Africa. But he was already in Johannesburg when the transition to deep-level mining occurred and had, from an early date, taken an interest in the economic potential of the Pretoria–Delagoa Bay railway.

As is often the case, it was the short gap between the Baring Brothers recession in the north and the swift take-off of Rand mining stock in the south that presented Lingham with inspiration and opportunity alike. He went into business in 1893 and, in keeping with ambitions that already transcended the timber trade, named the firm the Lingham Trading & Timber Company (LT&T). He could not have chosen a better moment. In 1892, the two largest mills on the south shore of Puget Sound, the St Paul & Tacoma Lumber Co and the Tacoma Lumber &

Manufacturing Co, had reached the crest of a boom. Indeed, they were already in danger of seeing supplies of the magnificent, irreplaceable, centuries-old Douglas fir and the ubiquitous Oregon pine outstripping demand. Oregon pine became part of Johannesburg's architectural and building heritage. The following year, 1893, the year of 'The Panic', saw a run on the banks in Tacoma and a severe contraction in lumber companies struggling to find hard-currency contracts.[82]

Part of the long-distance trade in lumber thus fell conveniently into Lingham's lap and, given the preferences of American mining engineers, he was soon also importing southern pine from Mobile, Alabama, and pitch pine from Pensacola, Florida. Both varieties provided surprisingly robust timber despite bearing names normally associated with less satisfactory softwoods. When the east coast rail link came into operation during the 'Kaffir Boom', Lingham employed steamers rather than ships under sail to transport increasing quantities of lumber from the southern and western American coasts to Mozambique. Having listed the company in London, Lingham had easy access to mid-decade speculative capital from the City, and two years later the 'Lingham Line' was operating in competition with the Karri Line. The boom year of 1895 also saw Lingham a willing participant in the plot to overthrow the Kruger government as LT&T landed lumber in Lourenço Marques valued at £200000 ready for dressing, marking up and onward sale on the Witwatersrand.[83]

With his credentials as an Anglophile-imperialist trader by then well-established in London, Lingham's ambitions soon extended beyond the importation of timber. His chance came in 1898 when the Foreign Office, without the prior knowledge of the Colonial Office, concluded the secret Anglo-German agreement on how, in the event of the Portuguese Empire collapsing, northern and southern Mozambique would be carved up between them. Exercising the 'pre-emptive rights' that had been renewed in 1891, the Foreign Office agreed to Portugal's granting two new concessions in Lourenço Marques. The first was largely unproblematic, allowing Lingham to develop the trading part of his company, including the erection of a mill to process imported Canadian wheat.

The second, however, known as the Eiffe-Catembe concession, was either a diplomatic blunder or part of an intentional oversight facilitated by the Foreign Office's former consul in Delagoa Bay, the Irish-born Roger Casement. Casement, an admirer of Colonial Secretary Joseph Chamberlain, had assumed his duties as consul-spy in Lourenço Marques in mid-1895, when Rhodes's plans for a coup d'état in the ZAR were gathering momentum. Sent to gather intelligence on the gathering tensions and imperial rivalries, Casement spent time fraternising with German officials and businessmen in the city, some of whom remained lifelong friends. Among those almost certainly known to him was a Franz Ferdinand Eiffe, a partner in a reputable local trading house.[84]

Casement, who was executed in 1916 for attempting to solicit German military aid for the Easter Rising in Dublin, must have been aware that Eiffe, who was well in with the Mozambican administration, was angling for a concession from Portugal. But be that as it may, it was on Casement's watch, while he was on the Foreign Office staff, albeit not based in Lourenço Marques, that Britain entered into a new understanding with Germany. 'The crucial problem, unrecognized at first by the Foreign Office negotiators' was that the agreement 'included a clause that permitted the development of port facilities at Delagoa Bay by rival commercial firms.' But it went much deeper. It allowed for a German-backed firm to establish a trading operation *and* a potential naval presence via the Eiffe-Catembe concession. By accident or design, Casement failed to pick up on the oversight, and Britain spent the remainder of 1898 and 1899 pushing hard to impede the Eiffe-Catembe concession and advance Fred Lingham's business interests. Lourenço Marques remained the playground of the Foreign Office, with Mozambique enmeshed in a regional economy of supposedly free enterprise.[85]

The Foreign Office, with the earlier support of Casement, ensured that Lingham's business in Delagoa Bay thrived throughout the Anglo-Boer War. Indeed, it was Lingham the British loyalist who, soon after the outbreak of the war, used his shipping expertise to help ensure adequate meat supplies for the British Army. The Anglo-American Livestock & Trading Company exported thousands of Texan cattle from the port of Galveston to Lourenço Marques, where they were unloaded at LT&T's Matola depot and given the time and space to recover from their transatlantic ordeal.[86] By then, Casement was back in southern Africa, exploring the possibility of sabotaging the Pretoria–Delagoa Bay railway line that his 1895 posting had made him so familiar with.

In southern Africa from the 1890s until at least the 1950s, the British government, its intelligence services, the Foreign Office, the Bank of England and the South African Reserve Bank, along with the South African government and the Witwatersrand mining houses, were always within hailing distance of one another, helping one another out in war and peace. At critical junctures, as in the turbulent 1890s and early 1920s, they cooperated to try and ensure that Mozambique remained a junior partner in a 'free enterprise' regional economic system that, at its industrial core, was partially dependent on imported indentured labour and a compliant port city. Fred Lingham and Karri Davies were business imperialists.

Lingham did much to assist the post-war Milner administration bring back to life and reconstruct the Rand mining industry by supplying it with American timber. With the east coast railway barely functioning, supplies of west-coast Oregon pine were diverted to Cape Town, as were the southern pine and pitch pine imported from Alabama and Florida. In September 1901, there were 12 American vessels waiting for their cargoes of lumber to be unloaded in Cape Town. The scale of this wartime effort outstripped LT&T's shipping capacity, and the Scandinavian merchant navy had to come to the rescue of importers. As the grateful Americans noted, in the year ended 30 June 1901, 'over fifty Swedish and Norwegian sailing vessels have left for our Southern Ports, to bring back Pitch Pine'.[87] LT&T remained a prominent importer up to World War I, but thereafter, as Lingham aged, and American mining engineers lost some of their influence, his Delagoa Bay business slowly declined.

The availability and presence of so many Swedish and Norwegian vessels under sail during the Anglo-Boer War was, however, neither an aberration nor a coincidence. Nordic countries had been providing southern African states with timber since the 1850s in quantities that only increased as the mineral revolution on the Highveld unfolded. It was an enduring business, based on the large-scale importation of sturdy European pine and spruce lumber. The business grew and firmed through the interwar years and persisted well into the 1950s.

The Nordic timber trade thus both predated and postdated that of Australia and North America and helped to build modern South Africa's economic foundations.[88]

From the start of deep-level mining, Swedish and Norwegian vessels dominated the number of sailing ships calling in at Lourenço Marques with lumber. Some idea of the volume of the early trade with the Rand is to be found in an 1895 report by Roger Casement in which he documents the importance and nature of trade with the ZAR. A typical three-masted barque carried about 1 500 tons of lumber, and in that boom year 28 sailing vessels and two steamers from Scandinavia earned their owners over £40 000 in freight charges and unloaded 31 600 tons, with a gross landed value exceeding £80 000 – a sum worth about £10 million today. In 1928, when the entire South African timber trade was worth about US$5 million, European pine and spruce accounted for 80 per cent of rough lumber imports.[89]

The Nordic countries' emerging dominance of the lumber trade, mostly through Delagoa Bay, was underpinned by a shrewd business strategy. Not only was the route from the Baltic to the Bay shorter than that from Puget Sound and the southern American ports, but the Scandinavian countries were slow to convert from sail to steam, a factor further retaining and enhancing their competitiveness. This comparatively slower conversion rate to steam was, in part, founded on climatic considerations. Baltic ports were frozen in the northern winter, which meant that lumber destined for the mining industry could only be transported during summer and landed in far-off Delagoa Bay during the southern winter – around mid-year.

The seasonal element to the northern lumber trade meant that the Baltic states often had spare merchant marine capacity, which, in turn, not only encouraged them to stay with sail for longer than did the Karri and Lingham lines but also allowed them to hire out vessels to the Americans in particular whenever possible. It was thus not by chance that Lingham hired Swedish and Norwegian sailing ships to fetch pitch pine from Mobile and Pensacola during the Anglo-Boer War.

The freezing of the Baltic ports, however, had financial implications not only for the Scandinavian shipping companies but also for the Rand timber merchants, landing companies and forwarding agencies in Lourenço Marques itself. The fact that Nordic timber was unloaded largely between June and September meant that it tended to accumulate in very large quantities at that time of the year. Moreover, because much of the lumber had a high moisture content, it had to be stacked and dried before it could be milled into industrial timber. Seasonal pressure therefore meant that space was often at a premium in the port.

The Rand timber industry's unending demand for unloading facilities, stacking and drying yards, sawmills and rail connections all helped push it out of the port and upriver to the industrial quarter in Matola. Some idea of the scale of these operations can be got from an inspection carried out at LT&T towards the end of the Anglo-Boer War. Lingham's timber yards, served by steam cranes on a specially constructed pier that could accommodate four railway trucks, formed part of a two-square-mile complex that included company housing, bonded warehouses, sheds for dressed timber, a large sawmill and a seven-kilometre rail link to the main line leading inland.[90]

The forwarding companies too, and for largely similar reasons, were constantly on the lookout for bigger, better, larger premises. The largest, like the Wernher-Beit-owned LMFC, was constantly in search of new properties to accommodate sawmills and timber yards. That search, in turn, led to further backward integration of the business. Its belated acquisition of the Delagoa Bay Lands Syndicate, from JCI during the buoyant 1920s, must be understood against this background. It was the Rand mining houses and timber merchants that did much – perhaps most – to shape the physical geography of Matola. In fair measure, then, Lourenço Marques constituted part of the Witwatersrand's mining warehouses-by-the-sea.

––––––––

The gold discoveries on the Rand destroyed the *raison d'être* for the Pretoria–Delagoa Bay railway line, officially opened in 1895. Instead of the railway linking largely underdeveloped neighbouring states of roughly equal financial stature, it became the vehicle for grossly unequal exchanges between a rapidly developing industrial, capital-ist economy and a backward, sluggish, rural, commercial economy built around the railway and port complex of Lourenço Marques.

Moreover, the insidious, predatory nature of the stronger 'partner' in the east coast line and the port traffic it generated was constantly reinforced so as to increase and/or perpetuate the dominance of the most advanced sector of the industrially strong capitalist economy on the Rand. Following the mineral discoveries, Mozambique entered the modern world with British hands around its throat and South African fingers in its pocket.

After the mineral revolution, the east coast line swiftly metamorphosed from iron horse to Trojan Horse. It played an important, if not a key, part in the curtailed development of a Mozambican economy only recently emerged from chattel slavery. Portugal sold the rights of the African majority in the Sul do Save – to freely enter the emerging southern African economy at negotiable rates in industries and locations they chose – to the WNLA, a subsidiary of the cartelised Chamber of Mines. Each month, the train exported tens of thousands of coerced, if not forced, black mine labourers to the Rand mines in return for a percentage of rail traffic being routed through the port of Lourenço Marques. It was the railway that not only helped to undermine the agricultural potential of the black peasantry in the southern part of the colony but also allowed cheap farm produce to enter the colony to the point where it could not provide even its largest market, at Delagoa Bay, with onions and tomatoes.

But because industrial capitalists seek to enhance and entrench their position, British and South African capital – mobilised around the gold-mining economy – was not content with its domination of the east coast railway line; it wanted more. In the early 1890s, with Portugal nearly bankrupt because of the collapse of Baring Brothers, capital gained control of the infrastructure of the port of Lourenço Marques. It was a position of dominance that took Lisbon more than two decades to wriggle free of. In similar fashion, Britain and South Africa ensured that the landing and forwarding agencies, shipping companies and timber companies in the Bay all came under the sway of the mining houses or their subsidiaries, with the LT&T, LMFC and Union-Castle companies constituting prime examples.

From the mid-1890s until at least the 1950s and probably beyond, the South African gold-mining industry exercised a stranglehold over Lourenço Marques and its hinterland, the Sul do Save, ensuring that its development potential remained restricted. A controlled and integrated chain of value ran all the way from the quayside, in Delagoa Bay, to the Witwatersrand via the port infrastructure, landing and forwarding agencies and the sawmills and timber companies. But this was no triumph of 'free enterprise', of 'free-market' capitalism or of 'open competition'. It was a special form of buttoned-down capitalism, one frequently structured around price-fixing agreements between 'gentlemen' in an age that prided itself on the superiority of its business and ethical codes. Those codes, adapted to an imperial and colonial setting, depended ultimately on cheap, coerced black labour.

Through the WNLA, the mining industry had a cartelised, monopolistic hold on black male labour throughout southern Mozambique. In the port, shipping was dominated by British and South African shipping lines notorious for operating a 'ring' that set freight charges. The port's forwarding agencies had an informal association that 'set prices so that competition is limited and fair'. In similar fashion, the Rand timber companies had an agreement that supposedly ensured fair trading, but all parties benefited from 'contracted' labour drawn from Lourenço Marques and beyond. Here, then, was a special form of colonially adapted industrialisation built around extractive industries, one in which costs were controlled and underwritten by a system of indentured labour and in which prices along extended chains of value were set by subsidiaries that, if they were not owned outright, as with the LMFC, were deeply aligned with the mine owners and their political programmers such as Karri Davies and Fred Lingham.

What is clear is that, for all its inherent limitations, Mozambique's entry into the new world was deliberately retarded by Britain and its imperial ally, South Africa. The Sul do Save was invited to a dinner but, alas, by cannibals.

PART III

COMMERCIAL BANKING, CURRENCY MANIPULATION AND CONTRACTED MOZAMBICAN WORKERS, CIRCA 1870–1950

I believe that banking establishments are more dangerous than standing armies.
THOMAS JEFFERSON

Bank robbery is an initiative of amateurs. True professionals establish a bank.
BERTOLT BRECHT

Long before the European voyages that 'discovered' what local inhabitants had known for centuries, coastal trading centres on the northeastern coast of the African continent were integrated into the wider western Indian Ocean economy. From at least the 9th century city-states along the coastline, such as Lamu in the north, in present-day Kenya, down to Kilwa, in southern Tanzania, and beyond, traded with Arabs, Indians and Persians. In a coastal culture heavily influenced by Islam, Swahili traders exchanged goods such as gold and ivory, along with human beings as slaves, for items as exotic as glass, porcelain and silk that sometimes originated from as far away as China. Much of this trade was already in decline by the time the Portuguese explorers sought a passage to India in the late 15th century.

Against that background, conceive of an ill-defined east African coastal universe, one extending even further south. Nominally controlled by the weakest of the European imperial powers between the 15th and 20th centuries, and sometimes reliant on cowrie shells as a store of value, a good deal of its long-distance trade remained aligned to the north and east, into the Arabian Sea and up India's Malabar coast. Imagine, too, that after being gripped by an ancient practice of production that mutated into institutions recognisably

African over hundreds of years, the colony was subjected to a century of predation by Western powers for slaves.

Slavery came to Mozambique as a frontal assault on its vital organs. Then, just as slave selling, heavily centred on the Atlantic world, was outlawed, in the latter part of the 19th century, the colony was subjected to a massive kick up the backside. In little more than three decades an economically feeble colony went from sending slaves into what passed for the 'civilised' new world to supplying contracted migrant mineworkers to the gold mines of a local emerging industrial power.

Then, think of how Portugal, out of step with advances in industrial production and modern technology and lacking domestic capital and raw materials after the loss of its prime colonial asset, Brazil, sought to prod its emaciated coastal enclave, Mozambique, into the 19th century. It ceded huge swathes of territory to chartered companies dominated by foreign capital that operated as states within a colonial state. This at a time when the previously unconnected diamond- and gold-mining frontiers of the interior merged to create an industrialising state commanding an internationally backed currency that appealed to most of the colony's African inhabitants, who had only recently been freed from slavery but who were still subject to forced labour in the colony.[1]

The same seminal change encouraged the colony's expatriate retail and wholesale trading establishments to turn their heads towards the hinterland and an emerging African working class for clients even as their hearts hankered after India and the old north–east alignment. An ocean-oriented economy, once reliant on trade conducted by Asians in a string of small ports linked by monsoon, dhow and sail, had to spread further inland and regroup. At small, geographically dispersed junctions, villages and 'towns', the fate of the traders was determined by steam and the steel skeleton of a modest railway system. Contemplate, too, how an enfeebled colony, lacking a metropolitan financial patron of substance and accustomed to trading in specie drawn from across the western Indian Ocean economy, might survive, let alone prosper, in the face of invading currencies drawn increasingly from an industrialising neighbour and the Atlantic world.

Designing, establishing and operating a colonial financial system in what was also an unpromising natural environment posed significant problems to an imperial power lacking in mere 'challenges'. How, in a coastal assemblage lacking a central bank, was legal tender determined, meaningful exchange rates set or foreign exchange accumulated? In a frontier-like setting, as short of human resources as it was of an ethically bound, adequately remunerated bureaucracy, how were the financial dealings of a shallowly rooted ethnic merchant elite set on repatriating most gains to the countries of their birth to be controlled?

Moreover, how was economic stability to be maintained when a successfully industrialising neighbouring state with explicitly stated expansionist objectives, including appropriating the colony's principal port, used its own greater international cachet to block the raising of loans in international markets? And, if problems associated with the 'normal' functioning of a domestic economy were somehow not enough, how was a bare-bones 'state' to cope with the vicissitudes of the global economy, deep economic depressions and two world wars?

In Mozambique, some of the roots of endemic poverty and chronic underdevelopment lay in a centuries-long history punctuated by gross misfortune. It was 'discovered' and colonised by an economically and militarily weak imperial power dominated by commercial thinking. Portugal, too, lacked the natural resources to make the transition into the age of industry possible, let alone tolerable. It tolerated, if it did not encourage, a century of slave-trading followed by decades of forced labour. Few colonies were as poorly equipped to enter the 20th century as was Mozambique. When it did, it had to endure the added misfortune of finding itself in the shadow of an emerging industrial dispensation dependent on huge supplies of domestic and foreign black migrant labourers who, at the points of production, were then racially segregated, tightly policed and denied any social and political rights.

Capitalist South Africa latched on to, and consciously sought to profit from, often directly and sometimes indirectly, Mozambique's miserable birthright. It deepened the plight of the Portuguese colony as it struggled to control and shape its banking, currency and financial structures. But client states, even those with unpromising dowries, do not enter the world fully formed. They have constantly to be created and recreated. How exactly, then, did this underdevelopment unfold?

Lisbon and the Banco Nacional Ultramarino:
Loincloths Among the Suits,
circa 1864–1899

For much of its existence, from the 16th to the 20th century, south-eastern Africa was a zone of Portuguese influence characterised by its liminality. It was an indeterminate coastal expanse forever in the making, one lacking formally defined boundaries and presided over by local rulers whose authority constantly waxed and waned. It was a 'possession', a nondescript 'colony' that much later aspired to become a 'province', hoping one day to become recognisable as a 'country'.

In a sleepy trading zone, where inland barter operated side by side with a few coastal outlets where specie circulated more freely and slave trading was widespread, calibrating monetary value precisely was always problematic. What constituted 'value' when brothers, some drawn from as far afield as the lower reaches of central Africa, might be traded more readily than beeswax in an economy that, from the mid-19th century was simultaneously being incorporated into a regional migrant-labour system? How could the value of a day's manual labour be locked into a coin that might be exchanged for a coin of lesser value?

Portuguese colonialists clearly understood the linkage between money and work, and sought to encourage the transition of Mozambique from a backward agricultural domain into something integrating with, and more closely approximating, a regional capital-ist economy. 'Work', in the case of Africans, excluded labouring for oneself, or ensuring the subsistence of the family, and 'was carefully defined as an activity completely integrated into the monetized colo-nial economy'.[2]

The earliest black Mozambican exposure to currency and exchange values was confined largely to the northern and central reaches of the coastal economy. From the 9th century, indigenous peoples were drawn into the western Indian Ocean trading economy through their interactions with Omani Arabs and Malabar Indians.[3] But the first mass exposure to the purchasing power of coins, and how this might vary, occurred among Africans in the far south, before slavery in the Portuguese colonies was legally abandoned, in 1879. Chopi and Thonga tribesmen, 'Shangaans' from the Sul do Save, undertook spells of voluntary migrant labour in southern Africa from the mid-1860s. They worked first in the sugar-cane fields of Natal and then moved on to the Kimberley diamond mines. By 1872, Chopi and Shangaan workers were repatriating so much of their wages, in coin, that the Natal government was forced to import specie to the value of £30 000 sterling in order keep the wheels of its booming sugar-cane economy turning.[4]

In the 19th century, most such cash earnings found their way back to the provinces of Gaza and Inhambane, the latter boasting the most prosperous of all southern black agriculturalists. However, as the inhabitants grew increasingly reliant on cash earnings, by the 20th century the migrants had mutated into an impoverished, subsistence-based, tax-paying peasant proletariat.[5] Inhambane, on the bay of the same name, saw a significant early inflow of British specie. But the port that lay 500 kilometres to the south, Lourenço Marques, saw a far bigger range of foreign currencies in circulation after the discovery of the richest goldfields in the world, along the Witwatersrand, in 1886.

The completion of the Suez Canal, in 1869, coincided serendipitously with the opening of the Kimberley diamond fields. Passage through the Mediterranean saw first a growing number of sailing ships and then, a decade later, North Atlantic steamers, being drawn directly into the Indian Ocean. Vessels called in at east African ports as far south as Cape Town. Delagoa Bay and Lourenço Marques – whose parentage and ownership had been settled by arbitration in 1875 – came to host captains and crews from around the world, not excluding the Far East.

The global dominance of oceanic trade in the imperial age was reflected in the number and variety of coins that circulated in the port – markers that can still be traced in Maputo's Museu Nacional da Moeda. Brazilian copper coins, French and German specie, and Mexican and Spanish dollars were all, but perhaps not equally, welcome in the bars and brothels that constituted a good part of the town's business.[6] But this laissez-faire dispensation came under strain as the gold discoveries in the interior prompted the realignment of the Mozambican economy, from north–east to south–west. The specie of the older Indian Ocean trade lingered on into the 1890s but was gradually, albeit never fully, replaced by British and South African gold coins, the *sine qua non* of early-20th-century black waged labour.

In 1889, it was noted how rarely Portuguese silver was seen in Lourenço Marques, and gold almost never. Lisbon had long lacked the resources necessary to mint coins for its Cinderella colony. This humiliating shortfall grew ever more apparent after 1892, as Portugal descended into near bankruptcy and the economy of the ZAR mounted the doorstep of prosperity, reaching a high point in the boom of 1895. Leading Asian traders were exporting gold and other coin to India as fast as the value of Portuguese currency was declining.

To maintain the level of liquidity necessary for the functioning of commerce, the Mozambican administration was forced to import increasing quantities of specie, at considerable cost, each month.[7] In 1891, it purchased specie worth over £100 000 sterling, making it the colony's fifth most important import, and by 1896 imported coinage was still among the largest items of expenditure in the colony. All these foreign coins, from Austrian thalers to Mexican dollars, were over-stamped locally with the letters 'PM' (Provincia de Moçambique).[8]

But foreign specie was not all of a piece. Closer examination of the coins in circulation in and around Delagoa Bay in the years leading up to the Anglo-Boer War bore witness to the economic transition taking place in the colony. A good number of Asian traders clung to the old port currencies of the north–east trade, while black migrant workers, newly exposed to the inland mining industry, were already adjusting to the emerging, stronger gold-backed currencies of the south and west. When it came to coin, it was the 'new' African consumers of retail goods who paved the way to change rather than older Indian suppliers.

The Maria Theresa thaler, first minted from silver bullion in Austria, in the 1770s, had been circulating in India, Muscat, Oman and elsewhere in the Arabian Peninsula for many years.[9] Long a minor trusty of dhow traders in the northern reaches of the Indian Ocean, the thaler slipped steadily south – beyond Inhambane and easy reach of the monsoon – as the mineral revolution in southern Africa unfolded. It was first officially accepted as legal tender and over-stamped 'PM', in 1889, and thereafter came to occupy a fairly important place in merchant houses up and down the coast.[10]

But, in the late 19th century, with coins backed by silver generally beating a slow retreat in the face of a challenge from those backed by gold, the future of the thaler was not assured. Nor was Austrian specie the sole silver-backed invader in the coastal colony. By the mid-1890s, at the height of the gold-mining boom in the interior, English specie in and around Lourenço Marques was rapidly giving way to silver coins minted in the ZAR – the new currency and work destination for black migrants from the Sul do Save. Uncomfortable with anything other than gold coin for taxes, the administration attempted briefly to ban *all* such silver coins in 1897.[11]

But the prince of trading currencies along the old north–east trade routes, the one most likely to resist the challenge by specie from the new economies of the south and west, was, of course, Indian. The rupee was the medium of exchange traditionally favoured by almost all Asian traders, along with many of their clients up and down the coast, including some peasant-proletarians in the Sul do Save. In 1893, amid a persistent shortage of Indian coins, Inhambane was turned into a thriving moneychanging centre offering returning miners in search of rupees, for use at inland trading stores, better rates of exchange for gold coin than those available in the remote northern coastal regions.[12] What smaller denominations of coins were still used is difficult to establish.

The Mozambican administration and its close banking ally, the Banco Nacional Ultramarino (BNU), struggled to control well-entrenched Asian traders who doubled as moneychangers and speculators. In the early 1880s, with upward of 60 per cent of the colony's trade in the hands of British Gujarati, as opposed to Portuguese Goan, Indians, the BNU attempted vainly to control the value of the rupee by imposing a ten per cent duty on the import of specie, thereby keeping the exchange rate artificially low and discouraging the repatriation of capital or profits.[13]

The first thunder on the Witwatersrand gold mines and drizzle of migrant remittances into the financially parched Sul do Save and waiting Asian trading stores saw a rising demand for rupees in the early 1890s. The turning point came in 1893, when, adding to the currency confusion, the Mozambican administration intervened, turning the rupee into a two-tier currency. All rupees remained legal tender, but those over-stamped 'PM' were exchanged at a premium, leaving the unstamped Indian specie to trade at a discount. Everywhere outside the colony, however, the value of the so-called British-Indian rupee

was determined by a daily rate quoted on the Bombay stock exchange.[14]
In a coastal zone with a long history of theft – of property and people alike – the value of the rupee proceeded to bob up and down according to tide tables supposedly set in Bombay, Lisbon, London, Lourenço Marques and Johannesburg. But what happened out in the informal, remote, liminal universe of black migrant workers, as experienced in the local Asian trading stores, defied time and tide alike.

In 'theory' – often the go-to tool in Satan's workshop – the situation was never meant to have reached so low a point. But in Lisbon, theory was about as far from practice as the stock exchange was from God. The Banco Nacional Ultramarino was a rather unusual financial institution.

The BNU had been founded in 1864 by Francisco Chamiço, brother of a leading Lisbon banker, just as Portugal embarked on two decades of relative prosperity. '[A] private bank controlled by the government', the BNU's objective was 'to improve the economic situation of Portugal's overseas possessions, by providing a stable currency and granting credit to business enterprises.' The bank had the sole issuing rights in the colonies. A private-public institution, the BNU became in effect the central bank in almost all Portuguese colonies, bar Macau.[15]

The Old Lady of Threadneedle Street, the Bank of England, did not bat an eyelid at this development, which would come to have considerable influence in the development of the southern African region. Lisbon was not London, and the Tagus was not the Thames. A shortage of investment capital, a hallmark of Portugal at the best of times, ensured that the BNU clung to the conservative-commercial, metropolitan-focused mindset, attuned to the needs of its upmarket metropolitan merchant clients. From the outset its interest rates were set at two per cent above those of its rivals. During the troubled 1890s, the BNU did well enough for wealthy clients invested in the cocoa of São Tomé plantations operating with forced labour – much of it from Mozambique – under conditions almost indistinguishable from slavery. But, other than that, it did not otherwise greatly distinguish itself as a driver of 'business enterprise'.[16]

The BNU's partners, the government of the day and the state, were not unduly concerned about so pedestrian an approach to investment in Portugal's colonies, choosing to intervene only when there was a crisis. Thus, in the wake of the alarm set off by the call for demonstrable development and occupation of colonies made at the Berlin Conference of 1884–1885, the Cortes Gerais scrambled to create the legal frameworks for the Companhia de Moçambique (1888), and the Companhia de Niassa (1889). The chartered companies, granted near-sovereign rights over enormous swathes of territory in colonial Mozambique and funded very largely by foreign capital, not only ignored the BNU as a potential partner but undercut a founding right of the bank when they were allowed to issue currencies of their own.[17]

In a coastal universe where a bewildering array of coins inhibited a clearer understanding of where the authority underlaying monetary exchanges lay, what the basis of interest was or how best to protect the value of manual labour, the chartered companies complicated matters. Operating in the central and northern regions of a colony only recently shed of chattel slavery, the companies paid African labourers in tokens redeemable exclusively in the company stores.[18] It was a classic form of demonetised double-dipping by corporations bent on the ultra-exploitation of workers held captive in remote locations far from authentic capitalist labour markets offering cash wages. The Mozambique Company, by far the more successful of the two entities, took its privileges even further and, shortly after World War I, floated the Banco de Beira, which issued a Beira pound and Beira silver escudo.[19]

The BNU was asleep on the watch and unable, or unwilling, to protect its backyard interests in Mozambique with much enthusiasm. The bank was slow to spot the stirrings of an industrial revolution on the regional periphery. The emergence of the Kimberley diamond fields, in the 1870s, and the significance of migrant workers returning with gold specie aroused more interest among Asian traders in the colony than it did the BNU. It took the bank more than a decade before it had agencies in Cape Town and Pretoria, and it was only in 1883 that it got around to opening a branch in Lourenço Marques. Not until 1912 did it establish its presence in the migrant hub of Inhambane.[20]

The Cortes, too, had reservations about the BNU's capitalisation and competence. When Portugal slumped into crisis in 1891, parliament revoked the bank's issuing rights, only to reinstate them shortly thereafter, but only up to 1899.[21] Industrial capitalists and their allies, often more alert and energetic than their commercial cousins, were quicker to respond to the changes in the subcontinent than was the BNU. Amid hesitancy in Mozambique, the South African banks moved in. Taking advantage of the recent arrival of the Anglophile Mozambique Company on the east coast, the Bank of Africa opened a branch in Beira in 1900, a lead followed by Standard Bank the following year. In 1894, a few months before the official opening of the Pretoria–Delagoa Bay railway, Standard Bank opened a branch in Lourenço Marques, the Bank of Africa bringing up the rear in 1902.[22]

But the deepest roots of currency and financial disorder in Mozambique lay not in the centuries-old colony. They lay in the commercial and ideological mindset of the Cortes and some wealthy Lisbon and Porto merchants. They were often willing to look to the City of London for capital or expertise, but they lacked the English banks' understanding of industrial underpinnings and opportunities. Unable to comprehend fully what was happening beyond the Bay of Biscay, and lacking capital in sufficient amounts, Portuguese notables were even less well-equipped than the BNU to pick up on the start of another industrial revolution, adjacent to remote and neglected Mozambique.

Imperial lassitude and conservative public and private banking policies made for a deadly combination. That, along with the lack of domestic capital in Portugal, long before the South African mining industry took off, contributed to some of the confusion and currency disorder in Mozambique that was frequently manipulated by traders. In a liminal universe, where a centuries-old agrarian order was forced to come to terms with the advance of a new industrial dispensation, change came relatively abruptly. In three decades, between about 1870 and 1900, a better understanding emerged of how specie could form the basis of seasonal credit and be a medium of exchange or a store of value.

The cross-border experience of tens of thousands of migrant labourers from the Sul do Save provided African peasant-workers with early mass exposure to racially demarcated labour markets, the vicissitudes of international capitalism and a preference for British and South African gold or silver specie. In Mozambique, as elsewhere, underdevelopment was a journey as much as it ever was a destination. A British victory in the Anglo-Boer War guaranteed an industrial-agrarian rather than an agricultural-industrial economy in South Africa and quickened Mozambique's journey into clientage.

Two Steps Back, One Forward: The BNU and African Labour, circa 1902–1914

Britain won the war of 1899–1902. The former Boer republics won the peace. By 1910, South Africa was a unitary state largely in control of its destiny and with new, white priorities. Seen against that backdrop, the post-bellum migrant miners of the Sul do Save were immediately placed on the back foot in a region where institutionalised racism was fuelled increasingly by the dynamics and pace of industry and urbanisation rather than agriculture and the countryside. It was the outcome of the war that did most to check the bargaining power of black Mozambicans.

Milner's post-war reconstruction team and the weak Portuguese administration collaborated to deliver indentured, legally bound black workers to the collieries of the eastern Transvaal and the Witwatersrand mines in increasing numbers. The wages of black workers, who were denied collective bargaining rights, declined consistently in real value for most of the first half of the 20th century. The 1902 modus vivendi was followed by the Mozambique Convention of 1909, which, in amended form, lingered into the 1960s. These agreements effectively reserved the south and east of the Sul do Save as the exclusive recruiting preserve of the Witwatersrand Native Labour Association, a subsidiary of the Chamber of Mines, an employers' cartel. Until at least World War I, a significant number of the WNLA's 'voluntary' indentured labourers – peasants being transformed into migrant proletarians – were delivered to Highveld mines in train coaches that were often barred and locked, to live their working lives in enclosed, well-policed mine compounds.[23]

The arrangement between the colonial administrations, entered into without the consent of the governed, was not entirely unproblematic, however. Constructing places of confinement for workers reduced

WNLA medical inspection of indentured Mozambican mine labourers, c. 1929.

employers' room for manoeuvre in the 'free' market if they wished also to safeguard their access to cheap indentured labour in more financially testing times. The compounds bound jailer and jailed alike, albeit in different ways. From the moment that the modus vivendi was signed, the Rand mine owners and the Sul do Save miners were bound by transnational cords linked by banks, gold and currency. It took two decades to show just how closely employers and employees had become intertwined.

The BNU, operating in Lourenço Marques since 1890, showed little outward appreciation of how most Sul do Save migrants were locked into an emerging industrial dispensation. It remained content to continue along its conservative, government-endorsed commercial pathway, lacking in capital. As historians of the evolution of Lusitanian financial institutions have noted, 'banking in an empire in the making had to follow the flag, not to precede it, and the Portuguese flag was not fully introduced everywhere until the end of the First World War'.[24]

Predictably, the Mozambican administration became the BNU's most important client in Lourenço Marques. The modus vivendi, the

fixed price of gold and the local Asian trading community encouraged the Portuguese administration to press the Chamber of Mines to
introduce a deferred pay system for black migrant workers, payable
in gold specie. The wish, which preceded the practice by more than a
decade, became incorporated but not acted upon in the renegotiated
Mozambique Convention of 1909. The start-stop delay in a deferred-
pay system for miners, only implemented fully and continuously after
1928, meant that for many years the southern part of the colony was
bleeding manpower as well as some income. Before World War I, the
BNU and the traders handled little of that third of the colony's cash
income that derived from the earnings of Sul do Save migrants.[25]

The BNU could not command the greater part of black workers'
remittances. The bank was unable, or unwilling, to provide mortgages
for homes or properties, or to underwrite the development of industries in or around Lourenço Marques. And, after the Anglo-Boer War,
the BNU was forced to compete with South African banks, including
a newcomer, the National Bank of South Africa, founded in Pretoria
during the republican era.[26] The old north–east trading pattern saw
Indian Ocean port currencies – including the thaler and rupee – still
circulating freely along the entire length of the Mozambican coast,
alongside an insurgent challenger from the new south – British sterling.

Even success at moneychanging in the port proved elusive. The
leaden-footed BNU was unable to compete with Lourenço Marques's
agile, street-smart Asian currency dealers and traders, such as the
Haji Essa, Haji Suliman Company. Then, in 'order to direct exchange
business towards the Portuguese bank', the BNU, in 1907, attempted
unsuccessfully to persuade the colonial administration to hike licence
fees for moneychangers to £25 or £30 sterling per annum.[27]

Not even the replacement of the old Portuguese *mil-réis* by the
new escudo, which marked the overthrow of the monarchy in Lisbon
in 1910, could render the BNU more competitive. The Mozambican
administration, however, did its best to be helpful. It exchanged the gold
coins that it harvested as taxes from returning migrants at the bank, but
this made little difference to the BNU's overall profitability because the
escudo held up reasonably well against the pound up to World War I.[28]

The advent of the Portuguese republic, in 1910, saw an upsurge in
nationalism in the small Portuguese community in Lourenço Marques

– not all of it necessarily born of a love for Lisbon. Some of it, such as insisting that the town be referred to by its name rather than as 'Delagoa Bay', or that shop signage in English be rendered in Portuguese, signalled a new, slightly more muscular approach to dealings with old-school Anglophone imperialists.[29] The formation of the Union of South Africa, in May 1910, four months before the advent of the republic, helped bring home to locals how the long-standing brutally direct dominance of the region by Britain was rapidly giving way to an imperial cousin who threatened to be almost as arrogant and demanding.

Cultural signals of a potentially muscular political approach to dealing with British imperialists by Mozambique's 12 000 Europeans were an external manifestation born of inner economic anxieties. Older urban residents and settlers in the countryside feared being overwhelmed by the new South Africa. Ongoing resentments around the modus vivendi had been revived by the signing of the 1909 Convention. Concerns about 'Anglicisation', 'clandestine migration' and 'denationalisation' of black migrants reflected deep-seated fears about becoming permanently dependent on an ever-stronger South Africa.[30]

To offset WNLA depredations and in the spirit of taking the fight to the latter-day slave-raiders, a patriotic Portuguese Native Labour Association (PNLA) was launched in 1911. But any organisation confined to whispering wishes in the wind was never going to receive a proper hearing, and the PNLA collapsed soon enough.[31] The truth was that, by then, the mining industry was already so powerfully entrenched that there could be no meaningful conversation among equals about how many black men from the Sul do Save were to be deployed on the Witwatersrand. The only question was how the wages of Africans might be distributed between 'Mozambique' and 'South Africa' – both terminological inexactitudes that denied workers themselves the first call on their earnings. The issue of deferred pay was duly reignited, which in turn prompted underlying questions about banking, currency and commerce in the captured coastal colony.

In 1911, amid mutterings about shortages of black labour at the derisory wages paid by Portuguese settlers, the WNLA launched a 'Commission of Enquiry' to gauge the mood and economic realities in the Sul do Save. It discovered the obvious. The administration in Lourenço Marques disapproved of wage differentials that encouraged 'clandestine migration'. It not only diminished its own pool of forced labour but threatened the size of an already modest tax base. Settlers, incapable of competing with the mining houses, resented the WNLA's privileged first call on black labour, while Indian traders bemoaned the fact that migrants spent most of their wages on the Rand before their homecoming.[32]

The lowest common denominator among the complaints received from Mozambicans was a plea for the introduction of a deferred-pay system for migrant workers. Black miners, who stood to forfeit half their gold coin if they failed to return to the Sul do Save, would be less inclined to be involved in 'clandestine migration'. The scheme might also make some African men less likely to sign up with the WNLA, benefiting settler farmers. The potential benefit for the many Asian retailers and wholesalers in the Sul do Save was self-evident.

Some officials in the Chamber of Mines and the WNLA had reservations about the wisdom of embarking on a scheme that might cause reputational damage. African miners had good reason to be suspicious about the fate of money passing through the hands of Mozambican officials on the Witwatersrand or in the Sul do Save. Not only were the colonial bureaucrats notoriously corrupt, but they were also perfectly willing to resort to theft as a way of supplementing their meagre salaries. It was estimated that barely 15 per cent of the existing mine-workers' modest 'remittances reached their destinations'. In Pretoria, the Secretary to the Department of Mines took a far more sanguine and reassuring view of the proposed change. He was convinced that implementing a deferred-pay scheme was unlikely to make much difference. The Chamber of Mines, assured of the government's backing, moved cautiously ahead. Within a year 'Mozambique' and 'South Africa' reached an agreement, in principle and in private.[33]

But Pretoria's tenor and Johannesburg's countertenor were not singing from the same song sheet. Not that the Chamber much cared. The ears of industry were more attuned to songs of the state than the humming of local players. When the implementation of the 50 per cent deferred-payment scheme was announced, publicly, in early 1913, there was an outcry from affected sections of the white community on the Witwatersrand. No one appears to have asked, or recorded, what the black wage-earners themselves thought about the sudden

The customs house (TOP RIGHT) and goods inspection (TOP LEFT AND ABOVE) of
returning miners – 'magaizas' – at Ressano Garcia, c. 1929.

change. No fewer than 4 000 storekeepers petitioned the government
to reconsider the scheme. But their pleas, heard clearly enough in the
Johannesburg City Council, where their votes mattered somewhat,
failed to reach Pretoria.[34]

The deferred-pay arrangement for new recruits from the Sul do
Save – miners with contracts of nine months or longer, contracts that
were criminally enforceable – went into operation in 1913. The success of the scheme, as measured against payments received, currency
exchanges and altered black consumer behaviour, was thus barely
in place before the effects of World War I began to course through
southern Africa. The resulting upheavals saw the scheme suspended,
and Portugal's entry into the war, in February 1917, was a disaster
for Lisbon and Lourenço Marques. It was followed by local banking,
currency and fiscal chaos.

The Financial Unravelling of Mozambique, circa 1916–1926

From a standing start, in 1886, when it produced less than one per cent of the world's gold output, and at a time when most international trade was underwritten by the gold standard, South Africa's share of the global output of the precious metal gathered speed at breakneck pace. On the eve of the Anglo-Boer War, it was already producing more than a quarter of global output, and a decade later that figure had risen to 40 per cent. It continued to climb well into the mid-1920s, by which time the country was producing slightly more than half of the world's gold.[35]

This extraordinary rise in output was facilitated by huge investments of capital and substantial technological advances. But it would not have been possible had it not also been for the exploitation of vast quantities of ultra-cheap, indentured foreign black labour, housed in prison-like working conditions for much of the 20th century.[36] Between 1903 and 1910, it was Chinese indentured labour that paid the greatest financial and physical price for South African economic ascendancy. After Union, in 1910, that burden shifted to what was becoming the long-term saviour of the South African gold-mining industry – black Mozambican workers drawn, overwhelmingly, from the Sul do Save. For most of that period, black Mozambicans accounted for between 50 and 60 per cent of the workforce, and as late as the 1950s, by which time their numbers had already fallen off considerably, about 30 per cent of the black workers still came from the Sul do Save trap.[37]

Those numbers were sustained throughout a time when, in cash terms and real purchasing power, the wages of African miners were falling steadily. The progressive impoverishment and underdevelopment of the sandy Sul do Save helped transform the pool of migrants in southern Mozambique from one primed by force to one of 'voluntary' labour, turning what had been a peasant base into a proletarian enclave. Between 1896 and 1911 the Chamber of Mines reduced black wages as a percentage of total cost to industry from 25 to 11 per cent. Likewise, the cash bill for black miners fell from 13.7 per cent of total revenue, in 1936, to 8.9 per cent in 1969. As has been noted, 'In real terms, using 1938 as the base year, black cash earnings in 1969 were no higher and possible even lower than they had been in 1911.'[38] As South Africa and the Rand mining industry rose, so the neighbouring Sul do Save sank slowly into economic nothingness.

But when it comes to understanding process, it is not enough to note where the pans of the scale come to rest. It is as important to chart the moment that first caused the scale to move before eventually settling. For a start, it makes sense to remember that, powerful as the Chamber of Mines was before and after the Anglo-Boer War, it was, after 1910, also locked into a developing South African state. The policies followed by the state's emerging bureaucracy and institutions could no more be read off the agenda of the mining industry than those of the Chamber of Mines could be read off the parliamentary order paper, even if the two overlapped more frequently than they did not.

When South Africa entered World War I, in September 1914, the state was 52 months old, barely out of its Union diapers. Although already politically hardened by armed contestations with ardent republicans and trade unionists, and with nationalist and imperialist tensions bubbling away within and between political parties, South Africa's most important financial flows remained linked largely to London.[39]

The underlying situation, however, was fluid. Wartime increases in gold production, although not always in profitability, and the emergence of new industries helped the country achieve fiscal stability. Military success in continental theatres fed into white South Africans' subconscious visions of what might, one day, become an expanded sphere of influence in central-southeast Africa. When the war ended, in November 1918, the country had a seemingly endless supply of ageing generals to call upon as future prime ministers. It did not take long for South Africa to develop financial fortresses capable of safeguarding its economic fortunes at home and a platform from which to launch political strikes against weaker neighbouring states.

A mixture of economic and political motives formed the conceptual foundations of three formidable new fortresses. Amid some vigorous contestation and debate, the foundations were poured during the war, and then set in the inflation-heated post-war environment. In little more than 12 months, between December 1921 and January 1923, South Africa acquired, in order, the Rand Refinery, the South African Reserve Bank and a branch of the Royal Mint. The refinery was a private company owned by the Chamber of Mines, the Reserve Bank an independent institution supposedly free of political influence, and the mint the only one in the British Empire authorised to issue gold as currency.[40]

The mint and refinery were part of an ineffectual attempt by General JC Smuts and his ruling South African Party to try and stem the growth in support for General JBM Hertzog and the National and Labour parties after he (Smuts) had led the brutal crushing of the white miners in the Rand revolt, in 1922. Nor did the establishment of a central bank with issuing rights satisfy Smuts's opponents, who wanted a state bank answerable to the government rather than an independent reserve bank.

In a volatile setting, with a general election due within 24 months, Smuts – seldom as interested in economic policy as he was in politics – looked around for the firmer, consensual, post-bellum terrain that might offer the South African Party a more secure footing.[41] Amid the political damage occasioned by the suppression of the miners' revolt, regional expansion presented itself as one way of beguiling an angry electorate. 'It would be a grand thing', he wrote, 'to round off the South African state with borders far flung into the heart of the continent.'[42]

Sensing almost from the outset that a successful push north and east along political pathways alone might prove to be a bridge too far, Smuts turned to South Africa's growing economic strength and new financial institutions to bolster his expansionist ambitions. Six months *before* white Southern Rhodesians were called upon to determine, in a referendum, whether they wished to become part of the Union, he was already actively engaging with the old British South Africa Company, Rhodes's powerful chartered company, 'to see whether we can arrive at an agreement on the expropriation of their assets'. The work, he noted, 'really means a financial review of the history of Rhodesia'.[43]

But Rhodesian voters, wary of being stranded between the political heat coming off the fires of Afrikaner nationalism and the icy economic blast of a Chamber of Mines that seemed capable of sweeping all the way to the equator, wanted more insurance. Besides being assured that they stood to eventually acquire the chartered company's mineral rights, they were offered 'strong financial support for the

TOP The newly established South African Reserve Bank, Pretoria, 1921.

ABOVE Workers in the melting department of the Royal Mint, Pretoria, c. 1930.

development of their transport system and other public works', and promised that 'their' black labour would not be recruited for South African industries.[44] It did not help; fire conquered ice. An October 1922 referendum sealed off the road north.

Smuts did not take kindly to the Rhodesian rejection, but, buoyed by earlier successful mischief-making in the London money market to stymie a possible loan to Mozambique, he returned to the fray.[45] Drawing on the wisdom of his predecessor, General Louis Botha, he looked around for other ways of skinning the cat. In November 1922, just weeks after a referendum that rejected his overtures, Smuts took it upon himself to educate the newly elected British prime minister, Bonar Law, about the realities underpinning South Africa's growing ambitions: 'It would not be good policy to extend any financial favours to Rhodesia, as she ought to seek relief for her financial troubles in the Union. Indeed, finance would be one of the principal causes to bring her into the Union, and the British government should not in any way lessen the force of that cause.'[46]

Drying up, when not positively sabotaging, prospective developmental loans destined for neighbouring states became an important part of South Africa's emerging 'foreign policy' in the wake of World War I. And, as we will see, Smuts, drawing on South Africa's new financial infrastructure, made ready use of the new weapons. The struggle for regional dominance was not through the free play of 'market forces'.

If Anglophone Rhodesians, tempted by a financial carrot, were respectfully dealt with by their southern sub-imperialist neighbour, then Lusophone Mozambicans got the stick. And plenty of it. Smuts's idea of coaxing wary white Rhodesians into the Union fold might not have appealed equally to Afrikaner nationalists and English-speaking voters back home, but when it came to the possible incorporation of Delagoa Bay, he was on electoral ground that had by then been ploughed by republican-minded South Africans for close on a century.

Ever since Louis Trichardt steered a party of pioneers fleeing the Highveld to the east coast as refugees, in 1838, Afrikaners viewed Delagoa Bay as a port potentially free from British influence that might one day serve the cause of Afrikaner nationalism. It was an aspiration that assumed even greater urgency during the era of high imperialism in the late 19th century. The seeds of that ambition, dormant but always alive, survived both the Anglo-Boer War and World War I.

In 1921, a newspaper columnist suggested that '[i]t is safe to assert that the vast bulk of South Africans, when thinking of Portugal in East Africa, have in their mind's eye nothing but Delagoa Bay'. The Afrikaner nationalist firebrand Tielman Roos predicted publicly that 'Delagoa Bay would also join the Republic the moment it was established here' (in South Africa).[47] The appeal of an electoral pitch from Smuts to acquire Lourenço Marques and the Sul do Save could be

Mozambican paper money issued by the Banco Nacional Ultramarino, Lourenço Marques, authorised in Lisbon and printed in London.

made to stretch effortlessly between Randlord and republican interests. The more immediate appeal behind the idea of appropriating the east coast could, however, be traced to Portugal's reluctant entry into World War I, in February 1917, and to Britain's growing wartime financial difficulties.

The financial vulnerabilities of Portugal and her colonies predated the Great War, but it took only weeks for new realities to manifest themselves in southern Africa. When hostilities in Europe commenced, in 1914, a pound in any of the sterling-bloc countries of the British Empire bought four escudos; by 1918 it could buy 40, and by 1922, 96.[48] In Johannesburg, just weeks after Portugal entered the conflict, a few misguided speculators, sensing that the Bank of Portugal and the Banco Nacional Ultramarino lacked the reserves necessary to fully back their notes, started hoarding escudos in the misguided belief that they might appreciate in the post-war period.[49] But in Britain, too, gold reserves were under pressure, a problem with consequences for South Africa.

The international gold standard system unravelled on the outbreak of war. Within months, the British government was buying sterling in the hope of maintaining the value of the pound against the dollar. Two years later, in 1917, it prohibited the export of gold, and within

South African bank note, the currency of choice in Mozambique during the post-World War I financial crisis.

four months of the war ending, in March 1919, it ceased buying sterling. The resulting stark fall in the value of the pound meant that South African gold could be sold at a premium that fluctuated. It usually came as a windfall, thus partly offsetting rising costs in an inflationary setting that lasted until April 1925, when Britain reverted to the gold standard.[50]

The major South African banks and the gold-mining industry had long-standing ties to the City. A network of hand-picked experts, working closely with the Bank of England, could always rely on the support of Smuts and his senior civil servants. Most domestic issues around balance-of-payment adjustments, credit, currency, money supply and arrangements for minting specie after 1917 were worked out jointly.[51] Amid all this reconfiguring of the country's financial architecture and shorter-term economic prospects, however, could be detected the largely hidden hand of an important party beyond easy reach of the mine owners and the state alike – the African miners of the Sul do Save.

Mozambican migrants with half a century's experience of southern African labour markets were familiar with the strengths and limitations of assorted currencies circulating along the east coast. They were also aware of the all-conquering monetary value of sterling earned in South Africa. For them, payment in British gold sovereigns was an essential part of labour contracts locked into a transnational colonial universe.

So, too, were the colonial Portuguese. The Lourenço Marques administration preferred its taxes settled in sovereigns. Asian traders, too, had a near insatiable appetite for gold that could be repatriated to India, where it sold at a premium at a time when silver was losing its lustre. Each year, five per cent of South Africa's supply of gold coins, carried back home to the east coast by African migrant workers, disappeared permanently from circulation via the Sul do Save drain.[52]

As is well known, the bulk of the capital invested into the South African mining industry came via European bourses. But what is often less well understood is that, through the wages paid to African workers, the gold mines formed part of a far wider global context. Earnings from the South African mining industry found their way directly from the Witwatersrand to the east coast of the continent and then on to India, while Mozambique, in turn, was also wired indirectly into Portugal. The wages of African miners were part of a financial quadrilateral spanning both hemispheres, connecting Johannesburg, Lourenço Marques, Bombay and Lisbon. Even the sleepy BNU had a branch in Bombay.[53]

By World War I, disgruntled Mozambican miners on the Witwatersrand were being hard-pressed by inflation, with the real value of their wages declining even more rapidly than usual. Migrant workers placed great store on the authenticity, durability and versatility of gold coin and were not well disposed to banknotes of uncertain provenance that were liable to physical degradation when stored in hot and humid conditions. By 1918, miners from the Sul do Save, and more especially those working in the very poorly paying collieries, had gone out on strike on more than one occasion for various reasons.[54] Already on the alert for signs of labour 'unrest', the Chamber of Mines became alarmed when it heard of the government's intention to relieve returning migrants of gold specie at the Komatipoort border post so as to keep South Africa in line with the latest imperial directive prohibiting the export of the precious metal.

Discussions to prevent the 'leakage' of specie were held in October 1919, well before the opening of the South African Reserve Bank. The

Chamber of Mines went into conclave with the Secretary of Finance, South Africa's Agent in Lourenço Marques, the Director of Native Labour, the General Manager of the National Bank of South Africa and almost all the senior officials of the mine owners' own recruiting operations on both sides of the border. It was an extraordinary array of South African economic and political firepower and probably the last occasion in the 20th century that the latent power of the Mozambican miners evoked such grudging respect, if not an entirely supportive response, from the captains of industry and a government that had previously ventured out only to rescue the Rand mine owners.

It was agreed that there could be no sudden withdrawal of gold coin specie, that the sovereigns might only be replaced, very gradually, by notes. Or, as one analyst noted pertinently, 'in the course of the 1920s African migrant mineworkers and their white bosses on the South African gold mines conspired to make gold coins the regional cornerstone of value'. The earliest financial architecture of the Union of South Africa was, in part, shaped by Mozambicans drawn largely from the Sul do Save.[55]

A unique configuration of forces meant that, for some months, the Chamber of Mines and African industrial soldiers marched in unison to the beat of the same distant drum – gold. The government, bringing up the rear, moved at a pace that did not initially threaten the integrity of the column. It was waiting on the right moment to break away and pursue its interests, after its own fashion. In March 1920, it set up a Select Committee to examine currency and banking reform, an investigation that also laid the groundwork for the establishment of the Reserve Bank. Once the Select Committee reported, the breakaway occurred within a matter of weeks. By August, both the House of Assembly and Senate had approved the Currency and Banking Act 31 of 1920, and the Act was promulgated on 17 December 1920.[56]

By then Prime Minister Smuts had the political momentum as well as sight of the emerging outlines of the state's financial infrastructure that might, hopefully, be aligned with his territorial ambitions. Two days before the promulgation of Act 31, he announced that black mineworkers would no longer receive their wages in gold coin. It would take four long years before African miners once again had their wages paid in gold specie. The mining companies attempted to soften the blow by paying at least twenty shillings of the wages due to each African mineworker in silver. But the new mode of remuneration failed to win the minds, let alone the hearts, of most of the black workers.[57]

The disappearance of gold coin from wage packets at a time of growing economic hardship was poorly received by black miners, and none more so than the Mozambicans. Protests were especially marked on the Witbank collieries where the WNLA's night trains dumped hundreds of labourers who had been 'recruited' in the Sul do Save, supposedly for work on the gold mines, but who then, through varying degrees of coercion, deceit and force, ended up working in the coal mines. For similar reasons, far East Rand mine managers, angered by the speed of the government breakaway, complained that Smuts's notice had left them with insufficient time to prepare workers for the great change.[58]

The choking-off of the supply of gold coins from Johannesburg, a source that accounted for a third of all revenue in Mozambique, was felt almost immediately in Lourenço Marques, Bombay and Lisbon. In Lisbon, yet another private-public enterprise, the Bank of Portugal, served as the country's central bank and enjoyed issuing rights. But it had been financially stretched ever since Portugal's entry into the war, in 1917. Lacking sufficient gold backing, the Portuguese escudo came under pressure, which had consequences in Lourenço Marques, where the currency situation was falling into even greater disarray.

In Mozambique, where the BNU's issuing right had been renewed in August 1919, currency problems were pervasive, bedevilling trading and feeding into wartime inflation in Lourenço Marques and Lisbon. Never able to stabilise its own, or the colony's, precarious finances through dealings solely in escudos of metropolitan origin – Bank of Portugal notes – or its own Mozambican 'provincial' escudos, the BNU had, ever since 1905, been issuing sterling notes of its own. Backed by gold, the *libra esterlina*, or 'Portuguese pound' – nominally of the same value as the British sovereign, convertible and supported in large part by the earnings of returning migrants – had long held up reasonably well.[59]

But, by 1919 the bank was mired in a serious problem of its own making that helped further to undermine the value of the *libra*. According to an inspector of the Standard Bank branch in Lourenço Marques, shortly after the war, and much like the speculators in Johannesburg, the BNU, in anticipation of a firming up of the value of the escudo, bought the latter currency freely to an enormous extent, and in doing so created heavy commitments on overdraft with their bankers in London. Their anticipations were not realised and the value of the escudo steadily declined, causing them serious financial embarrassment when their London bankers began to press for payment of their indebtedness. To relieve the situation it would appear that they considerably increased the issue of sterling notes [*libra*], with which they purchased British Sterling for transfer to London and, at the same time, declared their own note issues inconvertible ... it inevitably followed that these notes declined considerably in value.[60]

As BNU gold reserves eroded, so too did the value of the *libra*. By 1921, its value – once on a par with the pound – had depreciated by over 14 per cent.[61] Confidence in other BNU-issued notes had undergone earlier leaching when, four months *before* Smuts's announcement on specie, in August 1919, it was granted permission to issue 30 000 *contos* (thousands) escudos backed not by gold but by the paper issue of Portugal. This drew the Mozambican economy further into the slipstream of metropolitan Portugal, whose fortunes were declining more rapidly than those of the colony even though there were some forces pulling in the opposite direction. The BNU had been granted a monopoly in foreign exchange dealings and had become the de facto, if not the *de jure*, central bank of the colony. The tendency towards colonial decentralisation gathered momentum when, in 1920, Lourenço Marques was granted greater 'financial autonomy'.[62]

By 1920, the BNU was becoming a law unto itself and the stage was set for monetary chaos in Mozambique. Lacking gold cover, BNU notes were the first to fold. Later that year, exercising its new-found authority, the bank announced that foreign currency was no longer legal tender in the colony, although, in a thriving black market, British and South African currency circulated freely at a premium of at least ten per cent.[63]

In 1921, buckling beneath its post-bellum problems, the government in Lisbon – heading for an election – endorsed colonial policies that were at best confusing and at worst positively contradictory. The Cortes allowed the BNU to continue to run wild in terms of economic policy. Simultaneously, it sought to arrest a deteriorating political position by getting a strongman to prop up colonial autonomy in the face of South African financial aggression and territorial ambitions. In late February 1921, the government approved the appointment of Dr Manuel Brito Camacho as High Commissioner to Mozambique, giving him what seemed to be a free hand. Then, in March, it promptly hobbled him when it gave the BNU permission to issue *unbacked* notes for circulation in the colony for five years, paving the way for a prolonged period of inflation, gross currency speculation and political upheaval.[64]

BNU senior officials were well-connected in Portugal. In Lisbon, the tinkle of dividends often caught the ear of the political elite more readily than did squeaks of dissent from the colonies. The BNU soon had the measure of the reformist Camacho. Despite his often valiant defence of Mozambican interests in the face of insistent pressure from Pretoria, Camacho was unable to bring the self-serving policies of the hopelessly metropolitan-skewed BNU to heel.

Unable to sustain its *libra* currency-exchanging trick in Europe so as to fend off the demands of its creditors in the City, the BNU was forced to scour the hinterland in its search for loans. The National Bank of South Africa, commercial successor to a concession granted by Kruger in 1891, and itself saddled with post-war bad debts and poor management, opened its doors, if not its eyes and ears, to lending money to the BNU. But not even a walk-in heist, in Pretoria, yielded sufficient sterling to satisfy Lisbon or London. The BNU was constantly on the lookout for more pockets to pick. In September 1922, with gold coins remaining legal tender and highly sought-after, the BNU persuaded the Lourenço Marques administration – in debt to the bank – to force other commercial banks 'to accept its fiduciary circulation in exchange for the foreign notes that were, in theory, already illegal'.[65]

Besides contributing to pervasive currency confusion amid pernicious, chaotic inflationary pressures, the September decree added impetus to black market and other underworld activities. It allowed border officials and confidence tricksters to relieve black miners returning to the Sul do Save of sterling-based notes, earned in the Union, and to exchange them for escudos at rates that were criminal twice over.[66]

By the closing weeks of 1922, the complex, financially intertwined position of the Lourenço Marques administration and the flailing BNU had deteriorated to the point of no return. But only the High Commissioner was willing to break cover and acknowledge the extent of a crisis, which by then also involved the National Bank of South Africa pressing the BNU. In desperation, Camacho appealed to the equally poorly managed Bank of Portugal for a loan that might help free Mozambique from the attentions of the circling South African wolf. The appeal failed. He then set off to try and raise funds in other European markets, but the result was as predictable as was the sequel – his pleas again fell upon deaf ears. In December 1922, after less than two years in office, Camacho was recalled to a directionless Lisbon.[67]

Freed of the irksome Camacho, who appeared to be more interested in protecting the long-term prospects of the colony than the financial well-being of merchant capitalists in Lisbon and Porto, the BNU had the run of Lourenço Marques and the Sul do Save for the next 24 months. Camacho's successor as High Commissioner, VH Coutinho, only appeared in Lourenço Marques two years later, in November 1924. In Portugal, where political drift had long been the order of the day, German reparations for wartime damage had, by 1923–1924, eased financial pressures, but in Mozambique the situation had deteriorated.[68]

In 1925, despite the reappearance of gold coin in the wage packets of black miners on the Rand, the Mozambican economy was a shambles.[69] British and South African sterling were selling at a premium of 75 per cent, which meant that the provincial escudo had effectively been devalued by the same amount. It complicated and undermined trade and contributed directly to a violent strike by white railway workers in Lourenço Marques. In Whitehall, officials were sufficiently frustrated by the aimless drift in Portugal and Mozambique to suggest that the solution might lie in seeing 'British cruisers in the Tagus or off Lourenço Marques'. They were not alone in thinking of a military solution to years of political impotence. In Braga, General Manuel Gomes da Costa and a clutch of junior officers who would be cheered in the streets of Lisbon just months later were already toying with ideas of what a coup d'état might look like.[70]

Looking back, then, 1919–1924 was a period when African miners were forced to forego wages in gold coin. It was also, and not coincidentally, a time that witnessed the emergence of the starkest possible contrast between the interlinked economic and political fortunes of South Africa and Mozambique. It was, however, not an entirely new contest.

General Smuts, a witness at close quarters to British expansion in the subcontinent through military conquest, had long thought that southern Mozambique might one day fall South Africa's way in an imperial, post-bellum realpolitik settlement. General Botha's invasion of South West Africa, in 1915, had seen the former German colony being drawn into a South African orbit as a mandated territory, and Smuts occasionally dreamt of South Africa acquiring part of the rich, sprawling Belgian Congo.

But, when it came to Mozambique, it was Prime Minister Louis Botha who, drawing on a tactic first employed by Cecil Rhodes in the 1890s, reminded the ambitious Smuts that there was more than one way of skinning a cat. Money could sometimes do what mortars could not. 'Jannie,' Botha had told him, in 1918, 'there is no doubt about it, this is a matter which we must bring up and settle in our favour. The region must be bought out and we must pay for it.'[71] After that, Smuts appears to have been more open to thinking about other ways of extending South Africa's reach into listless southern Mozambique.

But old habits die hard. World War I had barely concluded when Botha died and the new prime minister, Smuts, signalled his no-nonsense approach to matters Mozambican. When the safety of British and South African citizens in Lourenço Marques was threatened in 1919, Smuts got a Royal Navy warship dispatched from Simonstown to Delagoa Bay in anticipation of a possible evacuation.[72] It was a potent reminder of the reach of raw imperial power, and, not surprisingly, throughout the early 1920s the Mozambican administration and the local inhabitants feared a South African takeover of Lourenço Marques and the adjacent reservoir of cheap black labour in the Sul do Save. But it was not the straight left of possible South African military intervention that needed watching so much as the hanging right that packed a financial punch.

After 1922, the South African refinery, mint and reserve bank – ostensibly independent, apolitical and market-driven institutions – were made to serve the new prime minister's territorial ambitions as he strove to shore up his increasingly vulnerable domestic political base. However, 'Smuts had an exaggerated view of the extent to which financial or economic pressures could induce fundamental political change' in southern Africa.[73] Having just overcome a revolutionary challenge by white miners in conflict with the Chamber of Mines on the Rand, his 'exaggerated view' may have been of recent vintage. Nevertheless, it caused him to misread how powerful nationalist sentiments could be – a strange weakness for a man who had himself been forged in the crucible of nationalist resistance to imperialism.

In October 1921, with the Mozambique Convention due for renewal and the prime minister keen to stay on side with the Chamber of Mines, Smuts fuelled anxieties in Lourenço Marques – and possibly Salisbury – by waving his right fist. In a speech to a meeting of the Associated Chambers of Commerce, in Pretoria, he appealed to Lisbon – a longtime friend of the Chamber of Mines – for Mozambique and South Africa to become 'one undivided country'.[74] A few days later, in a speech at Caledon, in the Cape, he returned to this theme with even greater vigour, causing more resentment in Portugal. It mattered not that these calls went unheeded, since the absence of gold coin and the gathering currency chaos were already forcing open some blocked ear passages.[75]

Little more than a month after crushing the Rand revolt on behalf of the Chamber of Mines, in March 1922, Smuts – like a puppy going at a sock – was back at his pet project, hoping to increase the prospects for a greater Union by subverting the chances of independent economic development in Portugal's east African colony. The negotiations around the possible renewal of the Mozambique Convention presented the prime minister with the opportunity of asserting South Africa's gathering economic dominance amid growing east coast vulnerability.

That April, a delegation led by Freire d'Andrade rather than the hard-nosed Camacho rejected out of hand Smuts's proposal for closer union. The prime minister then pushed for a joint board to take control of port and railway administration in Lourenço Marques, a project that the Rand gold-mining companies and their already dominant forwarding agencies along the wharf stood to benefit from more than most parties.[76] The joint-board suggestion was, at the very least, poorly timed. It came at a moment when Portugal had proudly just reclaimed ownership of most of the harbour infrastructure from entrenched foreign interests and been investing handsomely in the renewal of port facilities with funding generated entirely from within the metropole.

Not surprisingly, Camacho was not much taken with the idea of sharing control of the port facilities with an aggressive neighbour. But, eager to exercise South Africa's new institutional financial muscles, Smuts pushed on, rattling the cage of the currency crisis racking the embattled east coast colony. If, he suggested, Camacho were willing to accommodate South Africa on the joint-board issue, then 'the Union Reserve Bank would extend its operations to Mozambique. The BNU's sterling notes would be replaced by Union notes, backed by Union gold, which would constitute a Union government loan to Mozambique.'[77] But Camacho saw this for what it was – an iron fist in an iron glove – and Smuts's first attempt to use the Reserve Bank to help achieve foreign-policy objectives had tripped over nationalist pride. It was an exercise, as already noted, that was to be repeated in Rhodesia.

The prime minister was making it difficult for WH Clegg, the South African-born, Bank of England-trained Governor of the Reserve Bank, to maintain the fledgling institution's neutrality in the face of political pressures. Within weeks of having been stared down by the Portuguese delegation in a face-to-face meeting in Cape Town, Smuts was back at Clegg. That June, at his request, Clegg intervened with the Governor of the Bank of England to ensure that an attempt by Camacho to raise a loan for Mozambique in the City money market would be blocked.

The Old Lady of Threadneedle Street again peered briefly over her spectacles, coughed politely and reminded Clegg that she could only intervene 'for valid financial as opposed to political reasons'. But, when all was said and done, Clegg was a City man, a trusted member of the imperial family, and so he must have been relieved when, shortly thereafter, he received a telegram that he could show his prime minister – 'there is not much prospect of issue of Mozambique loan here or New York in the near future'.[78] It was the prime minister's first successful attempt, if muted, to employ financial sabotage as part of foreign policy in the region, and in 1923 he returned Clegg the favour by allowing him to bail out the National Bank from its Mozambican imbroglio.[79]

Camacho's intransigence had been suitably punished, but Smuts was astute enough to know that sneaking through the City's back door was a ruse that had to be used sparingly. When, later that same year, the Benguela Railway Company looked to raise a loan in the City, he seized the opportunity to apply more pressure on Portugal, and his objection, in Treasury circles in London, effectively sealed off the prospect of any funding. By the end of 1922, Smuts had used South Africa's post-war economic strengths, underwritten by gold and the implicit promise of support from the Reserve Bank, to pursue his expansionist dreams by offering financial inducements or handing out punishment right across the face of central Africa – from Angola and Rhodesia to Mozambique.

But Smuts's hope that, by applying pressure to neighbouring states and extending South African borders, the haemorrhaging of political support domestically might be arrested, proved to be misplaced. An aggressive approach to dealings with Mozambique failed to win the approval of even the Chamber of Mines. The signing of another modus vivendi, in 1923, merely saw the extension of the existing Mozambique Convention rather than the more robust agreement and incursions into the Sul do Save that the Chamber of Mines desired most.[80] When Smuts then lost the 1924 election to the Nationalist-Labour 'Pact' coalition, it eased some of the direct pressure on the Lourenço Marques administration but did little to remedy its ongoing currency chaos.

In Portugal, although the 'Democráticos' – the Republican Party – led a series of coalition governments so unstable that, for some, it suggested the need for urgent military intervention, the budgetary position had nevertheless improved fairly substantially by 1924.[81] The following year, a left-wing coalition, intent on further consolidating the position in Lisbon, took steps to rein in the power of the banks, including the BNU.[82] But, despite some progress, the overall metropolitan fiscal position continued to deteriorate, as it did, even more markedly, in Mozambique. The *libra* continued to decline in value, depreciating by 50 per cent and more. By late 1925, the possibility of the BNU's going insolvent was being debated in some South African banking circles.[83]

In late spring the following year, General Gomes da Costa led the May 1926 coup, and the junta appointed an ex-Mozambican military and civil administrator of 30 years' standing, João Belo, as its Minister of Colonies. Within five months the wings of the BNU received what was possibly their first serious clipping. The administration in Lourenço Marques administration was granted – quite independently of the bank – a substantial loan, and, more importantly, a series of deflationary measures were put in place. The fiduciary circulation of the BNU was reduced, and by early 1927 the value of the escudo against the pound sterling had improved by a remarkable 50 per cent.[84] Newly minted gold coins in the wage packets of Sul do Save miners helped to further stabilise the financial position in the colony, to the benefit of local retailers.[85]

The brief recovery of the Mozambican economy under Belo was, however, checked by three other developments. First, in 1928, Professor António de Oliveira Salazar of Coimbra University became Minister of Finance, going on to become prime minister in 1932 and then, effectively, dictator of Portugal. A neo-mercantilist, Salazar insisted on the balancing of the books not only in Lisbon but in Lourenço Marques. Second, with that in mind, Salazar supported the re-signing of the Mozambique Convention in 1928, reversing the tendency of earlier administrators such as Camacho and Belo to resist further South African financial encroachment in the east coast colony. Third, no sooner was the Convention back in place, with a guarantee of mine wages being paid in gold, than the Great Depression set in.

Global Economic Weakness and Regional Turbulence, circa 1928–1933

In 1970, a well-researched, reputably published guide contained a stark warning for arrogant South African visitors to Lourenço Marques. 'In Mozambique and Portugal', the overbearing were politely reminded, 'it is a *crime* to use words offensive to Portuguese currency.'[86] As we have already seen, there was a painful history to such nationalist clashes.

Shortly after World War I, when Smuts was still pursuing his aim of acquiring southern Mozambique, if not by outright means then by asserting control of the port and rail complex in Delagoa Bay, the hard-pressed Lourenço Marques administration was also having to cope with the fiscal madness of the faltering BNU. One of the Portuguese dreams, prompted by the hope of harvesting hard, gold-backed currency, was of turning the city and its surrounds into the subtropical holiday destination of choice for rich, as well as middle- and working-class, white South Africans. The centrepiece of that project was the construction of the finest of luxury accommodation in southern Africa.

The Polana Hotel, funded by the same South African speculators who had acquired much of the prime real estate in Lourenço Marques during the boom of the 1890s, opened in 1924 at a cost of a quarter of a million pounds sterling. The opening took place amid BNU-induced currency chaos, at a moment when relations between the countries were, arguably, at their most strained ever. But, as with the development of the harbour, or the selling-off of Sul do Save black labour to the Rand mining industry, the big-fish-eat-little-fish logic of capitalist exploitation was written into the Polana's business plan almost from the outset. The Portuguese administration had to indemnify the developer, the Delagoa Bay Lands Syndicate, against losses by way of a subsidy that eventually ended in 1948. The hotel ran at a loss throughout the 1920s and throughout the Depression. As a meaningful source of foreign exchange derived from tourists, Lourenço Marques only really came into its own after World War II.[87]

The port itself did not do much better as a source of revenue in the years immediately leading up to the Depression. By 1929, two out of every three ships calling at Lourenço Marques were loading South African coal for export, using modern facilities built from funds provided by Portugal. Along the wharves, too, the import-forwarding business was dominated by South African agencies, with one of the most prominent controlled by the largest of the Rand mining houses. In Mozambique, Salazar's severe neo-mercantilist strictures, demanding that all the colonies become self-supporting, never wanted for factual prompting.

Other factors did little to make Lourenço Marques a preferred destination for fixed direct investment. From November 1925 to April 1926, the port and railway complex was in a nearly continuous state of civil unrest. A four-month-long strike by Portuguese railway workers – an upheaval attributable directly to the financial crisis precipitated by the BNU's mismanagement of its depreciating sterling holdings and poor wages – saw armed forces pitted against strikers in street battles.[88] The city was awash with rumours of assassinations and bomb-throwing, and saw the deportation of strike leaders as well as the sabotage of some main-line trains.[89]

In part, the upheavals, which ended shortly before the Lisbon coup, mirrored some of the demonstrations of the late teens and early 1920s in Lourenço Marques. Those, too, had been triggered by a combination of the BNU's unrelenting focus on the need to deliver dividends for its metropolitan shareholders, rather than to increase the well-being of Mozambicans, and an inability to come to terms with regional fiscal imperatives. The prolonged railway strike of 1925–1926, however, prompted metropolitan Portugal to exercise more direct control over the private-public bank.[90]

The BNU's disastrous policies – formulated in Lisbon over many decades – invited, if they did not demand, a shift in influence and power from a private-public collaboration to one approximating more of a public-private partnership. The advent of Salazar's rule, followed almost immediately by the onset of the Great Depression, tilted the scales towards a greater public say in bank affairs. Within months the BNU, effectively the colony's central bank of issue, came under state control.

In 1933, a Standard Bank inspector in Lourenço Marques noted that '[t]he Banco Nacional Ultramarino has been under the control of the government for some two or three years past', and then, in the same sentence, went on to point out that, 'no balance sheet or statement is now issued'.[91] By then, however, Mozambique was long mired in a familiar banking, financing and currency crisis that dated back to at least World War I. The bank, the colony and the men of the Sul do Save – sold into indentured industrial labour en masse – appear to have been fated to lurch between the excesses of freewheeling commercial capitalism and the dictates of a new and repressive neo-mercantilist government.

Many of these problems arose from the way that Portuguese political culture reflected entrepreneurial ideologies and managerial practices that, in turn, could be traced to the roots of an economy still struggling to cast off the vestiges of feudalism. But not all obstacles to Mozambican economic development were metropolitan in origin. Some derived from the colony's proximity to the fields of force emanating from the regional heartland of industrial capitalism, South Africa, which, not unlike Mozambique, was closely linked to Britain.

After the Wall Street crash, in October 1929, and as the Depression unfolded, the British government was alarmed to find that the decline in UK exports did little to offset a huge public-sector wage bill. Unemployment insurance demands exacerbated the problem. Balancing the budget became increasingly difficult, placing pressure on the value of sterling, which proved impossible to protect solely through hikes in the interest rate.[92] On 21 September 1931, Britain came off the gold standard. Within days several South African banks, hoping to profit from an increase in value of the gold sovereigns that were still being freely minted in the country, immediately attempted to cut back on the number of gold coins that went into the wage packets of African miners. It took a swift intervention from the Curator of Portuguese Natives, in Johannesburg, and several mine managers to remind the banks about the provisions of the recently renewed 1928 Mozambique Convention and to have the decision swiftly reversed.[93]

In a replay of some features of South Africa's belated withdrawal from the gold standard, in the 1920s, the labour power of the Sul do Save miners – who still represented close on half the number of black labourers employed on the Witwatersrand – held sway for some time. When, in October 1931, white miners started receiving their wages in Union-issued notes, African miners continued to be reimbursed in gold coin.

The mine owners and government, not wanting their fortunes tied to sterling, clung to the gold standard until the downside was greater than the upside. On 27 November 1932, South Africa came off the gold standard. It was a date with destiny, one marking the beginning of the end of the prime position Mozambican workers had occupied in the South African gold-mining industry for half a century.

In those few months that South Africa remained on the gold standard – between the end of 1931 and late 1932 – the racially constructed, transnational, unfree 'labour market' continued to function as 'normal'. The Chamber of Mines was content to carry on paying black indentured workers in gold coin, and the Lourenço Marques administration to net the same sovereigns in the Sul do Save and elsewhere in the colony.[94]

But once South Africa came off the gold standard, in 1932, the Mozambican tax authorities and the BNU realised that there was easier money to be made. They became more diligent at harvesting hard currency from the returning migrant workers through taxes and then trading the specie against the weak metropolitan or provincial escudo.

During the post-World War I crisis, black miners returning to Mozambique with hard currency had been preyed upon by civilian fraudsters and a few officials at the Komatipoort terminus.[95] In the 1932–1933 crisis, a far more muscular Portuguese administration ensured that the state's official highwaymen enjoyed near-exclusive privileges when it came to systematically stripping returning migrants of the value of their labour.

The looting of migrant workers took two forms. First, as was noted in the Lourenço Marques branch of a South African commercial bank:

Deferred pay of Mozambique natives is paid over by the mines to the Portuguese Curator in Johannesburg and such money as they bring back, which was formerly in gold, is taken from them at the border and exchanged for escudos in which currency their deferred pay is also paid to them at a fixed rate of 109$00 [109 escudos] to the pound. In terms of the Convention this also was formerly paid to the natives in gold. The change has been to the detriment of the native and also the traders of the colony as the purchasing power of the natives has been considerably reduced thereby.[96]

Second, the Mozambican administration remained acutely aware of Salazar's insistence on balancing the books. It therefore demanded to be compensated for having lost access to the possible speculative gains that might have accrued to it from the collection of the miners' wages in gold coin rather than notes. The Chamber of Mines willingly bought the pup that any compensatory funding – to the state rather than the miners – would be used to benefit the colony's African population:

The sum of £135 000 was paid on behalf of the mining groups to the Portuguese Government as compensation for the substitution of Union currency for gold payment from the time the Union departed from the Gold Standard until the coming into force of the revised Convention. It is said that a large portion of this payment has been allotted to Native welfare.[97]

Never had the natives benefited more from welfare, having lost access to their wages in their specie of choice, gold coin, and having been stripped of their second choice, Union notes. The mining industry chose to compensate a third party who might, on a discretionary basis, use an unspecified portion of the hijacked funds for 'native welfare'.

The transnational manufacturing of rural poverty in southern Mozambique commenced with the signing of the modus vivendi in 1902. It operated steadily throughout the first half of the 20th century, churning out wages that, in real terms, were declining in value, and then managed to accelerate the process of creeping impoverishment in much of the Sul do Save during periods of enhanced economic hardship.

South Africa's departure from the gold standard ushered in a new era for currency speculators and the hundreds of licensed Asian money-changers in southern Mozambique. But unlike in the post-World War I period, renewed fervour in the legal and illegal foreign exchange markets now came under much closer scrutiny from a more centralised metropolitan and provincial state intent on enforcing Salazar's neo-mercantilist policies. To 'stabilise trade and ensure that a proper balance [of trade] was maintained' the Lourenço Marques administration established an 'Exchange Council'. But important parts of the old firm remained firmly intact. The Exchange Council's account was held by the BNU, and the colony's exporters were obliged to sell 80 per cent of all foreign exchange earned to the bank of privilege.[98]

Financial stability was an elusive target during a global financial contraction, and more so in a region where a neighbouring economy, buttressed by gold and operating counter-cyclically, was expanding. Signs of the crisis were evident even before South Africa abandoned the gold standard, in the shape of Exchange Decree No. 21.154 of 22 April 1932. In the words of a banker monitoring what was happening in Lourenço Marques:

> The effect of the Decree mentioned above has been to bring the export trade to almost a standstill and to discourage imports in every way. Exporters are compelled to deposit with the Banco Nacional Ultramarino, for credit of an Exchange Fund, exchange in the currency of the country to which their merchandise is

exported or notes of that country or the local equivalent in gold for 75% of the value of each consignment. No transfer of funds to places outside the colony may be made without the authority of the Government Banking Inspector whether such funds be for the use of the transferer or in payment for goods imported. Authority will only be given by the Banking Inspector or the Exchange Council when a balance is available in the Exchange Fund. The object of this ordinance was to control the balance of trade for the colony, but its effect has been so much more far-reaching than anticipated that in deference to the public clamour some modifications are now being contemplated.[99]

The 1932–1933 crisis matched, if it did not surpass, that of 1919–1922. The new decree caused little financial hardship for the British and South African firms who dominated the most important commercial business sector in Lourenço Marques – the forwarding agencies. These firms, locked into a price-fixing cartel, benefited from the favourable exchange rate and, whenever they sought a premium on sterling or Union notes, bypassed the BNU and reverted to what they referred to as the 'open market' – licensed Asian moneychangers who moved effortlessly between legal and illegal currency deals. The agencies also profited from paying their white and skilled employees of mixed race in gold, while their African employees, like other blacks working in the port, were fed the thin gruel of metropolitan or provincial escudos. It was a cynical practice that reinforced the contours of a liminal universe in which the colour of a man's skin determined the currency he was paid in and the value of his labour.[100]

Predictably, the decree pressed hardest on the port's Asian exporters and importers, traders celebrated for their contribution to the economy in good times and then dismissed as predatory aliens during downturns. One or two, including the respected owner of a sesame oil factory, SE Ginwala, were trapped in midstream. Contracts entered into before South Africa came off the gold standard were caught up in the maelstrom of the new regulations being enforced by the Exchange Council. Entrepreneurs without the necessary hard currency were caught short. Lack of gold-backed currency invited cross-border complications.[101]

In response to the April decree, leading Indian and other exporters withdrew as much gold-backed currency as swiftly as possible from their accounts with local banks. Then, using a legal provision entitling residents to operate bank accounts abroad, they opened accounts in Johannesburg, circumventing the requirement for hard-currency deposits demanded by the otherwise panoptical Exchange Council.[102]

For several months, the post-1932 regime further disrupted the time-honoured practice of local Asian moneychangers and traders of repatriating profits by exporting gold – in coin or other forms – to India. It was, in any case, by then a comparatively modest legal trade, one that had earlier been transformed by new international arrangements.

In the early 1920s, once the ban on the export of gold had been lifted, and especially after the return to the gold standard, South Africa, benefiting from its new refinery, mint and reserve bank, had begun exporting gold bars and coins directly to India, and on a grand scale. In October 1925, 'two steamers took between them £700 000 of gold in [sovereigns] from Durban to Bombay within a fortnight'. And, in the week ending 24 December of the same year, bullion worth £400 148 and coins to the value of £85 200 were exported to India.[103]

In Lourenço Marques, entrepreneurs, large export firms and currency speculators all helped keep up the demand for gold or gold-backed currency throughout the Depression and the remainder of the 1930s. In January 1933, SE Ginwala, who was apparently considering erecting an additional oilseed processing plant in Johannesburg – possibly to wriggle free of the excessive demands of the Exchange Council – was stopped at the South African border with 1 000 gold sovereigns.[104] It was only in the mid-1930s that something approaching 'normality' returned to the erratic money markets of southern Mozambique.

Settling into Structured Regional Disadvantage, circa 1934–1950

It may help if, for a moment, we pause to reconsider the *longue durée*. After centuries of gross exploitation and neglect by Portugal, the mineral revolution in southern Africa promised, albeit only briefly, to deliver Mozambique a set of modest developmental benefits centred on Delagoa Bay and the adjacent Sul do Save. But fortune dictated otherwise. Fierce imperial rivalries in the 1890s, a British victory in the Anglo-Boer War and the want of political direction and will in Lisbon after the turn of the century, along with measured financial strong-arming by South Africa after World War I, all but snuffed out the chances of Mozambique's constructing an economy that might meaningfully feed off, or properly into, the emerging industrial heartland on the Highveld.

Instead of assisting in the overall development of the colony, the Johannesburg–Lourenço Marques rail connection inhibited significant local agricultural and industrial production, leaving Portugal struggling to keep the South Africans from owning and commanding fully the infrastructure and associated businesses in the port and rail complex.[105]

In the Sul do Save, the African male peasantry was sold off to the Rand mining industry as cheap indentured labour – part of a black proletariat in the making largely for purposes of domestic tax collection. Most of these arrangements reached their apex formulation in the Mozambique Convention of 1928, which, within months, was followed by the Great Depression. By the end of the Depression southern Mozambique was, in economic terms, effectively a South African dependency. After that, it continued to expand and modernise slowly, but it did so marooned on an extended economic plateau from which there was no easy escape.

Lourenço Marques, increasingly important as a litmus for the economic fortunes of the southern coastal region and colony, came out of the Great Depression slowly and unevenly. The number of ships using the port rose from 848 in 1934 to 970 in 1935, and stood at 1 031 in 1936, before falling back during a downturn in 1937–1938. The largest of the industries, modest in number – cold storage, engineering and milling – were all South African-owned, while several smaller enterprises devoted to the production of beer, cement, macaroni and oil pressed from sesame seed were in local hands.[106] Lacking a robust, independently owned economic spine, the city on the bay was doomed to remain a somewhat flaccid entrepôt, a goods-handling, rent-seeking, secondary inlet and outlet linked by rail to the Witwatersrand.

The leading forwarding agency controlling the timber yards, feeding props into the open-mouthed underground workings of the gold mines and owned by a Johannesburg finance house, operated consistently at a handsome profit underwritten, in part, by a fair share of

This mill and macaroni factory in Lourenço Marques supplied Luigi Fatti's delicatessen in Johannesburg, which opened in 1896. In 1953, the enterprise evolved into the enduring firm of Fatti's & Moni's.

shibalo labour. All this while tariffs accounted for fully half the cost of landing timber imported from the west coast of the United States.[107]

Portugal's neutrality during World War II ensured that more shipping traffic passed through the Bay from 1939 to 1945, while modest post-bellum growth, constrained by the Exchange Council and neo-mercantilism, helped achieve a measure of financial stability, if not affordability, for the citizens. Lourenço Marques retained its standing as the city with the highest cost of living in southern Africa into the 1950s, a reputation that, by then, stretched back over half a century and, in its own way, spoke of deep, entrenched underdevelopment.[108]

Trying to stay afloat and simultaneously pay dividends throughout the financially tempestuous 1920s, the BNU had been forced to sell several promising assets in the colonies but was nevertheless unable to see off what effectively was a form of nationalisation that lasted until 1953.[109] Restrained by a short Lisbon leash ever since the Depression, the BNU was forced into more orthodox and predictable banking practices, which made for increased fiscal stability by the mid-1930s. In Mozambique, tightly allied to the administration, the

BNU dominated the Exchange Council and dominated the business of the Portuguese community.[110]

In the subcontinental race to reach a robust and stable financial destination, the South African hare had, for 50 years, been so far ahead that it was, for the most part, simply out of sight. But, from the 1930s to the 1950s and beyond, the Mozambican tortoise – having at last been set on a path across less rocky terrain – began to trundle along new Salazarist contours in meaningful fashion, even though other factors indicated that it could never win the race.

In the 1930s, South African notes were no longer accepted as legal tender and an attempt was made to dry up the supply, even though they continued to circulate widely in the Asian grey and black markets. The BNU helped steady the market when it gradually removed its own historically unmanageable, inflationary 'sterling' notes – the *libra esterlina* – from circulation. More progress was made when foreign exchange rates were fixed by the Council and the system simplified when the Portuguese and Mozambican escudos were placed on par. And the fact that the British and South African pounds were almost on a par for much of the decade further reduced turbulence in the market.[111]

It was the harsh April 1932 decree that did most to clear the thick currency undergrowth from the financial fields being ploughed by the Exchange Council. Five years after it, even the BNU's competitors – the British and South African commercial banks – were forced to admit that, insofar as foreign exchange was concerned, the situation had been transformed. 'That the Decree has achieved the desired purpose there can be little doubt', a Standard Bank official conceded, 'as the Exchange Fund has been steadily built up', and 'at 31 December last [1936] stood at £1688336.' As a result, exchange control regulations too were eased during 1935–1937, allowing foreign banks limited dealings in other currencies while gold coins circulated more freely.[112]

But, despite growing their share of the foreign exchange business, the commercial banks in Lourenço Marques fretted about competition from the few larger licensed Asian merchant houses and others. The largest foreign exchange operator, Kakoobhai, a well-connected founder of a retail banking cooperative, was so successful that his operation was the subject of unwanted envious publicity on the Witwatersrand.[113]

Sluggish commercial banks, specialising in death-by-form-filling, were simply no match for fleet-footed, savvy Indian moneychangers when it came to adjusting to changing rates for firmer currencies. British sterling, South African pounds and other notes of exotic provenance circulating in a port city were almost always traded at a premium against the languid escudo. The developing tourist trade, forwarding agencies that seldom hesitated to go to the grey market for their requirements and the large number of vessels calling in at the port when Portugal declared itself neutral during World War II, all helped bolster earnings in a large, usually trustworthy alternative financial sector.[114]

That sector was, of course, never confined to the port. A dense network of Asian traders acting as informal bankers and serving as bureaux de change extended through much of the Sul do Save, where their principal clients, since the 1870s, had been African migrant mineworkers. In strictly commercial terms, Indian storekeepers had been among the principal beneficiaries of the mines' deferred-pay system when it was reactivated through the revised Mozambique Convention in 1928.

Asian proprietors in remote rural settings, often part of extended families that stretched down to the coast and then across to India, reaped modest returns by providing banking and credit facilities to peasant-proletarians hoping to secure basic foodstuffs and items of apparel from wages that, in real terms, were declining for most of the 20th century. But for those trading in stereotypes, in search of 'profiteers', the heart of the problem of growing rural poverty in southern Mozambique lay not with the bush bankers of the Sul do Save but with metropolitan financiers in London, Lisbon and Johannesburg.

Fiscal constraints imposed in World War II encouraged Portugal to scour its possessions to find new ways of balancing its budget, and, not for the first time in its history, the imperial eye settled on Mozambique. Re-examining a provision in the 1928 Convention stipulating that the deferred wages of the Sul do Save miners were payable in gold, the Lisbon government revisited its arrangement with the Chamber of Mines. From 1940, the migrants' deferred pay was settled, in gold bullion, at a fixed price agreed upon by Portugal and South Africa. But, given the Chamber's expertise in marketing gold internationally and the hazards of war, the South Africans were instructed to sell the gold on the world market and the proceeds would then be transferred to the Lourenço Marques administration. Half the migrants' income – part of wages once paid, albeit intermittently, in the gold coin preferred by the miners and Asian traders, who, in turn, forwarded some of the specie back to India as profits – had been hijacked and then arbitrarily redirected for largely speculative purposes by a third party, Portugal.[115]

What had once been part of a labour quadrilateral linking South Africa, Mozambique and India to Portugal – one in which gold coins had passed directly through the hands of the discerning Sul do Save miners and appreciative local Asian storekeepers – had been reduced to an accounting triangle linking Johannesburg, London and Lourenço Marques, at considerable cost to Africans and to the benefit of Lisbon.

An iniquitous arrangement endorsed by the Chamber and the metropolitan government held for 37 years – from 1940 to 1977 – during which period, for most of the time, the difference between the official rate paid for the gold and the price that it fetched on the free market widened continuously. It meant that 'Portugal's gold holdings made a high – often spectacularly high – profit from the gold sales'.[116]

To date, no one in Portugal or South Africa, not even a politician, has advanced the argument that rural southern Mozambique was a notable beneficiary of windfall profits arising from the wages of migrant workers who had, in effect, advanced an interest-free loan to a predatory commercial-minded state and its partner, the Chamber of Mines.

By the late 20th century southern Mozambique was among the ten poorest regions on earth. Deep in the sandy scrubland of the Sul do Save, observers are now often struck by the ecological bareness of a coastal area that, over the centuries, has been visited regularly by climate disaster's vicious twins – flood and drought. For those unfamiliar with the complex history of the province and its deprived peoples, the inhabitants seem – like the indigent in many places – to have been overcome by forms of fatalism, lassitude and resignation. Trapped within the mental and physical borders of yet one more post-colonial pretend-state and governed by a well-fattened nationalist elite living off a diet of international aid, the locals appear to have had the inexplicable misfortune of having been raised in a place without prospects and – denied meaningful life choices – to be psychologically scarred if not broken. If the unfortunate people of the Sul do Save *do* have a history, it is, presumably, the familiar History of Hopelessness.

Yet nothing could be more misleading or further from the truth. If we peer beyond the present and invert the tyrannies imposed by place and time, a different picture emerges. When the Sul do Save is viewed sideways on – that is, when it is seen as being as much a historical part of what became 'South Africa' as it ever was of 'Mozambique' – an alternative perspective presents itself. The Sul do Save was part of an emerging region embedded in the web of invasive transnational industrial capitalism. Its people were not helpless, but rather were energised actors making intelligent choices in a warped labour market that was, at the behest of those holding power, constantly narrowing. Impoverishment was *not* an inevitable by-product of the poor soils of southern Mozambique, nor were its people born hopeless. In the Sul do Save those outcomes were openly constructed, by industrial capitalism and a colonial tax regime.

As one of many groupings in coastal Mozambique coming out of the misery of the capturing, selling or using of slave labour during the last quarter of the 19th century, the people of the Sul do Save demonstrated, from early on, an acute awareness of the advantage of the geographical location in which they found themselves. Once freed from predatory slaving, they were among the first African peoples to spot the emergence of agricultural and industrial capitalism and to respond to the demand for unskilled or semi-skilled black labour coming from the sugar plantations and diamond mines of a new Deep South. For the same reason, 'East Coasters' – as Thonga and Chopi migrants were known – were quick to understand how the value of a man's labour might best be captured and stored in gold coin and exchanged for life's essentials. Indeed, drawn from a coastal universe where specie from several different countries circulated freely, the men of the Sul do Save were perhaps better placed than most when it came to calibrating the value of new forms of money.

The enterprise and initiative shown by the first Mozambican plantation labourers and mineworkers in a search of gold in southern Africa – a metal that their predecessors knew from pre-colonial times to be an excellent store of value – are not surprising. The possibilities offered through migrancy encouraged them to operate relatively freely in new markets, leaving them to cope only with the various fees extracted by a tax-hungry Portuguese administration. From the late 1860s, men from the Sul do Save entering what, after 1910, became 'South Africa' had considerable choice as to which of the regional labour markets they wished to work in, for wages payable in gold coin. But much of this fluidity was lost as southern Africa moved from being a region marked by a slowly developing semi-feudal agricultural sector, with limited industrial offshoots, to one dominated by primary extractive industries relying on vast quantities of cheap black labour. As the net of industrial capitalism spread, eventually to include the slowly modernising farming practices needed to feed a growing urban population, so the relatively free flow of African labour – domestic and foreign alike – became subjected to increased channelling and direction by the state.

This process, of restricting the labour market choices of black workers in an increasingly racially stratified political economy, was already well under way by the close of the 19th century. The idea that race and class were somehow locked into an indissoluble marriage, ordained by the Bible and Darwin alike, was presented first by immigrant European workers fearful of African competition for 'their' semi-skilled jobs. It then became the policy of governments and industrialists in the region.

The coming of the Union of South Africa, in 1910, and the unusually rapid maturation of a diamond- and gold-powered capitalist state, was followed by the development of powerful new institutions. A gold refinery, mint and reserve bank, all founded in the early 1920s, presented the government and the most powerful cartel of employers in the region – the Chamber of Mines – with new instruments for managing the financial muscles of the state and industry. Being able to act in concert when necessary and to meaningfully influence, if not control, the supply of notes and specie, interest rates, the cost of living and the real value of wages widened the policy options open to both the government and the mining industry.

Ironically, this post-World War I strengthening of South Africa's financial architecture coincided, in large measure, with a decline in the state of the fiscus and relevant institutions in Lisbon and colonial Mozambique. Weakness inherent in the merchant-driven economy of

Portugal was compounded by the lack of a strong central bank. It was a metropolitan weakness passed on to Lourenço Marques via the colony's issuing bank, the Banco Nacional Ultramarino. Switching between its roles as now a private-public dividend-seeking bank, and then a public-private bank promoting fiscal stability, the BNU presided over chaotic inflationary monetary policies for much of the interwar period in Mozambique, leaving the colony extremely vulnerable economically.

Gross and growing regional disparities in the economic, political and social power of, on the one hand, an industrialising capitalist state forever in search of cheaper black labour and, on the other, an adjacent backward commercial colony whose financial horizons did not stretch much beyond tax- and tariff-collecting invited aggressive interventions. Neither the South African government nor its long-term ally, the mining industry – in search of a more proximate port to reduce the cost of imports – hesitated to exploit the glaring weaknesses in Mozambique's defences and poor negotiating positions.

Between the world wars, the South African government's regional foreign policy – and more specifically regarding Mozambique – was marked by its openly stated ambition to incorporate most of southern Mozambique into the Union. Its eager partner, the mining industry, aimed to entrench its monopoly of black migrant labourers from the territory at wages that, in terms of real value, were constantly declining.

To these ends, the South Africans successfully undermined attempts by the Lourenço Marques administration to raise loans in London and New York, encouraged its indebtedness, sought to exploit the weakness of the provincial escudo by attempting to draw it into the orbit of the Reserve Bank and tried to take control of its port and rail complex. The Chamber of Mines for its part, in 1928 and thereafter, pushed for the renewal of the Mozambique Convention's always punitive provisions.

The collective, tangible outcome of these policies was perhaps mirrored most starkly in the changing fortunes of the Sul do Save and its black migrants. When they first entered southern Africa in pursuit of gold specie, in the 19th century, the migrants of southern Mozambique could largely choose which of the emerging labour markets – agriculture or mining – they would engage in at wages partly determined by supply and demand. The 1902 modus vivendi, agreed by the unelected, post-war imperial British administration and agents of imperial Portugal, effectively limited the freedom of migrants to seek out labour markets of their own choice by designating the province a recruiting ground reserved for exclusive exploitation by the Chamber of Mines.

The Chamber's recruiting arm, the WNLA, used criminally enforceable contracts to bind indentured black miners to lengthy indentures at wages that lost real value consistently after World War I. Moreover, twice during the interwar period and, on the second occasion, permanently so, African miners lost their privileged access to wages paid in gold coin. Then, from 1940 to 1977, and again without their consent, the deferred wages of the African miners of the Sul do Save were forwarded to the province in the form of monies realised by the sale of gold bullion – at a premium in the world market – leaving Portugal with substantial profits that did not find their way back into southern Mozambique in meaningful ways.

Land that is inherently unpromising in terms of agricultural or pastoral production does not necessarily give rise to a defeated, lethargic or unskilled people, even if – when trapped by an encroaching industrial dispensation – it becomes a recruiting ground for capitalists in search of cheap migrant labour. Systemic, sustained backwardness of place and person is seldom a purely natural condition.

More frequently, growing impoverishment is the consequence of a set of policies and processes consciously imposed and pursued by powerful interested parties, either singly or in national or international combination, intent on transforming peasants into proletarians to facilitate consumption and revenue generation. As the harbingers of deep-seated, endemic poverty, the cry of 'Imperialism, Colonialism and Racism' can, all too readily, be incorporated into a political slogan. But the same descriptors can also reflect accurately the painful lived experiences of people in a politically, socially and economically deprived environment deliberately constructed over time. Ask almost anyone south of the Save River in southern Mozambique.

SELECT BIBLIOGRAPHY

All primary sources used in this study are listed, in full, in the end-notes of the relevant chapter.

Articles

Allen, R.B. 'European Slave Trading, Abolitionism, and "New Systems of Slavery" in the Indian Ocean', *Portal: Journal of Multidisciplinary International Studies*, Vol. 9, No. 1 (January 2012), pp. 1–21.

Alexander, P. 'Oscillating Migrants, "Detribalized Families" and Militancy: Mozambicans on Witbank Collieries, 1918–1927', *Journal of Southern African Studies*, Vol. 27, No. 3 (2001), pp. 505–525.

Alexopoulou, K. and Juif, D. 'Colonial State Formation without Integration: Tax Capacity and Labour Regimes in Portuguese Mozambique, 1890s–1970s', *International Review of Social History*, Vol. 62 (2017), pp. 215–252.

Bastos, S.P. 'Indian Transnationalisms in Colonial and Postcolonial Mozambique', *Wiener Zeitschrift für Kritische Afrikastudien*, No. 8 (2005), pp. 277–306.

Breckenridge, K. '"Money with Dignity": Migrants, Minelords and the Cultural Politics of the South African Gold Standard Crisis, 1920–1933', *Journal of African History*, Vol. 36 (1995), pp. 271–304.

Cahen, M. 'Slavery, Enslaved Labour and Forced Labour in Mozambique', *Portuguese Studies Review*, Vol. 21, No. 1 (Summer 2013), pp. 253–265.

Da Silva, F.R. 'Political Changes and Shifts in Labour Relations in Mozambique, 1820s–1920s', *International Review of Social History*, Vol. 61 (2016), pp. 115–135.

Hance, A. and van Dongen I.S., 'Lourenço Marques in Delagoa Bay', *Economic Geography*, Vol. 33, No. 3 (July 1957), pp. 238–256.

Harries, P. 'Mozambique Island, Cape Town and the Organisation of the Slave Trade in the South-West Indian Ocean, c. 1797–1807', *Journal of Southern African Studies*, Vol. 42, No. 3 (2016), pp. 409–427.

Harris, M. 'Emigration among the Moçambique Thonga: Cultural and Political Factors', *Africa*, Vol. 29, No. 1 (January 1959), pp. 50–66.

Henshaw, P. 'The "Key to South Africa" in the 1890s: Delagoa Bay and the Origins of the South African War', *Journal of Southern African Studies*, Vol. 24, No. 3 (September 1998), pp. 527–543.

Langhorne, R. 'Anglo-German Negotiations Concerning the Future of the Portuguese Colonies, 1911–1914', *The Historical Journal*, Vol. XVI, No. 2 (1973), pp. 361–387.

Mata, M.E. 'Foreign Joint-Stock Companies Operating in Portuguese Colonies on the Eve of the First World War', *South African Journal of Economic History*, Vol. 22 (September 2007), pp. 107–134.

Neil-Tomlinson, B. 'The Nyassa Chartered Company, 1891–1929', *Journal of African History*, Vol. XVIII, No. 1 (1977), pp. 109–128.

Newitt, M.D. 'The Portuguese on the Zambezi: An Historical Interpretation of the Prazo System, *Journal of African History*, Vol. 10, No. 1 (1969), pp. 67–85.

Nunes, A.B, Bastien, C., Valério, N., de Sousa, R.M and Costa, S.D. *Banking in the Portuguese Colonial Empire (1864—1975)*, Working Paper No. 41, Instituto Superior de Economica e Gestão de Lisboa, 2010.

Roesch, O. 'Migrant Labour and Forced Rice Production in Southern Mozambique: The Colonial Peasantry of the Lower Limpopo Valley', *Journal of Southern African Studies*, Vol. 17, No. 2 (June 1991), pp. 239–270.

Smith, A.K. 'The Idea of Mozambique and Its Enemies, c. 1890–1930', *Journal of Southern African Studies*, Vol. 17, No. 3 (September 1991), pp. 496–524.

Thomas, W.C. 'Outlines of the Timber Industry in Western Australia', in *Early Days Journal and Proceedings of the Royal Western Australian Historical Society*, Vol. 1, Part 5 (1929), pp. 31–55.

Vail, L. 'Mozambique's Chartered Companies: The Rule of the Feeble', *Journal of African History*, Vol. XVII, No. 3 (1976), pp. 389–416.

Vincent-Smith, J.D. 'The Anglo-German Negotiations over the Portuguese Colonies in Africa, 1911–1914', *The Historical Journal*, Vol. XVII, No. 3 (1974), pp. 620–629.

Chapters in books

Coates, T.J. 'The Long View of Convict Labour in the Portuguese Empire, 1415–1932', in C.C. De Vito and A. Lichtenstein (eds.), *Global Convict Labour* (Boston, 2015), pp. 144–167.

Kopone, J. and Heinomen, H. 'Africa in Finnish Policy – Deepening Involvement', in Wohlgemuth, L. (ed.), *The Nordic Countries and Africa: Old and New Relations* (Uppsala, 2002), pp. 15–28.

Schmitter, P.C. 'The "Regime d'Exception" That Became the Rule: Forty-Eight Years of Authoritarian Domination in Portugal', in L.S. Graham and M.H. Makler (eds.), *Contemporary Portugal: The Revolution and its Antecedents* (Austin, 1979), pp. 3–46.

Zamparoni, V. 'Colonialism and the Creation of Racial Identities in Lourenço Marques, Mozambique', in B. Barry, E. Soumonni and L. Sansone (eds.), *Africa, Brazil and the Construction of Trans-Atlantic Black Identities* (Trenton, 2008), pp. 20–43.

Books

Allina, E. *Slavery by Any Other Name: African Life under Company Rule in Colonial Mozambique* (London, 2012).

Ally, R. *Gold & Empire: The Bank of England and South Africa's Gold Producers, 1886–1926* (Johannesburg, 1994).

Alpers, E.A. *The Indian Ocean in World History* (Oxford, 2014).

Burbank, J. and Cooper, F. *Empires in World History: Power and the Politics of Difference* (Princeton, 2010).

Clarence-Smith, G. *The Third Portuguese Empire, 1825–1975: A Study in Economic Imperialism* (Manchester, 1985).

Crush, J., Jeeves, A. and Yudelman, D. *South Africa's Labor Empire: A History of Black Migrancy to the Gold Mines* (Cape Town, 1991).

Dos Santos, Rufino J. *Albuns Fotográficos e Descrítivos de Colónia De Moçambique, Vol. IV. Distrito de Lourenço Marques: Industrias, Agricultura, Aspectos das Circunscrições* (Hamburg, 1929).

Duffy, J. *Portuguese Africa* (Cambridge, Mass., 1959).

First, R. *Black Gold: The Mozambican Miner, Proletarian and Peasant* (New York, 1983).

Frankel, S.H. *Investment and the Return to Equity Capital in the South African Gold Mining Industry, 1887–1965* (Cambridge, Mass., 1967).

Galbraith, J.S. *Mackinnon and East Africa, 1878–1898: A Study in the 'New Imperialism'* (New York, 1972).

Hancock, W.K. *Smuts: Vol. 1, The Sanguine Years, 1870–1919* (Cambridge, 1962).

Hancock, W.K. *Smuts: Vol. 2, The Fields of Force, 1919–1950* (Cambridge, 1968).

Harries, P., *Work, Culture, and Identity: Migrant Laborers in Mozambique and South Africa, c. 1860–1910* (Johannesburg, 1994).

Ingham, K. *Jan Christian Smuts: The Conscience of a South African* (Cape Town, 1986).

Isaacman, A., *Mozambique: The Africanization of a European Institution. The Zambesi Prazos, 1750–1892* (Madison, 1972).

Isaacman, A. and B. *Mozambique: From Colonialism to Revolution, 1900–1982* (Boulder, 1983).

Jeeves, A.H. *Migrant Labour in South Africa's Mining Economy: The Struggle for the Gold Mines' Labour Supply, 1890–1920* (Johannesburg, 1985).

Katzenellenbogen, S.E. *South Africa and Southern Mozambique: Labour, Railways and Trade in the Making of a Relationship* (Manchester, 1982).

Kubicek, R.V. *Economic Imperialism in Theory and Practice: The Case of the South African Mining Industry, 1886–1914* (Durham, N.C., 1979).

Mitchell, A. *16 Lives: Roger Casement* (Dublin, 2014).

Munro, J.F. *Maritime Enterprise and Empire: Sir William Mackinnon and his Business Network, 1823–1893* (Woodbridge, 2003).

Newitt, M.D. *A Short History of Mozambique* (Cape Town, 2018).

Pallaver, K. (ed.). *Monetary Transitions: Currencies, Colonialism and African Societies* (London, 2022).

Penvenne, J.M. *African Workers and Colonial Racism: Mozambican Strategies and Struggles in Lourenço Marques, 1877–1962* (London, 1995).

Segal, R. *Islam's Black Slaves: The Other Black Diaspora* (New York, 2001).

Spence, C.F. *The Portuguese Colony of Moçambique: An Economic Survey* (Cape Town, 1951).

Vail, L. and White, L. *Capitalism and Colonialism in Mozambique: A Study of Quelimane District* (London, 1980).

Van Onselen, C. *The Night Trains: Moving Mozambican Miners to and from South Africa, circa 1902–1955* (Jeppestown, 2019).

Vaughan, E. *Portuguese East Africa: Economic and Commercial Conditions in Portuguese East Africa (Moçambique)* (London, 1952).

Warhurst, P.R. *Anglo-Portuguese Relations in South Central Africa, 1890–1900* (London, 1962).

Wilson, F. *Labour in the South African Gold Mines, 1911–1969* (Cambridge, 1972).

ACKNOWLEDGEMENTS

I have long aspired to be seen as a 'historian', rather than one knee-capped by a prefix or a suffix delineating a particular field of interest or subdiscipline. It is an arrogant aspiration. In truth, most historians have subject preferences and an appropriately narrowly honed repertoire of skills. Few of us are worthy of the encompassing accolade that licenses one to wander wherever your historical fancy might take you. In this instance, the first of three linked studies exploring the historical relationship between 20th-century South Africa and Mozambique, I would have been very pleased to be called an 'economic historian'. But I am not, and I have thus had to rely heavily on the advice and guidance of colleagues, friends and economic historians who know far more about the subjects explored here than do I. I regret that all remaining errors of fact or interpretation are mine. They should be more discerning when choosing intellectual company.

Some of those who have tried to help are repeat offenders who have come to my assistance in many ways over several decades. Fred Cooper, Johan Fourie, Hermann Giliomee, Albert Grundlingh, Jon Hyslop, Paul la Hausse and Jeremy Seekings all offered helpful comments or criticism, in passing, sometimes not only on the contents of this volume but over the two companion volumes that follow on this one. Jeanne Penvenne and Ian Phimister – specialist historians of the very highest calibre – were particularly helpful and supportive as I grappled with a new interest in regional history and a historiography that I was – and may still be – largely unfamiliar with. Thank you all.

I am also deeply indebted to Eugene Ashton, Annie Olivier and Alfred LeMaitre, editor, at Jonathan Ball Publishers for their encouragement and support for the extended and imaginative project that this book is but the first part of. My thanks to Phil Stickler for the maps, and to Cecilia Kruger for her help in procuring appropriate images.

This work was written under exceptionally difficult and painful circumstances that I will not dwell on. But as I worked through earlier drafts and read many of the constructive comments in the margins – some filled with bubbling good humour and tolerant asides – I was reminded of the true extent and nature of my debt to Belinda Bozzoli.

She left me surrounded with the finest of company and most loving support in the shape of our children. The saddest thing about clichés is that because they sometimes contain great truths, they render words so impotent. This book would not have been completed without the assistance of Matthew, Jessica and Gareth. But even love has its boundaries. I will not ask them to read it. Life is too bloody short.

Charles van Onselen
Parkview
March 2023

NOTES

Introduction to the Trilogy – Intersections of Church, Nation and State

1   '"History is the child of its time." So its preoccupations are the same as those which weigh on our own hearts and minds.' F. Braudel, *On History* (Chicago, 1982), p. 6 [as translated by Sarah Matthews, hereafter Braudel, *On History*]. As in the thinking of William James, see, for example, P.J. Ethington, 'Placing the Past: "Groundwork" for a Spatial Theory of History', *Rethinking History*, Vol. 11, No. 4 (December 2007), p. 475 [hereafter Ethington, 'A Spatial Theory of History'.

2   Braudel, *On History*, p. 4.

3   Braudel, *On History*, p. 30.

4   Braudel, *On History*, p. viii.

5   As cited in R.J. Mayhew, 'Historical Geography, 2009–2010: Geohistoriography, the Forgotten Braudel and the place of Nominalism', *Progress in Human Geography*, Vol. 35, No. 3 (2010), p. 409 [hereafter Mayhew, 'Historical Geography']. See also A. Moore, 'Rethinking Scale as a Geographical Category: From Analysis to Practice', *Progress in Human Geography*, Vol. 32, No. 2 (2008), pp. 203–225. See also J. MacArthur, *Cartography and the Political Imagination: Mapping Community in Colonial Kenya* (Athens, Ohio, 2016).

6   As cited in Mayhew, 'Historical Geography', p. 418.

7   Edward Said, as cited in D. Gregory, 'Edward Said's Imaginative Geographies', in M. Crang and N. Thrift (eds.), *Thinking Space* (Milton Park, 2000), p. 302 [hereafter Gregory, 'Imaginative Geographies'].

8   Gregory, 'Imaginative Geographies', pp. 302–348.

9   D. Sassoon (ed.), *Eric Hobsbawm on Nationalism* (London, 2021), p. 43 (emphasis on the word 'secular' added by this author) [hereafter Hobsbawm, *On Nationalism*].

10 Hobsbawm, *On Nationalism*, p. 39

11 Hobsbawm, *On Nationalism*, pp. 50, 57, 64–65.

12 F. Braudel, *The Mediterranean and the Mediterranean World in the Age of Philip II, Vol. 1* (New York, 1972), p. 18 [as translated by Siân Reynolds].

13 In this context, see also P. Lalu, 'Empire and Nation', *Journal of Southern African Studies*, Vol. 41, No. 3 (2015), pp. 436–450.

14 B. Anderson, *Imagined Communities: Reflections on the Origin and Spread of Nationalism* (London, 1991), p. 7.

15 J. Burbank and F. Cooper, *Empires in World History: Power and the Politics of Difference* (Princeton, 2010), p. 2 [hereafter Burbank and Cooper, *Empires*].

16 M. Wilson and L.M. Thompson (eds.), *The Oxford History of South Africa*, Vol. 2, 1870–1966 (Oxford, 1971), pp. 292–298 [hereafter Wilson and Thompson, *Oxford History*].

17 Wilson and Thompson, *Oxford History*, pp. 343–350.
18 Wilson and Thompson, *Oxford History*, pp. 390–395.
19 S. Schama, *Financial Times*, 5–6 March 2022.
20 G.H. Calpin, *There Are No South Africans* (London, 1941).
21 Broederbond Archives, Erfenisstigting, Pretoria, Box No. 7/1/7, AB 11/23, File 7/1952/PdR/Alg, Hoofstuk 7 P.J. du Plessis, Sec. Mooirivier Afdeling, to the Chief Secretary, 14 August 1952.
22 I. Chipkin, *Do South Africans Exist? Nationalism, Democracy and the Identity of 'the People'* (Johannesburg, 2007). See also E.S. Munger, *Afrikaner and African Nationalism: South African Parallels and Parameters* (London, 1967), pp. 9–10, for comments on 'The lack of unity and the absence of symbols of a single nationalism'.
23 Braudel, *On History*, p. 87.
24 V.R. Markham, *South Africa: Past and Present* (London, 1900), p. 146.
25 See, especially, A.K. Smith, 'The Idea of Mozambique and its Enemies, c. 1890–1930', *Journal of Southern African Studies*, Vol. 17, No. 3 (September 1991), pp. 496–524 [hereafter Smith, 'The Idea of Mozambique'].
26 On PIDE, the political police, see M.D. Newitt, *A Short History of Mozambique* (Cape Town, 2018), p. 135 [hereafter Newitt, *Mozambique*].
27 A.H. Jeeves, *Migrant Labour in South Africa's Mining Economy: The Struggle for the Gold Mines' Labour Supply, 1890–1920* (Jeppestown, 1985), pp. 196–197 [hereafter Jeeves, *Labour Supply*].
28 See C. van Onselen, *The Night Trains: Moving Mozambican Miners to and from South Africa, circa 1902–1955* (Johannesburg, 2019), pp. 37–69 [hereafter van Onselen, *Night Trains*].
29 See G. Clarence-Smith, *The Third Portuguese Empire, 1825–1975: A Study in Economic Imperialism* (Manchester, 1985), pp. 106 and 134 [hereafter Clarence-Smith, *Third Portuguese Empire*]; J. Duffy, *Portuguese Africa* (Cambridge, Mass., 1959), pp. 261 and 336 [hereafter Duffy, *Portuguese Africa*]; and J.M. Penvenne, *African Workers and Colonial Racism: Mozambican Strategies and Struggles in Lourenço Marques, 1877–1962* (London, 1995), p. 98 [hereafter Penvenne, *African Workers and Colonial Racism*].
30 See, for example, the deportation of Dr Alfredo Mendes de Magalhães, as reported in the *Rand Daily Mail*, 3 and 5 April 1913.
31 See S. Katzenellenbogen, *South Africa and Southern Mozambique: Labour, Railways, and Trade in the Making of a Relationship* (Manchester, 1982), pp. 73–74 [hereafter Katzenellenbogen, *Southern Mozambique*]; and L. Vail and L. White, *Capitalism and Colonialism in Mozambique: A Study of the Quelimane District* (London, 1980), p. 207 [hereafter Vail and White, *Capitalism and Colonialism*]; and G. Pirio, 'Commerce, Industry and Empire: The Making of Modern Portuguese Colonialism in Angola and Mozambique, 1890–1914', unpublished PhD thesis, Department of History, University of California, Los Angeles, 1982, p. 320 [hereafter Pirio, 'Portuguese Colonialism'].
32 See Clarence-Smith, *Third Portuguese Empire*, p. 214, and A. and B. Isaacman, *Mozambique: From Colonialism to Revolution* (Boulder, 1983), p. 40 [hereafter Isaacman, *Mozambique*].

33   A. Harvey, 'Counter-Coup in Lourenço Marques: September 1974', *International Journal of African Historical Studies*, Vol. 2, No. 2 (August 2010), pp. 139–153.

34   Although his focus lies on African liberation movements and his interests are contemporary, Michel Cahen makes several important suggestions about 'the confusion – widespread in the social sciences – between anti-colonialism and nationalism, between republic and nation, between nation and nation-state' that historians of settler nationalism in Mozambique would do well to pay heed to. See his 'The Anti-Luso Tropicalist Good Fortune of a Mozambican Dissertation', in *Kronos*, Vol. 39, No. 1 (January 2013), pp. 316–323, and, especially, 'Lutte d'émancipation anticoloniale ou mouvement de libération nationale? Processus historique et discours idéologique: le cas des colonies portugaises, et du Mozambique en particulier', *Revue Historique*, Vol. 315, No. 1 (January 2006), pp. 113–138.

35   Duffy, *Portuguese Africa, p. 261*. See also V. Zamparoni, 'Colonialism and the Creation of Racial Identities in Lourenço Marques, Mozambique', in B. Barry, E. Soumonni and L. Sansone (eds.), *Africa, Brazil and the Construction of Trans-Atlantic Black Identities* (Asmara, 2008), pp. 19–43 [hereafter Zamparoni, 'Racial Identities'].

36   See M. Newitt, 'Utopia in Portugal, Brazil and Lusophone African Countries' [review article], *E-Journal of Portuguese History*, Vol. 14, No. 2 (2016), pp. 108–110, and, more particularly, R. Williams, 'Migration and Miscegenation: Maintaining Boundaries of Whiteness in the Narrative of the Portuguese Colonial State in Angola, 1875–1912', in P.J. Havik and M. Newitt (eds.), *Creole Societies in the Portuguese Colonial Empires* (Bristol, 2010), pp. 155–170.

37   For examples, see Penvenne, *African Workers and Colonial Racism*, and Zamparoni, 'Racial Identities'.

38   See, for example, *Rand Daily Mail*, 23 January 1923, and Duffy, *Portuguese Africa*, p. 339.

39   See Duffy, *Portuguese Africa*, pp. 289–299 and 338.

40   F.J. Nance, 'A Holiday in Lourenço Marques', *South African Railways & Harbours Magazine*, December 1920, pp. 964–968 [hereafter Nance, 'Holiday at Lourenço Marques'], and *The City of Lourenço Marques Guide*, 'Authorised by the Municipality' (Lourenço Marques, 1960), p. 216

41   *The City of Lourenço Marques Guide*, pp. 207–216.

42   D. Alexander, *Holiday in Mozambique: A Guide to the Territory* (London, 1971), pp. 3 and 13.

43   But see also A. du Toit, 'No Chosen People: The Myth of the Calvinist Origins of Afrikaner Nationalism and Racial Ideology', *American Historical Review*, Vol. 88, No. 4 (October 1983), pp. 920–952.

44   See H. Giliomee, *Maverick Africans: The Shaping of the Afrikaners* (Cape Town, 2020), on the importance of decisions taken at meeting of the synod, in 1857, and on religious and political schisms, pp. 94–95 [hereafter Giliomee, *Maverick Africans*].

45   P.S. Gorski, *The Disciplinary Revolution: Calvinism and the Rise of the State in Early Modern Europe* (Chicago, 2003), p. xvi [hereafter Gorski, *Disciplinary Revolution*].

46   This summary of Calvinist precepts is drawn from several sources, most nota-
     bly Gorski, *Disciplinary Revolution*; A. Biéler, *Calvin's Economic and Social
     Thought* (Geneva, 2005); W. de Klerk, *The Puritans in Africa* (London, 1975);
     I. Hexham, *The Struggle for National Independence of Afrikaner Calvinism
     against British Imperialism* (New York, 1981); and T.B. Moodie, *The Rise of
     Afrikanerdom: Power, Apartheid, and the Afrikaner Civil Religion* (Los Angeles,
     1975) [hereafter Moodie, *Civil Religion*].

47   See Gorski, *Disciplinary Revolution*, p. 21; and for some of the wider South
     African context, M.R. Begg, 'A Weberian Analysis of Afrikaner Calvinism and
     the Spirit of Capitalism', DPhil thesis, University of Stellenbosch, 2011. For
     a fine fictional portrayal, see K. Schoeman, *'n Lug vol Helder Wolke* (Cape
     Town, 1967), pp. 82–87.

48   B. v. D. van Niekerk, '"Render unto Caesar": A Study of the Sunday Observance
     Laws in South Africa', *South African Law Journal*, Vol. 27 (1969), p. 31, f/n 18
     [hereafter van Niekerk, 'Sunday Observance Laws'].

49   See van Niekerk, 'Sunday Observance Laws', pp. 27–32, and, for an easily
     accessible tabulation of the earliest legislation and commentary, Union of
     South Africa, *Report of the Sunday Observance Commission* [UG 58-13] pp.
     6–7 [hereafter *Sunday Observance Commission 1913*].

50   Among others, see J.S. Ismail, 'South Africa's Sunday Law: Finding a
     Compromise', *Indiana International and Comparative Law Review* (2001–
     2002), pp. 563–585, and P. Farlam, 'Freedom of Religion, Opinion and Belief',
     in S. Woolman et al., *Constitutional Law of South Africa* (Cape Town, 2008),
     pp. 41–50.

51   The first, partial, exemptions came 15 years later; see *Sunday Times*, 5 April 1992.

52   J.D. van der Vyver, 'State-Sponsored Proselytization: A South African Expe-
     rience', *Emory International Law Review*, Vol. 14 (special edition, Summer 2000),
     p. 781.

53   See 'Sunday Observance', in H. van Coller, *Regulating Religion: State Governance
     of Religious Institutions in South Africa* (Abingdon, 2020).

54   This summary does not do justice to all the provisions of Law No. 16 of 1894,
     which attempted to deal with the agricultural as well as the urban commercial and
     industrial sectors of an economy in the early throes of a revolutionary upheaval.

55   For the response of white miners, see E. Katz, *A Trade Union Aristocracy*
     (Johannesburg, 2001), pp. 261 and 270.

56   Preamble, *Sunday Observance Commission 1913*. For evidence presented to
     the commission, see South African National Archives, Pretoria, K209, 'Sunday
     Observance Committee, 1909–1913'.

57   Clause 4, *Sunday Observance Commission 1913*, p. 38.

58   J.W. de Gruchy, *Christianity and the Modernisation of South Africa, 1867–1936*
     (Pretoria, 2009), p. 110.

59   See, especially, R. Elphick on 'Neo-Calvinism' in his *The Equality of Believers:
     Protestant Missionaries and the Racial Politics of South Africa* (Scotsville, 2002),
     pp. 238–257 [hereafter Elphick, *Equality of Believers*].

60   See Giliomee, *Maverick Africans*, pp. 146–154, and Moodie, *Civil Religion*,
     pp. 218–219.

61   Gorski, *Disciplinary Revolution*, pp. 63 and 130.
62   N. Roos, 'Work Colonies and South African Historiography', *Social History*, Vol. 36, No. 1 (February 2011), pp. 54–76.
63   For links between Calvinism and militarism in Dutch history, of the sort that characterised the Dutch revolt against Spanish Catholic rule in the 16th century, see, for example, Gorski, *Disciplinary Revolution*, pp. 67–75.
64   As with the Broederbond and the Dopper Church, see Elphick, *Equality of Believers*, pp. 246–249.
65   Giliomee, *Maverick Africans*, pp. 137–142.
66   See, more generally, J. de Gruchy, 'Calvin(ism) and Apartheid in South Africa in the Twentieth Century: The Making and Unmaking of a Racial Ideology', in J. Backus and P. Benedict (eds.), *Calvin and His Influence* (Oxford, 2011).
67   As quoted in Giliomee, *Maverick Africans*, p. 145.
68   G.B.A. Gerdener, *Handboek by die Katkisasie* (Cape Town and Pretoria 1968), pp. 253–254.
69   In some quarters, this was perceived as part of a wider, Cape-based campaign against Catholicism – see, for example, *Rand Daily Mail*, 21 May 1938.
70   These quotations are taken from C.C. Nepgen, *Die Roomse Gevaar* (Stellenbosch, 1917), p. 19; Driessen, *Die Roomse en Ons Kinders* (Cape Town, 1944), pp. 1–3; J.G. Strydom, *Die Roomse Gevaar en hoe om dit te Bestry* (Pretoria, 1938), pp. 15, 21 and 39; and A.H. Jeffree James, *Rome and the Reformed Churches* (Cape Town, 1962), p. 20. There is a fine collection of these and several other booklets along similar lines to be found in the archives of the NGK in Pretoria.
71   See Duffy, *Portuguese Africa*, p. 123.
72   P. Harries, 'Christianity in Black and White: The Establishment of Protestant Churches in Southern Mozambique', *Lusotopie*, No. 5 (1998), pp. 317–333 [hereafter Harries, 'Christianity in Black and White'].
73   See Clarence-Smith, *Third Portuguese Empire*, p. 185, and E.P. Antonio, 'Religious and Secular Aspects of Proselytization in Mozambique', *Emory International Law Review*, Vol. 14 (special edition, Summer 2000), p. 948 [hereafter Antonio, 'Proselytization in Mozambique'].
74   See Clarence-Smith, *Third Portuguese Empire*, p. 186, and Antonio, 'Proselytization in Mozambique', p. 939.
75   What follows relies heavily on É. Morier-Genoud's seminal essay, 'The Vatican vs Lisbon: The Relaunching of the Catholic Church in Mozambique, c. 1875–1940', *Basler Afrika Bibliographien: Working Papers* (Basel, 2002), pp. 1–16 [hereafter Morier-Genoud, 'The Vatican vs Lisbon'].
76   Morier-Genoud, 'The Vatican vs Lisbon', pp. 5–6.
77   See Duffy, *Portuguese Africa*, p. 105, and Morier-Genoud, 'The Vatican vs Lisbon', p. 9.
78   Morier-Genoud, 'The Vatican vs Lisbon', p. 10.
79   See J. Brain, 'Moving from the Margins to the Mainstream: The Roman Catholic Church', in R. Elphick and R. Davenport (eds.), *Christianity in South Africa: A Political, Social and Cultural History* (Cape Town, 1997), pp. 195–196 and 349.
80   Morier-Genoud, 'The Vatican vs Lisbon', pp. 11–12.
81   See Antonio, 'Proselytization in Mozambique', p. 945; Duffy, *Portuguese Africa*,

p. 105; and Morier-Genoud, 'The Vatican vs Lisbon', p. 14.

82   Elphick, *Equality of Believers*, p. 248.

83   Antonio, 'Proselytization in Mozambique', p. 946, and Duffy, *Portuguese Africa*, p. 310.

84   Antonio, 'Proselytization in Mozambique', p. 946.

85   In the case of the Portuguese, see, for example, Duffy, *Portuguese Africa*, p. 270.

86   C. van Onselen, *New Babylon, New Nineveh: Everyday Life on the Witwatersrand, 1886–1914* (Johannesburg, 2001), p. 57 [hereafter van Onselen, *New Babylon, New Nineveh*].

87   Van Onselen, *Night Trains*, pp. 25–56.

88   J. and J. Comaroff, *Of Revelation and Revolution: Christianity, Colonialism and Consciousness*, Vol. 1 (Chicago, 1991), p. 234.

89   *Africa's Golden Harvests*, September 1914, p. 119, and 'The Romish Perversion', September 1917, p. 22.

90   *Africa's Golden Harvests*, March 1915, p. 64.

91   See *Africa's Golden Harvests*, December 1913, p. 46, and June and July 1914, p. 100.

92   Harries, 'Christianity in Black and White', p. 329.

93   As cited in B. Hirson, 'The General Strike of 1922', unpublished seminar paper, available online.

94   See, among many others, reports in the *Rand Daily Mail* of 27 January and 15 July 1910, 2 and 26 January 1916, 29 March 1930, 24 January 1931, 6 February 1936 and 14 November 1950.

95   Van Niekerk, 'Sunday Observance Laws', pp. 49–50.

96   See, for example, reports in the *Rand Daily Mail* of 9 February 1935, 8 August 1936 and 16 February 1938.

97   *Rand Daily Mail*, 16 March 1950.

98   See, for example, *Rand Daily Mail*, 29 September 1940 and 15 June 1948.

99   *Rand Daily Mail*, 25 August 1955.

100   F. Wilson, *Labour in the South African Gold Mines, 1911—1969* (Cambridge, 1972), p. 70 [hereafter Wilson, *Labour in the South African Gold Mines*].

101   Bishop Malusi Mpumlwana, as quoted in *City Press*, 9 March 2022.

102   E.H. Gould, 'Entangled Histories, Entangled Worlds: The English-Speaking Atlantic as a Spanish Periphery', *American Historical Review*, Forum, June 2007, p. 766. For a fuller understanding of how Catholic and Protestant perspectives can shape historical narratives, see, especially, J. Cannizares-Esguerra, *How to Write the History of the New World: Histories, Epistemologies, and Identities in the Eighteenth-Century Atlantic World* (Stanford, 2001).

103   See J. de Vries, 'Playing with Scales: The Global and the Micros, the Macro and the Nano', *Past and Present*, Vol. 242, Supplement 14 (2019), pp. 29–36; and E.S. Carr and M. Lempert (eds.), *Scale: Discourse and Dimensions of Social Life* (Berkeley, 2016).

Part I

1   This pervasive sense of liminality in Mozambique has, in Anglophone literature at least, often been better captured by novelists than it has been by historians. See, especially, V.S. Naipaul, *Half a Life* (New York, 2001) and H. Mankell, *A Treacherous Paradise* (New York, 2011).

2   See, among others, Duffy, *Portuguese Africa*, pp. 216–218; Clarence-Smith, *Third Portuguese Empire*, pp. 6–8; and Pirio, 'Portuguese Colonialism', pp. 3, 41, 51–52, 76–79 and 205.

3   For the wider context, see E.A. Alpers, *The Indian Ocean in World History* (Oxford, 2014).

4   See R. Segal, *Islam's Black Slaves: The Other Black Diaspora* (New York, 2001), pp. 145–162 and 190–199 [hereafter Segal, *Islam's Black Slaves*].

5   See Duffy, *Portuguese Africa*, p. 48, and Newitt, *Mozambique*, p. 42.

6   See P. Harries, *Work, Culture, and Identity: Migrant Laborers in Mozambique and South Africa, c. 1860—1910* (Johannesburg, 1994), chapters 1–3 [hereafter Harries, *Work, Culture, and Identity*].

7   See G. Liesegang, H. Pasch and A. Jones (eds.), *Figuring African Trade: Proceedings of the Symposium on the Quantification and Structure of the Import and Long-Distance Trade in Africa, 1800—1913*, Kölner Beiträge zur Afrikanistik (Berlin, 1986), p. 59 [hereafter Liesegang, *African Trade*]; and Newitt, *Mozambique*, p. 136.

8   See van Onselen, *Night Trains*.

9   See, especially, Penvenne, *African Workers and Colonial Racism*, p. 32.

10   See Vail and White, *Capitalism and Colonialism*, p. 17.

11   See P. Harries's splendid 'Mozambique Island, Cape Town and the Organisation of the Slave Trade in the South-West Indian Ocean, c. 1797–1807', *Journal of Southern African Studies*, Vol. 42, No. 3 (2016), p. 426 [hereafter Harries, 'The South-Western Indian Ocean'].

12   See Duffy, *Portuguese Africa*, pp. 204–205, and Katzenellenbogen, *Southern Mozambique*, p. 10.

13   See Duffy, *Portuguese Africa*, p. 207; Newitt, *Mozambique*, p. 80; Katzenellenbogen, *Southern Mozambique*, p. 12; or Penvenne, *African Workers and Colonial Racism*, p. 32.

14   On the Berne decision, see A.M. Stuyt, *Survey of International Arbitrations, 1794—1938* (Berlin, 2013), No. 164, p. 172.

15   See Duffy, *Portuguese Africa*, pp. 209–210; Clarence-Smith, *Third Portuguese Empire*, pp. 83–85; and Newitt, *Mozambique*, pp. 81–89.

16   See Duffy, *Portuguese Africa*, p. 22; Katzenellenbogen, *Southern Mozambique*, pp. 23–24; Pirio, 'Portuguese Colonialism', p. 40; and Vail and White, *Capitalism and Colonialism*, p. 130. In keeping with the hegemonic economic ideas in Portugal, parts of the late-19th-century Lisbon elite were not averse to the idea of selling off one or more of the colonies – see Clarence-Smith, *Third Portuguese Empire*, p. 82. By 1890, however, Rhodes's early attempts to acquire Delagoa Bay via cheque book rather than cruisers were being hampered by

the British ultimatum to Portugal. The basic idea of buying part of southern Mozambique, however, remained in place until 1894–1895, by which time he had already helped arm Gungunhana for a confrontation with the Portuguese and was readying himself for a military takeover of the ZAR. On 10 October 1894, with the idea of what eventually became the 'Jameson Raid' already taking shape in Rhodes's mind, one James McIntosh, writing from Lourenço Marques, informed the Mozambique Island-based US consul, W. Stanley Hollis, that 'Rhodes is here and is trying to grab this port and the probability is that he will succeed'. See United States of America (USA), Stanford University, Despatches from the United States Consuls in Mozambique, 1854–1898', Roll 1, Vol. 1, 13 May 1854–31 December 1894 [hereafter USA, Stanford, Despatches].

17   On the ultimatum, see Duffy, *Portuguese Africa*, pp. 216–219; Clarence-Smith, *Third Portuguese Empire*, p. 9; and Newitt, *Mozambique*, p. 94; and for its impact on redefining Mozambique's northern and western borders, see Newitt, *Mozambique*, p. 93. On the southern and southwestern border, see Duffy, *Portuguese Africa*, pp. 20 and 207.

18   USA, Stanford, Despatches, Roll 1, W.S. Hollis to Assistant Secretary of State, Washington, 28 June 1894.

19   See C. van Onselen, *The Cowboy Capitalist: John Hays Hammond, The American West and the Jameson Raid* (Cape Town, 2017), p. 8 [hereafter van Onselen, *Cowboy Capitalist*].

20   See United Kingdom, Foreign Office, Annual Series, No. 2162, *Portugal, Report for the Year 1897 on the Trade and Commerce of Lourenço Marques and District*, p. 5 [hereafter UK FO].

21   See L. Vail, 'Mozambique's Chartered Companies: The Rule of the Feeble', *Journal of African History*, Vol. XVII, No. 3 (1976), p. 412, f/n 108 [hereafter Vail, 'Chartered Companies'].

22   See, especially, R. Langhorne, 'Anglo-German Negotiations Concerning the Future of the Portuguese Colonies, 1911–1914', *The Historical Journal*, Vol. XVI, No. 2 (1973), pp. 361–387, and J.D. Vincent-Smith, 'The Anglo-German Negotiations over the Portuguese Colonies in Africa, 1911–1914'; *The Historical Journal*, Vol. XVII, No. 3 (1974), pp. 620–629.

23   See Vail and White, *Capitalism and Colonialism*, p. 187.

24   Duffy, *Portuguese Africa*, p. 142. For an overview of this problematic relationship at the turn of the century, see also P.R. Warhurst, *Anglo-Portuguese Relations in South Central Africa, 1890—1900* (London, 1962).

25   USA, Stanford, Despatches, Roll 1, W.S. Hollis to Assistant Secretary of State, Washington, 20 October and 2 December 1899.

26   For a range of these prejudices as related to race, gender and sexuality in Mozambique, see R.G. Forman, 'Randy on the Rand: Portuguese African Labour and the Discourse on "Unnatural Vice" in the Transvaal in the Early Twentieth Century', *Journal of the History of Sexuality*, Vol. 11 (October 2002), pp. 600–602; and in film, N. Parsons, *Black and White Bioscope: Making Movies in Africa, 1899 to 1925* (Pretoria, 2018), p. 88

27   See Katzenellenbogen, *Southern Mozambique*, pp. 147–153, and van Onselen, *Night Trains*, pp. 37–56.

28   The first South African agreement of any significance to acquire African mine labour from Mozambique dated back to shortly after the Jameson Raid, when the government of the ZAR was taking meaningful steps to reform its administration in the face of long-standing opposition from the Chamber of Mines; see Jeeves, *Labour Supply*, p. 13. For President S.J.P. Kruger this was seen as a progressive move and it featured in his speech at his inauguration in May 1898; see J.S. Bergh (ed.), *Paul Kruger: Speeches and Correspondence, 1850–1904* (Pretoria, 2018), p. 735.

29   On Smuts, in 1908, see Katzenellenbogen, *Southern Mozambique*, p. 121; and on Botha's Mozambique ambitions, see W.K. Hancock, *Smuts: Vol. 1, The Sanguine Years, 1870–1919* (Cambridge, 1962), p. 553 [hereafter Hancock, *Smuts Vol. 1*].

30   For Smuts's ambitions in World War I and its aftermath, see Hancock, *Smuts Vol. 1*, pp. 408, 498 and 553, as well as W.K. Hancock, *Smuts: Vol. 2, The Fields of Force, 1919–1950* (Cambridge, 1968), pp. 151–152 [hereafter Hancock, *Smuts Vol. 2*]. On his desire to take over Lourenço Marques, see also Smith, 'The Idea of Mozambique', pp. 515 and 519–520.

31   See Katzenellenbogen, *Southern Mozambique*, p. 125.

32   See Vail and White, *Capitalism and Colonialism*, p. 210.

33   Vail and White, *Capitalism and Colonialism*, p. 210.

34   Vail and White, *Capitalism and Colonialism*, p. 202.

35   The lack of Portuguese capital and the limitations of rentier notions of development as played out in Lourenço Marques are well laid out in Chapter Two of J.M. Penvenne, 'A History of African Labor in Lourenço Marques, Mozambique, 1877–1950', DPhil thesis, Department of History, Boston University, 1982 [hereafter Penvenne, 'A History of African Labor'].

36   See, for example, the reforms in northern Portugal, under the liberal Mousinho da Silveira, as described in Vail and White, *Capitalism and Colonialism*, p. 14.

37   This switch in economic and geographical orientation was, of course, not without historical precedent. In the 18th century the French economy 'detached itself from the Mediterranean, despite its increased trade, and turned towards the Atlantic: a turning which entailed important transformations in trade routes, markets, and cities' – Braudel, *On History*, p. 87.

38   On the origins of the *prazo* system, see Duffy, *Portuguese Africa*, pp. 82–85, and Newitt, *Mozambique*, pp. 25–27. The emergence of the *prazo* system, its functioning and its utilisation of labour are perhaps best laid out in F.R. da Silva, 'Political Changes and Shifts in Labour Relations in Mozambique, 1820s–1920s', *International Review of Social History*, Vol. 61 (2016), pp. 115–135 [hereafter da Silva, 'Political Changes and Shifts'].

39   As in several other fields, Portugal played a pioneering role in developing intensely exploitative labour colonies in its expanding seaborne empire. See T.J. Coates, 'The Long View of Convict Labour in the Portuguese Empire, 1415–1932', in C.C. De Vito and A. Lichtenstein (eds.), *Global Convict Labour* (Boston, 2015), pp. 144–167. For the role of convicted criminals – *degredados* – seizing and then laying claim to land, see, for example, Vail and White, *Capitalism and Colonialism*, p. 8.

40 See Duffy, *Portuguese Africa*, pp. 82–85; A. Isaacman, *Mozambique: The Africanization of a European Institution. The Zambesi Prazos, 1750—1892*, (Madison, 1972), pp. xi–xiv [hereafter Isaacman, *Africanization of a European Institution*]; M.D.D. Newitt, 'The Portuguese on the Zambezi: An Historical Interpretation of the Prazo System', *Journal of African History*, Vol. 10, No. 1 (1969), pp. 72–76 [hereafter Newitt, 'Portuguese on the Zambezi']; and Vail and White, *Capitalism and Colonialism*, p. 8.

41 See Isaacman, *Africanization of a European Institution*, pp. 138–139, and Newitt, 'Portuguese on the Zambezi, p. 74.

42 See Newitt, 'Portuguese on the Zambezi', pp. 73–75.

43 See, among others, Duffy, *Portuguese Africa*, pp. 84–85; Newitt, 'Portuguese on the Zambezi', p. 76; and Vail and White, *Capitalism and Colonialism*, p. 10.

44 See, for example, Isaacman, *Africanization of a European Institution*, p. 127.

45 L. Chewins '"Stealing Dingane's Title": The Fatal Significances of Saguate Gift-Giving in Zulu King Dingane's Killing of Governor Ribiero (1833) and Piet Retief (1838)', seminar paper presented to the Department of History, University of Johannesburg, February 2022. On the ongoing attempts at *prazo* reform during these times, see Isaacman, *Africanization of a European Institution*, pp. 121–123 and, more generally, pp. 36–171.

46 This paragraph is derived entirely from Vail and White, *Capitalism and Colonialism*, pp. 13–15.

47 See Newitt, *Mozambique*, p. 71.

48 See Newitt, 'Portuguese on the Zambezi', p. 79, and Vail and White, *Capitalism and Colonialism*, p. 13.

49 Newitt, 'Portuguese on the Zambezi', p. 85.

50 On the Middle East trade, see Segal, *Islam's Black Slaves*, pp 13–34 and 190–199; and on the slave trade in India, Clarence-Smith, *Third Portuguese Empire*, pp. 34–35; and S. Hassell's important 'Beyond the Numbers: The Slave Trade from East Africa to Portuguese India' – an essay currently under revision for publication.

51 See, especially, Vail and White, *Capitalism and Colonialism*, pp. 22–37.

52 Vail and White, *Capitalism and Colonialism*, p. 17. After 1810, much of the Portuguese slave trade north of the equator had also been outlawed by the Anglo-Portuguese Treaty of Amity and Friendship – see Harries, 'The South-Western Indian Ocean', p. 423. But for continuities between the old northerly Omani trade in slaves and shipments south to the Portuguese in Mozambique, see Clarence-Smith, *Third Portuguese Empire*, p. 35.

53 See Clarence-Smith, *Third Portuguese Empire*, p. 36; Harries, 'The South-Western Indian Ocean', pp. 409–427; Newitt, *Mozambique*, pp. 53 and 67–69; Vail and White, *Capitalism and Colonialism*, pp. 22–37.

54 Vail and White, *Capitalism and Colonialism*, p. 19.

55 See Liesegang, *African Trade*, p. 460; Newitt, *Mozambique*, pp. 54–55; and Vail and White, *Capitalism and Colonialism*, pp. 16–22.

56 Harries, 'The South-Western Indian Ocean', p. 410; and Vail and White, *Capitalism and Colonialism*, p. 18.

57 Clarence-Smith, *Third Portuguese Empire*, p. 35.

58 Newitt, *Mozambique*, p. 54. There are also some suggestive figures to be derived from the Trans-Atlantic Slave Trade Database as put forward in R.B. Allen's 'European Slave Trading, Abolitionism, and "New Systems of Slavery" in the Indian Ocean', *Portal: Journal of Multidisciplinary International Studies*, Vol. 9, No. 1 (January 2012), pp. 8 and 12.

59 On the *prazos* of Zambezia as a source of slaves, see, for example, Harries, 'The South-Western Indian Ocean', p. 422, and Vail and White, *Capitalism and Colonialism*, pp. 17 and 27.

60 See Clarence-Smith, *Third Portuguese Empire*, p. 36.

61 Newitt, *Mozambique*, p. 69.

62 For ongoing slaving operations between Angoche and Madagascar, just south of Mozambique Island, see, for example, USA, Stanford, Despatches, Roll 1, USA Consul, E.H. Smith to Secretary of State, Washington, DC, 21 February 1889, and another excellent account from same primary source, EH Smith to Secretary of State on 18 May 1889, coupling the arrival of armed dhows to the strengthening monsoon and the regional trade in African bodies.

63 Newitt, *Mozambique*, p. 8.

64 See especially, Vail and White, *Capitalism and Colonialism*, p. 17, for the post-1811 opening of southern ports to Brazilian slave traders.

65 See Clarence-Smith, *Third Portuguese Empire*, pp. 34–36.

66 Harries, 'The South-Western Indian Ocean', pp. 423–424.

67 See Duffy, *Portuguese Africa*, p. 149; and Clarence-Smith, *Third Portuguese Empire*, pp. 35–36.

68 Harries, *Work, Culture, and Identity*, p. 1.

69 See Duffy, *Portuguese Africa*, p. 150, and, more especially, Vail and White, *Capitalism and Colonialism*, pp. 24–34. 'There was unquestionable evidence as late as 1890 of practices in Moçambique which could only be called slaving' – suggests Duffy, at p. 145.

70 See Newitt, *Mozambique*, pp. 67–68.

71 USA, Stanford, Despatches, Roll 1, Vol. 1, W.S. Hollis to the Assistant Secretary of State, Washington, 23 November 1894.

72 See Vail, 'Chartered Companies', pp. 398–399, and 'A Slavery Lie', *Rand Daily Mail*, 2 February 1910.

73 See van Onselen, *Night Trains*, p. 80.

74 See Burbank and Cooper, *Empires*, pp. 14–15.

75 See Duffy, *Portuguese Africa*, pp. 140–147, and Newitt, *Mozambique*, pp. 54 and 75–76.

76 Da Silva, 'Political Changes and Shifts', p. 128.

77 On the post-slavery labour regulations and regime and the continuities it represented in the African colonies see Duffy, *Portuguese Africa*, pp. 152–157, and, for its South African connection, van Onselen, *Night Trains*, pp. 37–56.

78 See, especially, E. Allina, *Slavery by Any Other Name: African Life under Company Rule in Colonial Mozambique* (London, 2012), pp. 1–16 [hereafter Allina, *Slavery*].

79 Da Silva, 'Political Changes and Shifts', pp. 124–127.

80 See Allina, *Slavery*, pp. 23–25, and Vail, 'Chartered Companies', pp. 391–393.

81 See Allina, *Slavery*, p. 24, and Vail, 'Chartered Companies', p. 393.

82   See Clarence-Smith, *Third Portuguese Empire*, pp. 101–102, and Isaacman, *Mozambique*, p. 37.

83   See van Onselen, *Night Trains*, pp. 37–56

84   See van Onselen, *Night Trains*, pp. 114–132.

85   See van Onselen, *Night Trains*, pp. 114–132.

86   Van Onselen, *Night Trains*, p. 41.

87   In this sense the speculative fortunes of the Mozambican chartered companies were simply locked into the far larger market dynamics manifesting themselves in regard to other southern African enterprises and as expressed in the stock exchanges of Europe and Johannesburg. See, especially, I.R. Phimister's outstanding 'Bears, Bulls, Boers and Brits: Market Mining and Southern African Mining Finance, 1894–1899' [forthcoming; hereafter Phimister, 'Bears, Bulls'].

88   As Allina has noted, the chartered companies were neither one thing nor another but an elision of state and commercial enterprise with the consequent blurring of vision – see Allina, *Slavery*, pp. 4 and 62. On the resulting changes in boards, financial failures, rumour and market manipulations, see Vail, 'Chartered Companies', pp. 394–416.

89   Vail, 'Chartered Companies', p. 401.

90   Vail, 'Chartered Companies', p. 399.

91   See, especially, Allina, *Slavery*, pp. 142–143.

92   On the modest success of the political – as opposed to the economic – objectives of the Niassa Company, see especially, B. Neil-Tomlinson, 'The Nyassa Chartered Company, 1891–1929', *Journal of African History*, Vol. XVIII, No. 1 (1977), pp. 109–128.

93   See Vail, 'Chartered Companies', p. 415.

Part II

1   The background to Burgers's initiatives are outlined in van Onselen, *Night Trains*, pp. 25–27; for one of the important unintended consequences of the Treaty of Commerce (1875), see, for example, van Onselen, *New Babylon, New Nineveh*, p. 57.

2   Van Onselen, *Night Trains*, pp. 26–27.

3   Van Onselen, *Night Trains*, p. 27.

4   Van Onselen, *Night Trains*, p. 28.

5   See especially C. van Onselen, 'Randlords and Rotgut, 1886–1903: The Role of Alcohol in the Development of European Imperialism and Southern African Capitalism with Special Reference to Black Mineworkers in the Transvaal Republic', in *New Babylon, New Nineveh*, pp. 47–108.

6   See van Onselen, *Cowboy Capitalist*.

7   See da Silva, 'Political Changes and Shifts', pp. 115–135.

8   See also Katzenellenbogen, *Southern Mozambique*, p. 97: 'There was also a general feeling that Mozambique gave much more in the modus vivendi than it got and this was simply one aspect of British/South African dominance in the country.'

9   Van Onselen, *Night Trains*, pp. 37–56.

10   Wilson, *Labour in the South African Gold Mines*, p. 46, quoted in van Onselen, *Night Trains*, p. 40.

11   Van Onselen, *Night Trains*, pp. 37–56.

12   There is a summary of early African subsistence farming practices to be found in O. Roesch, 'Migrant Labour and Forced Rice Production in Southern Mozambique: The Colonial Peasantry of the Lower Limpopo Valley', *Journal of Southern African Studies*, Vol. 17, No. 2 (June 1991), pp. 245–252.

13   This paragraph is based on materials drawn from the reports complied by the Inspectors of the Standard Bank reporting on the financial well-being and viability of its Lourenço Marques branch; see Republic of South Africa (RSA), Johannesburg, Standard Bank Archives and Historical Services (A&HS), Inspection Reports for 1904 and 1908 [hereafter RSA, JHB, SBA & HS]. On Africans selling surplus maize to Indian traders for onward sale to Lourenço Marques see also US Department of State, Bureau of Foreign Commerce (1854–1903), *Commercial Relations of the United States and Foreign Countries* (Government Printer, Washington, DC, 1903), Vol. 1, p. 248.

14   See RSA, JHB, SBA & HS, Inspection Report of the Lourenço Marques Branch for 1926.

15   See C.F. Spence, *The Portuguese Colony of Moçambique: An Economic Survey* (Cape Town, 1951), p. 50 [hereafter Spence, *An Economic Survey*].

16   On maize failures and importation and female hardship in the Sul do Save during famine times, see 'Delagoa Bay Trade – Natives in a Bad Way', *Rand Daily Mail*, 28 August 1922.

17   On the inability of white farmers in Mozambique to compete with the more capital-intensive white farmers of South Africa, see, for example, Clarence-Smith, *Third Portuguese Empire*, pp. 135 and 177.

18   Paragraph based on UK FO, Annual Series, No. 1760, *Report for the Year 1895 on the Trade of the Consular District of Mozambique*, pp. 8–10.

19   See J. dos Santos Rufino, *Albuns Fotográficos e Descrítivos de Colónia De Moçambique, Vol. IV. Distrito de Lourenço Marques: Industrias, Agricultura, Aspectos das Circunscrições* (Hamburg, 1929), p. 7 [hereafter Rufino, *Lourenço Marques: Industrias, Agricultura, Aspectos das Circunscrições*].

20   RSA, JHB, SBA & HS, Inspection Reports pertaining to the Lourenço Marques Branch for 1907, 1911, 1914 and 1915.

21   As early as 1902, settlers were poorly disposed to the modus vivendi – see Katzenellenbogen, *Southern Mozambique*, p. 52. In 1911, at Xai-Xai, in Inhambane, the Governor was implacably opposed 'to the emigration of natives, on the grounds that they ought to be kept in this country so as to develop the farming industries'. See Republic of South Africa (RSA), National Archives of South Africa (NASA), NTS, File 7565/1011/F473, 'Report of the WNLA Enquiry Commission', pp. 2–5 [hereafter RSA, NASA, 'Report of the WNLA Enquiry Commission, 1911']. See also Vail and White, *Capitalism and Colonialism*, p. 207, and *Rand Daily Mail*, 8 January 1913. On the consequent underdevelopment of the Sul do Save, see Smith, 'The Idea of Mozambique', pp. 506–507.

22   See Katzenellenbogen, *Southern Mozambique*, pp. 150–152, and for the objections of the Lourenço Marques Chamber of Commerce to the WNLA's drawing down

the local labour supply, pp. 73–74. The quotation comes from Clarence-Smith, *Third Portuguese Empire*, p. 177.

23 On the prohibitive cost of capital and resultant undercapitalisation, see Pirio, 'Portuguese Colonialism', p. 67.

24 See, for example, M Harris, 'Emigration among the Moçambique Thonga: Cultural and Political Factors', *Africa*, Vol. 29, No. 1 (January 1959), p. 64; Harries, *Work, Culture, and Identity*, p. 149; and M. Newitt, 'Migrant Labour and the Development of Mozambique', *Societies of Southern Africa in the 19th and 20th Centuries*, Vol. 4, pp. 67–76.

25 Among others, see Clarence-Smith, *Third Portuguese Empire*, pp. 177–178; and Duffy, *Portuguese Africa*, pp. 262–265.

26 See Duffy, *Portuguese Africa*, p. 336; and Isaacman, *Mozambique*, p. 43.

27 See A. MacDonald, 'Colonial Trespassers in the Making of South Africa's International Borders, 1900 to c. 1950', PhD thesis, Faculty of History, Cambridge University, p 183; and Penvenne, *African Workers and Colonial Racism*, pp. 98–99.

28 On categorisation and related problems in the colony as regards the *mestiçagem* (miscegenation) – but not numbers – see Duffy, *Portuguese Africa*, p. 261, and, especially, Zamparoni, 'Racial Identities', pp. 20–43; and Penvenne, *African Workers and Colonial Racism*, p. 109.

29 See RSA, JHB, SBA & HS, Inspection Reports, Lourenço Marques Branch for 1907 and 1915.

30 See also Rufino, *Lourenço Marques: Industrias, Agricultura, Aspectos das Circunscrições*, p. 7.

31 See 'The Union and Mozambique – What Portugal has Done', *Rand Daily Mail*, 5 August 1922, and Rufino, *Lourenço Marques: Industrias, Agricultura, Aspectos das Circunscrições*, pp. 23–24.

32 On the prospects and problems of the meat-chilling business see RSA, JHB, SBA & HS, Inspection Reports, Lourenço Marques Branch for 1933, 1937 and 1935. The collapse of the later cold-storage business is reported on in Spence, *An Economic Survey*, pp. 64–65, and, on later developments, in Penvenne, *African Workers and Colonial Racism*, pp. 118–122. On persistent problems around dairy and meat products in the city see also A. Hance and I.S. van Dongen, 'Lourenço Marques in Delagoa Bay', *Economic Geography*, Vol. 33, No. 3 (July 1957) p. 251 [hereafter Hance and Van Dongen, 'Lourenço Marques'].

33 See A. van Niekerk, 'The Use of White Female Labour by the Zebediela Citrus Estate, 1926–1953', MA thesis, Faculty of Arts, University of the Witwatersrand, 1988, p. 26.

34 On the abortive Limpopo settlement scheme, see Clarence-Smith, *Third Portuguese Empire*, p. 177.

35 Paragraph based on material drawn from UK FO, Annual Series, No. 855, *Report for the Year 1890 on the Trade of the Consular District of Mozambique*, p. 22, and Spence, *An Economic Survey*, pp. 64 and 71. Some of the earliest fruit and vegetables produced for the market in Lourenço Marques were supplied by Chinese gardeners operating on the town's outskirts. After World War I – perhaps earlier – a limited amount of fresh fruit and vegetables, presumably the produce of African farmers, was brought in to the town by boat from Catembe;

see Nance. 'Holiday at Lourenço Marques', p. 966.

36   UK FO, Annual Series, No. 995, *Report for the Year 1891 on the Trade of the Consular District of Mozambique*, p. 10, and Annual Series, No. 1904, *Report for the Year 1896 on the Trade and Commerce of Lourenço Marques*, p. 14.

37   See USA, Stanford, Despatches, Roll 1, Vol. 1, W.S. Hollis to the Assistant Secretary of State, Washington, DC, 8 February 1896 [emphasis added].

38   The early history of the development of Lourenço Marques, between 1886 and 1899, cannot be divorced from, or understood without appreciating, the great speculative 'Kaffir Boom' of 1895 and the spillover into Delagoa Bay. See Phimister, 'Bears, Bulls'.

39   See also Hance and van Dongen, 'Lourenço Marques', p. 245.

40   On the speculative pedigree of the Delagoa Bay Development Corporation, see R.V. Kubicek, *Economic Imperialism in Theory and Practice: The Case of the South African Mining Industry, 1886—1914* (Durham, N.C., 1979), pp. 163–168 [hereafter Kubicek, *Economic Imperialism*].

41   See, for example, the case of Transvaal Consolidated Coal Mines Ltd, as cited in UK FO, Miscellaneous Series, No. 398, *Report on the Port and Railway of Lourenço Marques*, June 1896, pp. 6 and 15.

42   P. Henshaw, 'The "Key to South Africa" in the 1890s: Delagoa Bay and the Origins of the South African War', *Journal of Southern African Studies*, Vol. 24, No. 3 (September 1998), p. 528 [hereafter Henshaw, 'Delagoa Bay and the Origins of the South African War'].

43   See USA, Stanford, Despatches, Roll 1, Vol. 1, W.S. Hollis to Assistant Secretary of State, Washington, DC, 3 and 19 September 1895.

44   See 'Commercial Advertiser and Shipping Gazette', and 'The Block at Delagoa' in the *Natal Mercury*, 27 and 29 August 1895.

45   Penvenne, *African Workers and Colonial Racism*, p. 35.

46   Henshaw, 'Delagoa Bay and the Origins of the South African War', pp. 527–530.

47   See Penvenne, *African Workers and Colonial Racism*, p. 35, and, especially, USA, Stanford, Despatches, Roll 4, Vol. 2, W.S. Hollis to Assistant Secretary of State, Washington, DC, 8 July 1903, 'Lourenço Marques, Province of Mozambique, River and Harbor Improvements'.

48   For 1905–1906 improvements to port infrastructure, see especially RSA, JHB, SBA & HS, Inspection Report, Lourenço Marques Branch, 1906.

49   This paragraph based on Penvenne, *African Workers and Colonial Racism*, p. 35, and 'Chamber of Trade', *Rand Daily Mail*, 19 January 1910.

50   The period 1918–1928 saw the greatest increase in coal exports; see Katzenellenbogen, *Southern Mozambique*, pp. 120 and 130.

51   On Torre do Valle's business, see, for example, an advertisement placed in the *Rand Daily Mail*, 5 February 1903, and, more importantly, RSA, JHB, SBA & HS, Inspection Report of the Lourenço Marques Branch, 1912.

52   South African complaints dated back to 1916–1917; see, especially, RSA, NASA, Governor General (GG), Vol. 1353, File 39/153, Minute 343, Prime Minister's Office, Cape Town, 9 March 1917. But, on recognition of port improvements, see also 'Mozambique as a Neighbour', *Rand Daily Mail*, 26 January 1921.

53   There is a fine description of the operation of the new plant – side by side by

with remnants of an older system of loading, done manually, with Africans carrying coal on their heads for tipping into a skip – in Nance, 'Holiday at Lourenço Marques', p. 967.

54 The memorandum appears to have been reproduced, almost in full, in 'The Union and Mozambique – What Portugal has Done', *Rand Daily Mail*, 5 August 1922. For a report on the regular functioning of the port at the time –including ships arriving and departing – see also 'Delagoa Bay Trade', *Rand Daily Mail*, 28 August 1922. On coal-handling facilities into the 1950s, when oil was beginning to replace coal as fuel for ships, see also Hance and Van Dongen, 'Lourenço Marques', pp. 247–248.

55 For an overview of the port in the 1950s, see Hance and Van Dongen, 'Lourenço Marques', pp. 238–256.

56 The early weakness of Portuguese shipping is noted, in passing, in UK FO, Annual Series, No. 995, *Report on the Trade of the Consular District of Mozambique 1891*, p. 3. See also W. Stanley Hollis, 'Steam Communication with Southeast Africa', in US Board of Manufacturers, *Monthly Consular and Trade Reports*, Vol. 73, Issues 276–279 (US Government Printing Office, 1903), pp 327–329.

57 On Mackinnon, see especially J. Forbes Munro, *Maritime Enterprise and Empire: Sir William Mackinnon and his Business Network, 1823–1893* (Woodbridge, 2003), and J.S. Galbraith, *Mackinnon and East Africa, 1878–1898: A Study in the 'New Imperialism'* (New York, 1972). On the BISNC push into south-eastern Africa, see also A. Porter, *Victorian Shipping, Business and Imperial Policy: Donald Currie, the Castle Line and Southern Africa* (Woodbridge, 1986) [hereafter Porter, *Victorian Shipping*], and UK FO, Annual Series, No. 742, *Report for the Year 1889 on the Trade of Mozambique and District, the Consular District of Mozambique*, p. 8.

58 For the initial strengthening of the triangular Britain–India–Mozambique coastal trade after the opening of the Suez Canal and until the discovery of gold on the Rand, see Vail and White, *Capitalism and Colonialism*, pp. 63–64.

59 On Currie's many and varied investments in southern Africa, see Porter, *Victorian Shipping*, pp. 144–152 and 154–157.

60 See Porter, *Victorian Shipping*, pp. 204–210.

61 The struggle between Currie and Mackinnon for east coast mastery can be followed in Porter, *Victorian Shipping*, pp. 204–210, 213 and 256–257.

62 See also Penvenne, *African Workers and Colonial Racism*, p. 17.

63 Data in this paragraph drawn from Clarence-Smith, *Third Portuguese Empire*, pp. 95–96 and 156–157.

64 See J. Crush, A. Jeeves and D. Yudelman, *South Africa's Labor Empire: A History of Black Migrancy to the Gold Mines* (Cape Town, 1991), p. 142 [hereafter Crush et al., *South Africa's Labor Empire*], and Isaacman, *Mozambique*, p. 36.

65 See especially Phimister, 'Bears, Bulls'.

66 Landing agents and forwarding agents are listed in, for example, UK FO, Annual Series, No. 1537, *Report for the Year 1894 Trade of the Consular District of Mozambique*, pp. 337–338. The shortage of lighters, rerouting and cargo-dumping problems can be traced in a special report, UK FO, Miscellaneous Series, No. 398, *Report on the Port and Railway of Lorenzo Marques, 1896*, pp. 3 and 23.

67 See Penvenne, 'A History of African Labor', p. 38. The subsequent fortunes of the Rand-Delagoa Bay Landing Company can be tracked in RSA, JHB, SBA & HS, Inspection Reports of the Lourenço Marques Branch for 1896 and 1898, and, RSA, Grahamstown, Rhodes University, Cory Library, Gold Fields Collection, MS 14 909, Rand-Delagoa Bay Landing Company, Letter Book.

68 Kubicek, *Economic Imperialism*, pp. 53–55.

69 See RSA, Johannesburg, University of the Witwatersrand, Cullen Library, Barlow-Rand Archives, H. Eckstein & Co. Collection, H.E. 257, File 142 (l) Nos. 1–27, Lourenço Marques Forwarding Co. Ltd., Extract from a letter to Messrs. H Eckstein & Co. to Messrs. Wernher, Beit & Co, London, 23 October 1905; and Box 64, File 152, Memorandum to C.L. Read and LMFC shareholders, 20 March 1928 [hereafter RSA, Barlow-Rand, LMFC]. On the Rand mining machinery importers, see USA, Consular Reports, *Commerce, Manufacturers*, Vol. LXI, Nos. 228–231, September–December 1899 (Government Printing Office, Washington, DC).

70 RSA, Barlow-Rand, LMFC, File 142 (l) Nos. 1–27, 'Remarks by Chairman at General Meeting of Shareholders, held at Company Offices', Johannesburg, 5 July 1907.

71 RSA, Barlow-Rand, LMFC, Box 65, Dr Alfredo Reis to 'My Dear Martin' [recipient unknown], 6 April 1939.

72 RSA, Barlow-Rand, LMFC, Box 65, File 152/e, J. Clark (Manager LMFC) to J.D. Massey, 19 August 1932.

73 RSA, Barlow-Rand, LMFC, Box 64, File 152, statement on issued share capital, profits and dividends, 25 September 1919.

74 RSA, Barlow-Rand, LMFC, Box 64, File 152, Chairman LMFC to Prime Minister JBM Hertzog, 20 September 1925.

75 See Penvenne, *African Workers and Colonial Racism*, p. 87, and Vail and White, *Capitalism and Colonialism*, p. 229.

76 See Hance and Van Dongen, 'Lourenço Marques', p. 245, and Penvenne, *African Workers and Colonial Racism*, p. 119. On Santos Gil's early but limited interest in timber see *Rand Daily Mail*, 15 June 1941.

77 The best overview of the southern African timber industry between the two world wars is the U.S. Bureau of Foreign and Domestic Commerce's *Methods of Handling Lumber Imports in South Africa* (Government Printer, Washington, DC, 1931) – see especially pp. 9–11 [hereafter US, *Methods of Handling Lumber Imports*].

78 See J. Kopone and H. Heinomen, 'Africa in Finnish Policy – Deepening Involvement', in L. Wohlgemuth (ed.), *The Nordic Countries and Africa: Old and New Relations* (Uppsala, 2002), p. 17, and, on tariffs, RSA, Barlow-Rand, LMFC, Box 65, J. Clark, Manager, to J.D. Massey, Central Mining, 19 August 1932.

79 A bare-bones background to the Karridale industry can be found in W.C. Thomas, 'Outlines of the Timber Industry in Western Australia', in *Early Days Journal and Proceedings of the Royal Western Australian Historical Society*, Vol. 1, Part 5 (1929), pp. 31–55; and D. Sanders, 'From Colonial Outpost to Popular Tourist Destination: An Historical Geography of the Leeuwin–Naturaliste Region, 1829–2005', PhD thesis, Murdoch University, 2005.

80 On Karri Davies and early imports of Australian timber to the Rand, see especially, UK FO, Miscellaneous Series, No. 398, *Report on the Port and Railway of Lorenzo Marques, 1896*, pp 9–12; and for the continuity via other firms working out of Bunbury, WA, see 'O.B.' on 'Lourenço Marques', *The West Australian*, 24 July 1937.

81 See van Onselen, *Cowboy Capitalist*, p. 43.

82 See I.W. Clogston, 'The City of Destiny's Darkest Hour: Tacoma and the Depression of the 1890s', undergraduate thesis, Department of History, University of Washington, 2015, pp. 10–17.

83 On Lingham, see, for example, UK FO, Annual Series, No. 1760, *Report for the Year 1895 Trade of the Consular District of Mozambique*, pp. 7–8, and UK FO, Miscellaneous Series, No. 398, *Report on the Port and Railway of Lorenzo Marques, 1896*, p. 9.

84 On Casement's German friendships in Lourenço Marques, see A. Mitchell, *16 Lives: Roger Casement* (Dublin, 2014), p. 25; and on F.F. Eiffe, UK FO, Annual Series, No. 1537, *Report for the Year 1894 Trade of the Consular District of Mozambique*, p. 37; and M. Seligman, *Rivalry in South Africa, 1893—1899: The Transformation of German Colonial Policy* (Berlin, 1998), p. 43.

85 See, especially, Henshaw, 'Delagoa Bay and the Origins of the South African War', pp. 527–529; and A.N. Porter, *The Origins of the South African War: Joseph Chamberlain and the Diplomacy of Imperialism* (Manchester, 1980), p. 126.

86 See an item from the *Gold Fields' News*, 30 June 1903, as reproduced in USA, *Consular Reports: Commerce, Manufacturers Etc.* (US Government Printing Office, Washington, DC), Issues 276–279, p. 446.

87 See USA, *Railroad Gazette*, Vol. 33, 27 September 1901, p. 657.

88 See, for example, US, *Methods of Handling Lumber Imports*, p. 48; Nance, 'Holiday at Lourenço Marques', p. 966; and RSA, Barlow-Rand, LMFC, Box 66, H.D. Hoyle, Manager's Report, LMFC, for the month of January 1940.

89 Paragraph based on material drawn from UK FO, Annual Series, No. 1537, *Report for the Year 1894 Trade of the Consular District of Mozambique*, p. 35; and UK FO, Miscellaneous Series, No. 398, *Report on the Port and Railway of Lorenzo Marques, 1896*, pp. 3–5; and US, *Methods of Handling Lumber Imports*, p. 24.

90 See an undated, unsourced press cutting headed 'Lourenço Marques' as part of an addendum to USA, Stanford, Despatches, Roll 4, Vol. 2, W.S. Hollis to Assistant Secretary of State, Washington, DC, 8 July 1903, 'Lourenço Marques, Province of Mozambique, River and Harbor Improvements'.

Part III

1 Portugal did not ratify the International Labour Organization's agreement on the abolition of forced labour in the colonies until 1956 – see K. Alexopoulou and D. Juif's 'Colonial State Formation without Integration: Tax Capacity and Labour Regimes in Portuguese Mozambique, 1890s–1970s', *International Review of Social History*, Vol. 62 (2017), p. 222 [hereafter Alexopoulou and Juif, 'Tax Capacity and Labour Regimes'].

2   M. Cahen, 'Slavery, Enslaved Labour and Forced Labour in Mozambique', in *Portuguese Studies Review*, Vol 21, No. 1 (Summer 2013), p. 261 (emphasis in the original) [hereafter Cahen 'Slavery, Enslaved and Forced Labour']. See also da Silva, 'Political Changes and Shifts', pp. 115–135.

3   See K. Pallaver (ed.), *Monetary Transitions: Currencies, Colonialism and African Societies* (London, 2022), and, more especially, A. De Cola, 'The Maria Theresa Thaler in Italian Eritrea: The Impact of Colonial Monetary Policies during the First World War', p. 81–106; C. Eagleton's, 'How and Why did the Rupee become the Currency of Zanzibar and East Africa?', pp. 211–238; and A. Mseba, 'Beyond Imperial Interests: Settler Regimes, Capital and Africans in Colonial Southern Africa's Currency Politics to 1920', pp. 139–160 [hereafter referred to only as the work of the author as cited in *Monetary Transitions* and the relevant page numbers].

4   See Harries, *Work, Culture, and Identity*, p. 89. On the demand for coins in southern Africa after the opening of the Kimberley diamond mines, see also Mseba, *Monetary Transitions*, pp. 146–147.

5   On Inhambane's shift from a town with 'few prospects', in 1885, to one where its migrants took the steamer to Durban before going to Natal and then on to work in Kimberley, in 1889, and to one where by 1893 they constituted the most prized miners, navvies and porters in the Sul do Save, and where the district was the only one in the colony where revenue exceeded expenditure, see the following: UK FO, Series No. 60, Report for the Year 1885 on the *Consular District of Mozambique*, pp. 2–8; UK FO, Series No. 742, *Report for the Year 1889 on the Trade of Mozambique and District*, p. 10; UK FO, Series No. 1963, *Report for the Year 1893 on the Trade of Mozambique*, p. 13; and UK FO, Series No. 2630, *Report for the 1901 on the Trade of Inhambane*, p. 6. On the wider context and importance, see also Alexopoulou and Juif, 'Tax Capacity and Labour Regimes', pp. 231 and 239.

6   See, for example, UK FO, Annual Series, No. 855, *Report for the Year 1890 on the Trade of the Consular District of Mozambique*, p. 10. On struggles around the use of silver coinage and American trade down the east coast in the 1860s see especially Eagleton, *Monetary Transitions*, pp. 222–223.

7   See UK FO, Annual Series, No. 855, *Report for the Year 1890 on the Trade of the Consular District of Mozambique*, pp. 19–20, and, more importantly, UK FO, Annual Series, No. 1537, *Report for the Year 1894 on the Trade of the Consular District of Mozambique*, p. 18.

8   Paragraph based on material drawn from: UK FO, Annual Series, No. 742, *Report for the Year 1889 on the Trade of Mozambique and District*, p. 6; UK FO, Annual Series, No. 855, *Report for the Year 1890 on the Trade of the Consular District of Mozambique*, p. 10; UK FO, Annual Series, No. 1312, *Report for the Year 1892 on the Trade of Mozambique*, p. 4; and UK FO, Annual Series, No. 1904, *Report for the Year 1896 on the Trade and Commerce of Lourenço Marques*, p. 3.

9   The longevity of the thaler as currency in the Horn of Africa can be traced in De Cola, *Monetary Transitions*, pp. 81–101.

10   On recognition of the thaler, see USA, Stanford, Despatches, Roll 1, Vol. 1, E.W. Smith to Assistant Secretary of State, Washington, DC, 11 February 1889;

and, for its circulation in Lourenço Marques, UK FO, Annual Series, No. 1463, *Report for the Year 1893 on the Trade of Mozambique*, pp. 29–30. See also Vail and White, *Capitalism and Colonialism*, p. 203.

11   See UK FO, Annual Series, No. 2162, *Report for the Year 1897 on the Trade and Commerce of Lourenço Marques and District*, p. 9.

12   UK FO, Annual Series, No. 1463, *Report for the Year 1893 on the Trade of Mozambique*, p. 30.

13   UK FO, Annual Series, No. 1463, *Report for the Year 1893 on the Trade of Mozambique*, p. 30; and Vail and White, *Capitalism and Colonialism*, p. 84.

14   Vail and White, *Capitalism and Colonialism*, pp. 17 and 29–30.

15   See A.B. Nunes, C. Bastien, N. Valério, R.M. de Sousa and S.D. Costa, *Banking in the Portuguese Colonial Empire (1864–1975)*, Working Paper No. 41, Instituto Superior de Economica e Gestão de Lisboa, 2010, p. 7 [hereafter Nunes et al., *Banking in the Portuguese Colonial Empire*]. See also Vail and White, *Capitalism and Colonialism*, p. 202.

16   See Clarence-Smith, *Third Portuguese Empire*, pp. 97–98; Smith, 'The Idea of Mozambique', pp. 511–517; Pirio, 'Portuguese Colonialism', pp. 67–68; and Vail and White, *Capitalism and Colonialism*, p. 202.

17   See Vail, 'Chartered Companies', pp. 391–399.

18   The differences between chattel slavery and enslaved and forced labour are explored in Cahen, 'Slavery, Enslaved and Forced Labour', pp. 262–265.

19   On company tokens, see, for example, Vail and White, *Capitalism and Colonialism*, p. 119; and on the Banco de Beira, US Bureau of the Mint, *Annual Report of the Director of the Mint*, 1924, p. 209.

20   See Nunes et al., *Banking in the Portuguese Colonial Empire*, p. 8.

21   See Clarence-Smith, *Third Portuguese Empire*, pp. 97–99, on the revocation, and, for the reinstatement, FO, Annual Series, No. 1463, *Report for the Year 1893 on the Trade of Mozambique*, p. 17.

22   See Nunes et al., *Banking in the Portuguese Colonial Empire*, p. 42.

23   Van Onselen, *Night Trains*, pp. 37–56 and 71–90.

24   Nunes et al., *Banking in the Portuguese Colonial Empire*, p. 13.

25   See Crush et al., *South Africa's Labor Empire*, pp. 1–11, and Katzenellenbogen, *Southern Mozambique*, pp. 49 and 75–76.

26   On the dominance of the incoming British-South African bank and the BNU's unwillingness to underwrite industrial development, see, for example, Clarence-Smith, *Third Portuguese Empire*, pp. 137 and 176; and on mortgages in Lourenço Marques, Pirio, 'Portuguese Colonialism', p. 68.

27   On early competition in the moneychanging sector of the economy, see, for example, RSA, JHB, SBA & HS, Inspection Report on the Lourenço Marques Branch, 2 November 1907; and, for the longevity of the problem, RSA, Barlow-Rand, LMFC, J. Clark, Manager, Lourenço Marques Forwarding Agency, to G.D. Massey, Johannesburg, 26 June 1932.

28   See Clarence-Smith, *Third Portuguese Empire*, p. 137, and Vail and White, *Capitalism and Colonialism*, p. 203.

29   *See Rand Daily Mail*, 26 September 1911, and Katzenellenbogen, *Southern Mozambique*, p. 101.

30   See *Rand Daily Mail*, 8 January 1913, and Katzenellenbogen, *Southern Mozambique*, pp. 93 and 103.

31   Katzenellenbogen, *Southern Mozambique*, pp. 101–102.

32   See RSA, NASA, 'Report of the WNLA Enquiry Commission, 1911'.

33   See Katzenellenbogen, *Southern Mozambique*, pp. 112–113.

34   See *Rand Daily Mail*, 8 and 9 January, 24 February and 4 March 1913.

35   Van Onselen, *New Babylon, New Nineveh*, pp. 1–2; and K. Breckenridge, '"Money with Dignity": Migrants, Minelords and the Cultural Politics of the South African Gold Standard Crisis, 1920–1933', *Journal of African History*, Vol. 36 (1995), p. 275 [hereafter Breckenridge, 'The South African Gold Standard Crisis, 1920–1933']; and T.E. Pogue, 'The Evolution of Research Collaboration in South African Gold Mining, 1886–1933', unpublished PhD thesis, University of Maastricht, 2006, p. 141.

36   See S.H. Frankel, *Investment and the Return to Equity Capital in the South African Gold Mining Industry, 1887—1965* (Cambridge, Mass., 1967), p. 3; Wilson, *Labour in the South African Gold Mines*, pp. 9–10, 40 and 46; and van Onselen, *Night Trains*, pp. 38–39.

37   See van Onselen, *Night Trains*, pp. 41–42.

38   F. Wilson, quoted in van Onselen, *Night Trains*, pp. 39–40.

39   See S. Gelb, 'The Origins of the South African Reserve Bank', African Studies Seminar Paper No. 157, September 1984, pp. 1–7 [hereafter Gelb, 'The South African Reserve Bank'].

40   See R. Ally, *Gold & Empire: The Bank of England and South Africa's Gold Producers, 1886–1926* (Johannesburg, 1994), pp. 47–101 [hereafter Ally, *Gold & Empire*].

41   On Smuts's hesitancy and reluctance to deal fully with financial and economic policies, see K. Ingham, *Jan Christian Smuts: The Conscience of a South African* (Cape Town, 1986), pp. 139–140.

42   See Hancock, *Smuts* Vol. 2, p. 152.

43   Hancock, *Smuts* Vol. 2, pp. 151–152. This initiative had British backing; see R. Hyam, *The Failure of South African Expansion, 1908—1948* (London, 1972), p. 48 [hereafter Hyam, *The Failure*].

44   Hancock, *Smuts* Vol. 2, p. 153.

45   See, especially, Ally, *Gold & Empire*, p. 93, for Smuts's June 1922 intervention to thwart a loan for Mozambique.

46   Hancock, *Smuts* Vol. 2, p. 154.

47   See, 'Ignotus', 'Mozambique as a Neighbour', *Rand Daily Mail*, 26 January 1921.

48   See especially Vail and White, *Capitalism and Colonialism*, pp. 230–231.

49   See 'Cases in the Courts', *Rand Daily Mail*, 27 July 1917.

50   See Breckenridge, 'The South African Gold Standard Crisis, 1920–1933', p. 276, and Wilson, *Labour in the South African Gold Mines*, p. 36.

51   The principal figure behind the reconfiguration, the man invited by Smuts to assume a leading role, was the Austrian-born Anglophile London banker Henry Strakosch, a close confidant of Lionel Phillips, who controlled the Corner House group that dominated Rand gold mining. See Ally, *Gold & Empire*, pp. 49–50, and Gelb, 'The South African Reserve Bank', pp. 15–16.

52   See Breckenridge, 'The South African Gold Standard Crisis, 1920–1933', p. 278.

53   Nunes et al., *Banking in the Portuguese Colonial Empire*, p. 15.
54   See especially P. Alexander, 'Oscillating Migrants, "Detribalized Families" and Militancy: Mozambicans on Witbank Collieries, 1918–1927', *Journal of Southern African Studies*, Vol. 27, No. 3 (2001), pp. 505–525 [hereafter Alexander, 'Mozambicans on Witbank Collieries'].
55   See Breckenridge, 'The South African Gold Standard Crisis, 1920–1933', p. 277.
56   See Ally, *Gold & Empire*, pp. 90–91.
57   See Breckenridge, 'The South African Gold Standard Crisis, 1920–1933', pp. 279–280.
58   See Alexander, 'Mozambicans on Witbank Collieries', pp. 505–525; Breckenridge, 'The South African Gold Standard Crisis, 1920–1933', pp. 280–281; and van Onselen, *Night Trains*, p. 80.
59   US Bureau of the Mint, *Annual Report of the Director of the Mint*, 1924, p. 209. It is worth noting that 'during the war and for some years thereafter, the Union effectively ceased to have an independent currency, the South African pound becoming virtually indistinguishable from sterling' – Ally, *Gold & Empire*, p. 85.
60   See RSA, JHB, SBA & HS, Inspection Report of the Lourenço Marques Branch, 1923. Lisbon's demand for BNU sterling at this time is noted in Katzenellenbogen, *Southern Mozambique*, at p. 127.
61   US Bureau of the Mint, *Annual Report of the Director of the Mint*, 1924, p. 209.
62   See Duffy, *Portuguese Africa*, p. 250; Katzenellenbogen, *Southern Mozambique*, p. 125; and Vail and White, *Capitalism and Colonialism*, pp. 203–204.
63   Vail and White, *Capitalism and Colonialism*, pp. 204–205.
64   See Vail and White, *Capitalism and Colonialism*, p. 205, and Smith, 'The Idea of Mozambique', p. 510.
65   Vail and White, *Capitalism and Colonialism*, p. 205.
66   See, for example, Katzenellenbogen, *Southern Mozambique*, pp. 134–135, and van Onselen, *Night Trains*, pp. 158–159.
67   See, especially, Smith, 'The Idea of Mozambique', pp. 516–517.
68   See Clarence-Smith, *Third Portuguese Empire*, p. 123, and Breckenridge, 'The South African Gold Standard Crisis, 1920–1933', p. 286.
69   Vail and White, *Capitalism and Colonialism*, p. 229.
70   On the devaluation, see RSA, JHB, SBA & HS, Lourenço Marques Branch, J.P. Gibson, Senior General Manager to The Secretary, Standard Bank, London, 31 December 1925; and on the direct link between BNU policies and the railway workers' strike, *Rand Daily Mail*, 24 December 1925. The quotation is from Vail and White, *Capitalism and Colonialism*, p. 232.
71   As cited in Hyam, *The Failure*, p. 32.
72   Katzenellenbogen, *Southern Mozambique*, p. 125.
73   Katzenellenbogen, *Southern Mozambique*, pp. 123–124.
74   Katzenellenbogen, *Southern Mozambique*, p. 126.
75   See Hyam, *The Failure*, p. 31.
76   Katzenellenbogen, *Southern Mozambique*, pp. 129–133.
77   Katzenellenbogen, *Southern Mozambique*, pp. 130–131.
78   Ally, *Gold & Empire*, p. 93.
79   Ally, *Gold & Empire*, p. 97.

80   See Katzenellenbogen, *Southern Mozambique*, p. 132, and Smith, 'The Idea of Mozambique', p. 517.

81   See P.C. Schmitter, 'The "Regime d'Exception" That Became the Rule: Forty-Eight Years of Authoritarian Domination in Portugal', in L.S. Graham and H.M. Makler (eds.), *Contemporary Portugal: The Revolution and its Antecedents* (Austin, 1979), p. 32.

82   See Vail and White, *Capitalism and Colonialism*, p. 232.

83   See, RSA, JHB, SBA & HS, J. Jeffrey to The Secretary, Standard Bank, London, 6 November 1925.

84   See, Vail and White, *Capitalism and Colonialism*, p. 234, and *Rand Daily Mail*, 10 January 1927.

85   'The free circulation of gold within the territory during the past 12 to 18 months has tended to create a sounder position, and a number of firms are now quoting prices on a gold basis only' – RSA, JHB, SBA & HS, Inspection Report of the Lourenço Marques Branch, 6 January 1927.

86   D. Alexander, *Holiday in Mozambique: A Guide to the Territory* (London, 1971), p. 13.

87   On the earliest financial history of the Polana Hotel, see, for example, items in the *Rand Daily Mail*, of 13 March 1914, 8 and 22 November 1922, 17 March 1926 and 20 March 1928.

88   On the contributory role of the BNU to the unrest, see, for example, the *Rand Daily Mail*, 24 December 1925. The Manager of the Standard Bank, too, saw currency problems as lying at the root of the disturbances. 'This continued depreciation of the Banco Nacional Ultramarino Sterling issue [the *libra*, depreciated by 42 per cent] is giving rise to a feeling of unrest, as a result of which the railway employees at Lourenço Marques, have come out on strike'; see RSA, JHB, SBA & HS, J. Jeffrey, Joint General Manager, Lourenço Marques, to the Secretary, Standard Bank, London, 20 November 1925.

89   See, among others, reports in the *Rand Daily Mail* of 24 November, 10 December, 16 December, 18 December and 24 December 1925, and 15 March and 26 April 1926. For the wider context of the strike, see, especially, Penvenne, *African Workers and Colonial Racism*, pp. 86–87.

90   See Penvenne, *African Workers and Colonial Racism*, p. 32.

91   RSA, JHB, SBA & HS, Inspection Report on the Lourenço Marques Branch as at 31 March 1933.

92   See M. Kitson, 'End of an Epoch: Britain's Withdrawal from the Gold Standard', Judge Business School, University of Cambridge, June 2012.

93   See, especially, Breckenridge, 'The South African Gold Standard Crisis, 1920–1933', pp. 296–297.

94   'Gold sovereigns and half-sovereigns were in circulation until 21 December 1932, on which date the Union suspended gold payments' – S. Steinberg (ed.), *The Statesmen's Year-Book: Statistical and Historical Annual of the States and the World for the Year 1958* (New York, 2018), p. 267.

95   See van Onselen, *Night Trains*, pp. 158–161.

96   RSA, JHB, SBA & HS, Inspection Report on the Lourenço Marques Branch as at 31 March 1933.

97 RSA, JHB, SBA & HS, Inspection Report on the Lourenço Marques Branch, as at 25 September 1935.

98 See Spence, *An Economic Survey*, p. 124, and G.E. Vaughan, *Portuguese East Africa: Economic and Commercial Conditions in Portuguese East Africa (Moçambique)* (London, 1952), pp. 3–4 [hereafter Vaughan, *Economic and Commercial Conditions*].

99 RSA, JHB, SBA & HS, Inspection Report on the Lourenço Marques Branch as at 31 March 1933.

100 See, for example, RSA, Barlow-Rand, LMFC, Box 63 – one undated and two other letters dated 20 July 1933 and 24 June 1934 from the WNLA port agents, Breyner & Wirth, working side by side with the Lourenço Marques Forwarding Agents (in turn a subsidiary of the Corner House, Rand Mines group) to the Secretary, Central Mining, Johannesburg. For other dual-currency, racist, wharf-side payment systems, see Penvenne, *African Workers and Colonial Racism*, p. 84.

101 See 'Order to Attach a Man', *Rand Daily Mail*, 10 February 1933. The best account of the history of Asian traders in Mozambique is that of S.P. Bastos, 'Indian Transnationalisms in Colonial and Postcolonial Mozambique', *Wiener Zeitschrift für Kritische Afrikastudien*, No. 8 (2005), p. 283 [hereafter Bastos, 'Indian Transnationalisms'].

102 RSA, JHB, SBA & HS, Inspection Report on the Lourenço Marques Branch as at 31 March 1933.

103 *Rand Daily Mail*, 27 October and 31 December 1925. For the historical background to gold exports to India, see also Ally, *Gold & Empire*, p. 69.

104 See *Rand Daily Mail*, 31 January 1933.

105 See Part II, above.

106 See RSA, JHB, SBA & HS, Inspection Reports on the Lourenço Marques Branch as at 6 November 1931, 25 September 1935, and 27 Februray 1937. See also Penvenne, *African Workers and Colonial Racism*, p. 98.

107 On tariffs, see, for example, RSA, Barlow-Rand, LMFC, Box 65, File 152/e, J. Clark (Manager, Lourenço Marques Forwarding Agency) to J.D. Massey, 19 August 1932.

108 On the cost of living, see, for example, RSA, NASA, Pretoria, BTS, File 37/17 – 'Copies of Secret and Confidential Communications, Union Consul-General to Union Government, E.K. Scallan to the Secretary of Finance, Pretoria, 18 October 1941, or, in 1950, Vaughan, *Economic and Commercial Conditions*, p. 45.

109 On the sale of BNU assets in the 1920s and its subsequent successful trajectory into the 1960s, see Clarence-Smith, *Third Portuguese Empire*, pp. 170 and 213. Decree No. 39221 of 25 May 1953 made it clear that the BNU was to remain in essence 'a private bank controlled by the government' – Nunes et al., *Banking in the Portuguese Colonial Empire*, p. 24.

110 See, especially, RSA, JHB, SBA & HS, Inspection Reports on the Lourenço Marques Branch as at 27 February 1937 and 29 April 1941.

111 Paragraph based on information drawn from, among others, RSA, NASA, Pretoria, Treasury File 114/9 – 'Copies of Secret and Confidential Communications, Union

Consul-General to Union Government', D. Steyn, Union Consulate-General to Secretary for External Affairs, Pretoria, 9 January 1933 and 26 October 1933; and RSA, JHB, SBA & HS, Inspection Reports on the Lourenço Marques Branch as at 27 February 1937.

112   See RSA, JHB, SBA & HS, Inspection Reports on the Lourenço Marques Branch as at 25 September 1935 and 27 February 1937.

113   On Kakoobhai, see, for example, *Rand Daily Mail*, 25 April 1952.

114   For the legal and illegal trade in currency, see, for example, RSA, JHB, SBA & HS, Inspection Reports on the Lourenço Marques Branch as at 25 September 1935 and 23 April 1941; and on wartime profits by Asian money traders, see Bastos, 'Indian Transnationalisms', p. 285.

115   See van Onselen, *Night Trains*, p. 40.

116   R. First, *Black Gold: The Mozambican Miner, Proletarian and Peasant* (New York, 1983), pp. 25–26; and Katzenellenbogen, *Southern Mozambique*, pp. 153–154.

INDEX

Note: Entries in *italics* indicate photographs.

Ingram Content Group UK Ltd.
Milton Keynes UK
UKHW020236210623
423745UK00017B/511